365 Excuse Me . . .

365 Excuse Me . . .

Daily Inspirations That Empower and Inspire

MINA PARKER

Cover design by Jane Hagaman
Cover art: Freeing Bird by © iStockphoto.com / Carlos Benigno;
Summer Flowers and Circles Background by © iStockphoto.com / Dean Turner;
Summer Pattern by © iStockphoto.com / Tom Nulens
Interior Art by © iStockphoto.com

All the introductory quotes in this book are taken from *Excuse Me, Your Life Is Waiting* or *The "Excuse Me, Your Life Is Waiting" Playbook,* both by Lynn Grabhorn and published by Hampton Roads Publishing Company.

Hampton Roads Publishing Company, Inc.
1125 Stoney Ridge Road • Charlottesville, VA 22902
434-296-2772 • fax: 434-296-5096
e-mail: hrpc@hrpub.com • www.hrpub.com

If you are unable to order this book from your local bookseller, you may order directly from the publisher. Call 1-800-766-8009, toll-free.

Library of Congress Cataloging-in-Publication Data

Parker, Mina.
365 excuse me-- : daily inspirations that empower and inspire / Mina Parker.
p. cm.
Summary: "A book of daily meditations and essays based on Lynn Grabhorn's Excuse Me, Your Life Is Waiting"--Provided by publisher.
ISBN 978-1-57174-602-3 (5.25 x 6.75 tp : alk. paper)
1. Spiritual life--Miscellanea. 2. Inspiration--Miscellanea. I. Title.
II. Title: Three hundred sixty five excuse me.
BF698.35.O57P35 2009
158.1'28--dc22
2009003285

ISBN 978-1-57174-602-3
10 9 8 7 6 5 4 3 2 1
Printed on acid-free paper in the United States

For my mother

and, as always,

for D and B

Introduction

Lynn Grabhorn's landmark book *Excuse Me, Your Life Is Waiting* appeared on my doorstep one day, the gift of a friend of the family. I did not seek it out, I did not ask for it, but my vibrations must have been sending out the message that I needed this book. I picked it up not knowing what to expect. I had heard bits and pieces about the law of attraction: the idea that *like attracts like* in all aspects of the universe and that we can create our own destinies through acceptance and mastery of this concept. Some of this seemed to resonate for me and some of it seemed completely bogus. So with curiosity, excitement, and a degree of skepticism, I plunged in. Lynn's voice rings from each page—authentic, worldly, and wise—and I quickly found myself wrapped up in the start of a amazing and challenging journey.

Soon after I opened *Excuse Me, Your Life Is Waiting,* stories started to pour into my life—stories of people's experiences with the law of attraction, whether they called it that or not. Some were thrilled that something they'd been wanting, hoping, and working for seemed to float into their lives on a cloud. Some were excited by the new directions their lives had taken as a result of some unexpected stroke of luck. But a recurring theme in many of the stories was the difficulty of living these principles day after day and finding the inspiration to reclaim that initial spark when the going got rough.

The law is simple: like attracts like. There are many straightforward ways to put the idea into practice. Sure, it all made sense while you were reading, and, yes, there were initial leaps and bounds and many saw results right away. But then old habits would resurface, sometimes in insidious ways. Lynn talks about finding ways to open our valve, that inner part of us that flows energy freely or stops it up completely. People would manage to pry it open a tiny bit and then after some success they would inexplicably begin to clamp down, judge themselves, and shut the valve completely. I wondered why. Shouldn't this get easier as you go? If it's really such a simple concept, why is it so difficult to live by on a daily basis?

In my own experience, as I played around with some new ways of thinking and feeling, several amazing things came down the pike—along with some miserable ones. I thought, "This isn't any better; it's just a life pushed to the extreme and the end result is about the same (or worse, given the exhaustion of going back and forth between good and bad)." How was I going to find consistency and comfort in a whole new way of being?

I came up with the idea to make a book to help people, including myself, navigate the slumps and pitfalls of the daily practice of living through the law of attraction. It is essential to me (as it was for Lynn) to take all of this stuff with a grain of salt, to continuously find the joy and the levity in this ongoing life adventure, and to lighten up on and take care of ourselves. To me, the law of attraction is about finding and holding on to the inspiration, passion, and connection to what you love that makes your life meaningful. There are all sorts of ways to do this, and I mean *really* do this, but our old habits and our fear will more often than not lead us to the *least effective* strategies. So these 365 meditations are meant to serve as a guidebook, a source of inspiration and encouragement throughout the year and again and again. The law of attraction is best learned through practice, and 365 times seems like a pretty good way to do that.

When my life is going along at a happy clip, I now attribute it largely to the fluidity and inspiration of the ideas in Lynn's books, as well as a special rule that correlates to the law of attraction. I call it the law of plenty. We operate on a model of scarcity all too often, worrying about what will come next and how we will struggle to get what we need. The law of plenty assures us that *we already have anything we will ever need.* Everything we need is at our fingertips, and the law of attraction is the information superhighway that brings it to us.

There is no concept more relevant to our lives than what Lynn calls the law of attraction. It goes far beyond the immediate, self-gratifying milestones of unblocking your energy and getting the stuff, jobs, and relationships that you want (though that's pretty great too!). This is about tapping into the energy that connects all of us, that defines the goals and the wisdom and the trajectory of the human race.

We are disconnected from our deepest selves in our daily lives. We are steeped in chaos and anxiety. It doesn't have to be this way. This book brings together ancient wisdom and new concepts in a way that applies to our hectic, overstuffed, frenetic lives—lives in which we seem to be *doing more* than ever and *getting less* out of it all. The principles laid out in *Excuse Me, Your Life Is Waiting* and *The "Excuse Me, Your Life Is Waiting" Playbook* are explored in this book. If followed in an earnest and open way, these principles provide a complete reversal of what makes our modern lives crazy without taking the drastic steps of moving off the grid and into the hills to weave our own clothing and raise our own food (unless that is your lifelong dream, in which case, go for it). This is simple, revolutionary, and completely suited to the lives we want to lead, the lives that will make us happy if we only let them.

Lynn dedicates her book to "every one of us who finally . . . maybe . . . possibly . . . believes they have the right to perpetual happiness." What is perpetual happiness? How can I get a double order of it right away? Perpetual happiness doesn't mean you're never going to be sad or upset or frustrated again. If that's your goal, then you might want to consider a vegetative state, though I wouldn't recommend it. Perpetual happiness, to me, can best be defined as embracing the big picture of what makes you feel good, what feels important and vital to your concept of yourself in the world, and what challenges and renews you on a regular basis. There are happy janitors and happy bankers; it has been proven by scientists that one's individual circumstances make almost no difference. Through the daily meditations of this book, I hope you will find the courage to embrace that belief and find the strength and inspiration to open up to the possibility of that happiness saturating every part of your life.

I have picked up and used some of Lynn's phrases that may be unfamiliar to you. Even if you haven't read her work, most of these simple concepts will become clear through the meditations in this book. In addition to the inner "valve" I just mentioned, she talks about "feeeeeling" and getting into a "feeeeeling place"—an alternate spelling to convey emotion that is the result of wonderful, positive, focused energy. She writes about "flip-switching," a way she devised to turn off negative vibrations as you would a light switch, which enables you to quickly move into a better state. She talks about "prepaving," a method of sending out your positive energy so that instead of fretting about future events you can simply send your good vibes ahead of you to generate the best possible outcome. Some other vocabulary may be new to you, but I urge you to trust yourself and go with the flow, and you'll soon come to your own, greater understanding.

I hope this book will be a resource for you. I encourage you to use it any way you wish—set it on your bedside table or close to your desk; read it daily and incorporate it into your routine; pick it up now and then to get a jolt of inspiration or reawakening (even just close your eyes and open it to the page you need!). Simple as these concepts are, as Lynn says, they are completely foreign to us, and a daily practice to remind us of what we're meant to be doing, or the suggestion of a new way to look at something, is often indispensable. So welcome to the next phase of your journey, and here's to *365 Excuse Me . . .*

. . . a year of letting it happen
. . . a year of staying calm
. . . a year of practice
. . . a year of abolishing fear
. . . a year of desires
. . . a year of forgiveness
. . . a year of resilience
. . . a year of beating boredom
. . . a year of comfort in small things
. . . a year of stumbling
. . . a year of new beginnings
. . . a year of honesty
. . . a year of giving over but never giving up.

1

"Step 1. Identify what you DON'T want.
Step 2. From that, identify what you DO want.
Step 3. Get into the feeling place of what you want.
Step 4. Expect, listen, and allow it to happen."

These four steps are the gateway to a new life. They are simple, even deceptively so, as all true and life-changing things tend to be. They are also practical, by which I mean, they form a basic, simple exercise that you can practice again and again. You can practice this series of steps about anything—from finding a prime parking spot to moving beyond the resentment of a miserable childhood. They can and should form a daily practice, like prayer, or washing, or stretching. They provide some structure for this nebulous world of feelings, and, at the same time, they will help you release some of the old thought patterns that you think are helping you get what you want, when, in fact, they are most likely doing just the opposite.

When I'm in a moment of distress or disorganization, when I'm sick or can't sleep, or can't focus, these steps at a very minimum serve to calm me down and help me refocus. When I can use these steps on a daily basis, they help me unlock problems that I could never even begin to think or muscle my way through. These steps bring solutions in the strangest and most wonderful ways.

In small ways and large, enfold these four steps into the practice of living.

2

"Step 1. Identify what you DON'T want."

This is the easiest step for most of us. We come up with laundry lists of things that annoy, flummox, or grind on us all day long. We mull them over. We attach blame to those lists. We try to think of ways to fix, push, and pull our way to understanding and controlling those lists. We feel out of control, and our list of problems feels like the culprit. It is our list of things standing in the way of our happiness and fulfillment. So, we try to tackle the list head on and wrestle back that control, or we slump in a heap, feeling like we'll never get there. And the only reason we have to do any of this is that we have inexplicably handed control of our lives to our list of Don't Wants. It's like having a free election and unanimously voting in a repressive dictator. How did this happen?

It happened because we never think about this list of Don't Wants as what it is: the biggest gift we can get from ourselves. We think that it controls us, when in fact its true purpose in our lives is to feed us important information. Looked at this way, we take away the power of this list to control our lives.

We must know what we don't want before we can learn what we do. It's a great place to start, so stop treating it like the finish line.

3

"Step 2. From that, identify what you DO want."

Figuring out what you don't want is the easy part. The second step is also simple, but a bit tougher. We rarely let ourselves really want anything. There are plenty of reasons for this: we're afraid if we really want it and we don't get it that we'll be disappointed (or worse), we feel that we don't deserve to want certain things, or we feel like wanting in and of itself is not a worthwhile or meaningful activity.

Again, we have to remember that Wants and Don't Wants, in and of themselves, don't have any moral value. They cannot be bad or wrong, or good or right. They are just Wants—basic, pure paths to feeling. Try as best you can to let go of the thoughts that block you from really wanting anything, or that encourage a kind of feeble wanting of things that aren't really connected to your core self.

Use your long list of Don't Wants to formulate a new parallel list of Wants. Let the two correspond directly for now—don't start a listing of Wants out of the blue—"I want a house, I want a new job, I want, I want." That's a kind of desperate wanting and you might as well throw coins down a well. Use each Don't Want to lead you to a Want that feels right to you.

Just make the list, and do your best to avoid feeling anything about those Wants for now, because that invites your old thinking about wanting.

4

"Step 3. Get into the feeling place of what you want."

This is the step that looks so simple on paper, even a little silly. As if you could hear some kind of rhythm of what you want and just start bobbing your head in time. Or as if you could pretty easily fake it by deciding, "oh yeah, this feels great, I'm really getting into that place," even though you feel like crap. Good luck with that.

This feeling place is hard to talk about and think about because we rarely get a chance to visit it for real. The subject is not taught in school, it's not instilled in us by our parents and mentors, it's not even considered real by most people in the world. This "feeling place" is only ever talked about in its most extreme forms—inspiration, passion, rapture. We leave the "feeling place" to artists, mystics, and spiritual leaders. But we don't have to. It's free to everyone, and there's no special training or education to it that we can't provide for ourselves.

There are all sorts of ways to get into the feeling place of what you want. Your imagination is your best tool, and, if you feel silly using it, you're going to want to get over that starting now. Go slowly—even though we've all felt moments of excited inspiration, it will feel strange to get into that place deliberately. The very consciousness of getting there often can pull us right out of it.

Get used to the idea that you can easily get into the feeling place of just about anything.

5

"Step 4. Expect, listen, and allow it to happen."

Now, most of us can at least sort of figure out the first three steps. They make sense in a sort of "alright, it's crazy, but I'll give it a go" sort of way. And then there's the last one. Our normal pattern is to figure out what we want. Then, if we must, we could try to add step three about feeling something (but we're not sure how to really do that), but, then, for step four, it seems, we'd better get to business, and that (we think) means *doing.* Quick! We've got to make a plan; throw all our mental and physical weight behind it, trying to make that plan a reality; and, sooner or later, it'll all come together. Therein lies the secret of happiness, right? *Wrong.*

This step is the most infuriating one of all. Do all this work to figure out what we want and get into a place where we feel like we might actually get it, and then stop? Just grind to a halt and do nothing? *Yep.* Well, sort of. Expecting takes a leap of faith. Listening is no small task. And allowing is maybe the hardest thing we can ask ourselves to do. But other than that, nothing much is needed.

These three things together can subvert our whole way of being in the world up to this point. They can break the cycle of wanting things we'll never get. They can end the damaging tug-of-war between what we desire and what we deserve. They can clear the way for intuitive, inspired solutions to the worst problems we face.

Shh! Just listen. Listen and expect until you see the beginnings of change.

6

"Don't think your reactions. Feel them."

I can't stress this enough and Lynn Grabhorn couldn't, either: *thoughts* won't do it. Your brain can only get you part way. If you're not feeeeeling it, you might as well forget about it.

Lynn uses the word feeeeeling, adding extra "e's" because she really had to invent a new word, one we don't have in the English language, and that I don't know of in any other language, either. The closest we have is intuition, awareness, instinct, gut. These are all approximations and you know why? Because feeeeeling is beyond word-using intelligence. There are some things that you just can't talk about. This is soul intelligence channeled through the intelligence of a single atom.

Frankly, once you get your brain involved in your reactions, you are (most often) short-circuiting and shutting down that beautiful, pure energy that manifests whatever you want into the world.

Now, I'm not saying that the brain is some enemy—it's an amazingly resourceful part of who we are. It's by far the best tool we have, but we're too busy whacking away at our problems with it to notice. That's why scientists tell us we're only using some puny percentage of our brains: we're using them like blunt instruments, a prehistoric rock tied to a stick. And that's like using a perfectly calibrated telescope to bash a nail into the wall and hang up a picture. Come on.

The brain is whole, and our consciousness is only a small part of it. Don't forget that our own minds can encompass infinite perception (even if not consciously).

7

"We create by feeling, not by thought!"

Feelings are probably the least understood thing about humanity. We know what it's like to have certain feelings, but the color palate is all primary: sad, happy, angry. The few variations on the theme all come out of those basic three, and most of what we do every day, we don't label with any feeling at all. Which, more often than not, means we're walking around in one of those three colors—sad, happy, or angry—all day long with no access to the rainbow we could be experiencing.

Beyond that, we treat feelings as though they are some great, unknowable force. They overtake us; we think that they are a product of forces outside our control. Or, most powerfully, they are the opposite of thoughts and, therefore, are unknowable and impossible to examine except maybe in memoirs years after the fact. But still we're obsessed with how we're feeling, hitching the events of days or years on some vague notion about our inner state.

Feelings are not thoughts, and they are not the opposite of thoughts. Feelings are not about social mores or structures, though it is an age-old pastime to try and squeeze different kinds of experiences into a box labeled "good" or "bad," "grace" or "sin." Feelings are the vibrational core of your body and soul.

I create by feeling and I create my feelings.

8

"What's so new to us is grappling with this seemingly backwards concept that real Life is about feeling first and performing second. That's just utterly backwards to us. Only practice will bring the fruits of that outrageous new concept into being."

We spend most of our lives thinking that consequences are something you get because of something you did—you work really hard so you get a raise, or you slack off and get fired. And the world seems to make sense in this system, except for all the times that you work hard and get fired anyway, or the guy next to you does nothing and is promoted to the top of the heap. Then we say, "life's just not fair sometimes," and we feel we're meant to soldier on as best we can.

But action and reaction, doing something to get something, are all just one way of telling the story. Usually, we watch the big performance of events around us and play our parts in the show, and then wait for the feelings to wash over us. But, what happens if we rearrange things a bit and make the opening number all about feeling? Of course, it's not enough just to feel, but if the feelings are real and specific, and we invest in them, we almost cannot help ourselves playing out the rest of the story to our extreme delight. It's not the narrative we're used to, but why not give it a try?

Instead of thinking, "I gotta do, do, do, and that will make me feel," rewrite your script and say, "I gotta feeling in me that's got a lot of living to do, so let's see how this unfolds."

9

"Didn't you ever feel that there's some secret part of you that knows everything there is to know but just doesn't stick its head out? There is."

The day you call in sick (though you feel okay) and miss the major accident on the freeway. The day you hand in your resignation and a headhunter calls to offer you the job of your dreams. The day you buy a winning lottery ticket (even though you don't believe in buying lottery tickets). Call it psychic powers, serendipity, or sixth sense, or just call it your birthright. Here are five easy ways to encourage that inner you to come on out and share the secrets.

1. *Get jazzed.* No matter where you are, you can usually get excited about some aspect of your situation. If you hate your job, visualize how great things are going to be when you're your own boss.
2. *Dream.* Usually a problem doesn't need an everyday solution. Or even a daytime one. Spend some time writing about what you'd like to attract into your life before you go to sleep, and keep a notebook by the bed to jot down your dreams as soon as you wake up. You might get some helpful messages.
3. *Get physical.* Pretty sure your brain is the smartest thing in your body? Think again. Your body has the answers, and it needs plenty of blood pumping through it to generate results.
4. *Let it go.* Ever notice how you can't find your keys until the moment someone brings you the spare set? Take your focus off something you don't want and onto something you do (even something totally unrelated) and many problems will sort themselves out.
5. *Bless it.* Bless as many rotten conditions as you can think of in your life. Thank them, for without them you'd never know what you don't want.

Quit burning up gas trying to figure everything out; it's time to let your intuition take the wheel.

10

"Knowledge or no, 'getting more out of life' wasn't happening and it was beginning to tick me off. Something was missing, and I flat-out couldn't put my finger on it."

How often do we feel this? Nothing's wrong, per se, but it doesn't seem like enough is really right, either. Whole generations of Americans have grown up in this feeling to a greater or lesser degree, and many of us just take it for granted, as though feeling unfulfilled, unchallenged, and unexcited were somehow the true expression of who we are. Or sometimes this feeling coincides with a major life change—the death of a family member, or retirement, or a new baby. In this case, we blame the event itself and tend to disregard the fact that it's not our circumstances that create our feelings, it's the other way around.

I, for one, have always tried to assail this feeling in one of two ways: staying in the house all day reading until my eyes hurt or flailing myself into action that may or may not be appropriate or helpful (usually *not*). By reading, I figure, I can get smart enough to push through my malaise. By doing something (anything!), I think I can at least shove the boringness out of my life, but I'm rarely thrilled with the results of my fits and starts of uninspired action.

There is a third option, one so simple, it is easily overlooked; so radical, it seems impossible: learn to control how you are vibrating energy. All life is energy; all life is vibration. There is more to get out of life, and the possibilities are infinite. You are not the sum of your grievances and dissatisfactions, there are more important things to play at and do, so it's time to get started.

Are you ready to find the missing piece?

11

"How do we do it? Don't laugh; it all comes from . . . *how we're vibrating!*"

When we think about a Want, we often take a little side trip by asking the question *How?* "How is this going to happen?"

"How will I ever manage to accomplish this?"

"How should I get started and how will it all turn out?"

How is a trick question, a meandering path that will dump us a long way from our original Want. Surely to get anything done we must think about what to do and how to do it, right? Wrong. *How* is a question for the history books, it's a tool of hindsight masquerading as a tool of preparation.

We employ *How* before the fact only when we're trying to cheat at the game, count the cards, predict the outcome. But as a means to an end, *How* will cheat us every time. We open up our valve to a clear Want, we are happily buzzing along thinking about the great things that are on their way, and then blam! Things slam to a halt. Go back to the source of those screeching brakes, and you'll probably find a *How* lingering there in the shadows.

You don't have to solve the issues on your way to the fulfillment of a Want. You could not guess or divine the exact steps that will get you from point A to point B and what will happen along the way. So stop trying. Just get back to the place or original desire and get buzzing about it again. And don't worry, the *How* detour won't set you back far—when you get back on track, you'll probably be even further invested in your goal with no time lost, so don't beat yourself up about it.

When *How* leads us astray, all we have to do is remember: those aren't our problems to solve.

12

"You are the ongoing energy of Life scampering around down here right now on this particular playground. You are the pure positive energy of well-being, and *you cannot kill energy!*"

"Energy. Well-being. What, who, me? Nah, I'm just ground down and tired. I haven't scampered in what feels like a century." Now, there is an attitude. That and a blanket to pull over your head will buy you a bucket of misery. What does it take for us to look at life as a playground rather than a purgatory of work, tired, work, grief, tired some more?

Really, all it takes is one simple little thing—a change of heart.

It takes looking around to find the swing, the merry-go-round, the slide of this particular playground. (Sure, we may get a scraped knee now and then if we're having fun. But we're still having fun.) It takes paying attention and participating. Reaching out to others with something as simple as a smile—a little piece of positive energy shared.

"Energy? What? Who, me?" Well, yes. I find if and when I stop to think about it, when I stop to count the positives and smile when I can, even though I know there are major negatives "out there"—poverty, war, financial worries—I can visualize the positive, pure energy in my own heart. I can send it out to others, get it back, and watch it romp.

Take five minutes to play in the playground of your heart today—a quiet meditation, a walk, whatever feeds you.

13

"The reality—the *real* reality—is that we are already worthy, there is no test to pass."

You are complete—nothing less than a whole being. Your being-ness is above and beyond body, ability, intellect, social or economic position. The fact of your being makes you inherently whole, since all you have to do to be in a state of being is to exist here on this planet, which you're doing very well right this moment.

We spend so much time wanting to be different, deriding or regretting what we are or have been, feeling hopeless, all because we've tied our value to our circumstances and our attributes, and that's not really who we are. Our ideas about identity may be wrapped up in the careers we've chosen, our families, our ages, but none of those things form the cores of our being.

Sure, we live here on this plane in this life story, and there are lots of "rules" that govern our lives. There are lots of ideas that feel very real because they affect us every day—social mores, religious teachings, ideas about success and failure. We do inevitably pay a good deal of attention to these rules and live by them. In doing so, we sometimes forget that some rules are helping us and some are pulling us apart, and we don't have to let them. Rules are made to be broken, so which ones are you going to break today? Which ones are you going to break through, not just for the sake of doing it, not to take advantage of or hurt someone else, but to give yourself the gift of a true *breakthrough?*

There is no test to pass, the point at which you can be deemed to have earned your worthiness, sacredness, or joy—you are already at that place now.

14

> "Think of asking and receiving as the same thing. If you say, 'Throw me the ball,' you have already affirmed you are ready to receive it."

I am ready to catch what comes my way, as soon as I ask for it. This is a simple affirmation and meditation that can make a huge change in your life. So often when you ask for things, when you express a Want, you then go on to subvert or undermine it. Guilt or blame comes into the equation. Subconsciously, you think you're not deserving of the receiving Want you ask for, and that feeling derails the whole process.

Think of watching a really fast volleyball game. People play certain positions, and they are meant to hit the ball in their territory. But, it doesn't always work that way. And, since a player can only touch the ball once, if it doesn't go back over the net on the first hit, another player has to jump in. Usually they call out some sort of signal, "Got it," or, "It's mine."

So when I'm asking the universe for something, what kind of signal can I call out? What can I do to let myself feel the asking and feel the receiving? Visualize the receiving, act "as if," ask with a clear heart, stay in tune with my Guidance—and then asking and receiving become one flowing motion.

My Want is mine only if I ask for it *and* receive it.

15

"Engaging (which is Inspired Action) breaks old patterning. Engaging spawns the joy and excitement necessary to magnetize . . . Engaging keeps your mind off your Don't Want. Engaging in some way, every day, is absolutely mandatory for manifestation!"

So much of what we're talking about has to do with our inner life—taking the focus off your Don't Want, and then flowing some feel good energy to your Want. So you get into that feeeeeling place, and you're managing to stay out of your own way, and expecting it to come, and all the rest of it. Now what? Engage! Engaging is all about making it physical. You've laid the groundwork, and now it's time to put things into motion.

Why engage? Because while it's true that you create through the flow of your energy, that doesn't mean that you can sit back and leave it to the universe with no action on your part. That sitting back would be curtailing your energy and action, and pulling it away from your desires. No, when you get a sign, or a feeling, or an inspiration, you *must* pick it up and follow it where it leads you, throwing the full force of your intelligence and physical strength behind it.

This doesn't mean you have to move mountains tomorrow. Keep your response in line with and in proportion to what the universe sends you. You don't have to force anything. Your physical action one day may be to write a letter, the next day to start your training to run a marathon.

Now is the time to go into action! I will engage whatever in me is called upon to act.

16

"Having desires—wanting—is no more a sin than breathing. Never again think you have to justify your Wants. Just don't! You cannot be justifying, defending, or rationalizing—which is all negative flowing—and remain connected to your core energy."

How many times a day do you judge yourself worthy, or, more likely, *unworthy?* Whether it comes from our upbringing, religious background, or the images and stories around us, we are flooded with mixed messages about who deserves what. We judge ourselves and others against a standard of qualities and attributes that ought to be upheld before we get this outcome or that reward. *I won't be loved if I'm not good looking. I must be sweet and personable in order to be liked. I have to be tough to keep danger at bay. Good things come to those who wait.*

Sometimes, we get what we feel we deserve, and then the system seems to work okay. Yet if we feel we live up to the standards we've set for ourselves but still don't get what we want, we feel slighted, get defensive, and spin out negativity, which we all know is not going to lead us anywhere.

Here's the answer: desire without judgment. Not judging yourself or anyone else; give it a go and see how you feel. You'll save a lot of time and energy, and, believe it or not, you're going to see results as the people around you become more comfortable, more productive, and more willing participants in life. Let go of what you feel you *should* do or *should* be, and tap into the energy source of your own powerful barometer. If you trust in and listen to your own energy source, and not some useless, outdated moral code, your true feelings cannot lead you astray.

Tune in to your own sense of what's right for you by tossing the judgments and nixing the guilt.

17

"Replace your 'things to do' list with a 'things to feel' list."

I keep a to-do list on my computer so that I can constantly update it, removing things and replacing them with new things. That way, I don't have to rewrite the list over and over, and waste time that could be used getting things done. But that also means I never get the satisfaction of completing the whole list and tossing that piece of paper into the recycling bin.

But what would happen if I dropped that file into the trash can on my desktop and then emptied it, losing that unfinished list forever? Frankly, I would panic. I'm not quite ready for that yet. In the meantime, I could definitely start a new, parallel list—a "things to feel" list. Because, without the feelings in place, I can plod away forever on my things to do and never make much progress.

So here's the start of my Things to Feel list: passion, excitement, energized, organized, hopeful, unstoppable. If I can check off even three of those in any given day, I think I'll be way ahead of the game, and I could probably check off a ton of stuff on my to-do list through the inspired action that ensues. Maybe I'll even consider throwing that list away altogether, and do the actions as they come to me, and trust that everything will get done through feeeeeling.

Today I will trust that I can do what needs doing by focusing on how I'm feeling.

18

"Don't ever forget, you are not Joe or Sally, you are not a carpenter or secretary, you are a force of Life. Act like it! Become it!"

You are not your name, date of birth, your social security number. The value of your *youness* is entirely unconnected to your credit score, your net worth, or even to the number of people who love and care about you. You need not be defined by your social status or your job. You cannot list your life force on a resume, you cannot measure your energy flow with a thermometer or arm cuff.

We think that society runs better if we can categorize ourselves into small enough boxes that we can be organized, put away, and expected to do what we are told. But we all know what it feels like to be labeled into a kind of oblivion. We become invisible to others and shut down to ourselves.

There's nothing wrong with your name, or your occupation, or your family status. Those things are all part of you in some way, even more so if they reflect something about your core values. But never forget that you are a powerful life force, a creator, a being that goes far beyond the current moment, into the past and future, far beyond the physical space you take up.

Your life force can break any societal mold. You're here to be you, not to be shoved into categories!

19

"Don't Wants are how we view the world, and they feel no different than what we think life is."

Get ready for the single biggest block you've ever faced, the massive thing that shuts down almost every joyous inspiration we could ever have: reality. Well, not even *real* reality. It's your perceived reality, and it's your own bit of real estate in the worldwide landmass of perceptions about what exists and what is true.

The disconnect between us and our Wants can almost always be traced back to a fundamental, almost inescapable belief that *this is the way things are.* However it got into us, that belief informs almost everything about our lives, for better or worse. But interestingly almost every one of the most admired and accomplished people in history figured out at some point, usually early on, that they had to forge an utterly new thought: *things can no longer be as they have been.* This feeling would be impotent if it weren't for the corollary: *I am the one to change those things that must change.*

We surround ourselves with a tornado of Don't Wants and keep them swirling around us all the time, until we feel that this is the way things have always been. This is our normal environment, so ingrained that we call it "reality." Exploration of Wants and learning how to harness our powers to get them are the change we have been seeking.

Your true reality is yours to make, but you are the only one who can say, "I am the one to change."

20

"Never had it entered my head that it was possible to live life without some degree of concern, not to mention full-blown stress or outright panic."

There's a wonderful bit in *Alice in Wonderland,* where the Queen of Hearts says she believes seven impossible things every morning before breakfast. Since the Queen of Hearts is a drama queen given to shouting "Off with her head!" one of those seven is probably NOT that it's possible to live a panic-free life. Too bad for her.

Our culture—not to mention our economy—is built on concern, fear, and panic. Will you get rid of bad breath? Will you be ready for the coming earthquake, flood, or economic downturn? Will we be safe from terrorist attack? Will we get stuck in traffic? Will our dandruff show? Stress, hypertension, overweight, cholesterol. Phew, there's a very long list of things to get stressed out about. They're on TV commercials every day—just in case we were inclined to not turn our attention toward them.

So, how do we go about letting the message enter our heads that despite the existence of all these things and more and ones we haven't even heard of yet—we don't have to get our knickers in a twist? One way is to think about the odds of any or all of that disaster befalling us. Another is to think about relative worth. Simple comparisons. Is being late for work the end of the world? No. And yet another is to let the realization in—when bad things happen (and they will), I'm going to be more prepared to deal with them if I'm not stressed out.

In the meantime, take time to smell the flowers.

21

"We are what we look outside ourselves to find. We are the love we seek, the joy for which we yearn, the fervor of life we think we have lost. Our longing is but the pressing call of our soul to wake up, and to remember. This, then, is our grand journey home."

If you're anything like me, you're pretty sure that you need something to drop out of the sky for things in your life to *really* change. You're waiting patiently for an epiphany you're almost certain will never happen, and, in the meantime, you're just trying to make do with whatever cards you've been dealt.

While you wait for a life change to drop on your head, you hear a steady, low, repetitive noise. It's your internal alarm clock, and it's coming from very deep inside you. You hit Snooze and go back to waiting. It rings, you hit Snooze, go back to waiting. Again it rings, you hit Snooze, go back to waiting, this time with some anxiety—maybe some bitterness—*"where is it already?"*

We can't see it because we are convinced it's coming from somewhere outside us, and this conviction comes from our feeling that we are somehow not up to the task that our own souls require of us, and nothing could be further from the truth. What a comfort it is to learn that your own longing (which feels like a problem) is the wake-up call you've been waiting for (the first step to a solution).

Let the alarm ring. Don't reset it; don't turn it off.

22

"We cannot find the light until we acknowledge the darkness. This is called owning!"

So many of my plans for a new way of being have failed miserably I can't even count them. When I want a change, I want it wholesale—no partway shimmying around it—and I've often convinced myself that the only way to do that is to cut ties with whatever I hate about my "old life" and embark with a clean slate on a new one. Of course, this is pretty much impossible (at least overnight) and so I work myself up into a frenzy to convince myself that I'm, in fact, on the right path and I've suddenly found the light.

And then a few weeks or months later, it comes crashing down, or I wake up and go, "What was I thinking?" Most often this is because I have skipped a crucial step: the one where I embrace whatever it is that I feel like I have to change so drastically.

That embracing, as Lynn says, is owning. "Owning is: Taking hold of your past, and owning it all. Welcoming your past, and owning it all knowing no one's responsible but you. Getting rid of 'If Onlys.' Knowing you can create it any old way you want it. Stopping stuffing."

If we never really take the time and energy to dive into the feelings of the past, we can never create a future that is free of those horrible old patterns and we will be destined to rehearse and repeat them forever.

The darkness of what you hate about yourself, your past, or your current situation is the best key to a future free from that hate.

23

"Which is why it feels so good to feel good. *You're vibrating closer to your real self.* You and your nonphysical self are in sync."

I can't think of a single religious or cultural tradition that equates the mind and the soul. The mind is physical and of the body; if not totally contained in the brain, then, at least, strongly linked to it. The soul seems to reside in the body in a temporal sort of way, and its energy extends beyond the here and now, as well as backward and forward in time. Many of us feel more comfortable in the realm of the mind—where we are linked to this physical, provable world. Many of us try to ignore or suppress our nonphysical selves because we don't understand something we can't see or analyze.

When you are in a feeeeling place and feeling good, "you're vibrating closer to your real self." That real self is your mind and soul in harmony and on the same path. Though this feeling is usually pretty foreign to us (because we avoid it so often), it can be pure bliss while it lasts, and we ought to grab every chance we can to experience it.

Getting these two in sync will solve a huge number of the problems in your life, without you having to fret or plan or push. Why? Because when your mind and soul are aligned, your energy can flow purely and forcefully out of you. When your mind and your soul are in conflict, your energy is trapped, bouncing between the two and not getting much accomplished in all the confusion. But put those two together, and you will be amazed as the results seem to arrange themselves.

Are you ruled by your mind or your soul? Get out of your own way by aligning the two, and prepare to be amazed.

24

"When we're not connected to our Guidance, we have no real sense of what we're doing or where we're going. So we become conformists (better known as sheep). We go along with the crowd, and believe in our limitedness."

Imagine a roomful of people with a project in mind. Now imagine there is one "leader" and he is going to tell them how the project will be done. The project will start at a certain time every day. One person will be responsible for opening up the room. She will have to be there before the others. She gets her assignment. The others will all arrive at the same time, pick up their pencils, and go to work. They will take a break at the same time, and they will go home at the same time. At the end of three months, if they accomplish their six square inches every single day, they will have a huge drawing ready to be painted. Sounds like an inspiring way to make art, doesn't it? Or, as we used to say in middle school, NOT!

I'm not here to say that doing art or any other purposeful, inspired work doesn't need a lot of thought and planning. It does. If it's being done by a group, it may even need a leader. But it doesn't benefit from a lock-step, top-down, follow-the-rules sort of person. And we, individually, don't benefit by treating ourselves as if we're both leader and follower to rote rules we think someone would like us to follow.

So, take a minute. Put down your pencil. Step out of the sheep's holding pen, aka office, or wherever it is that's stifling you, and connect to what you're doing and why you're doing it. Tune in. How does your body feel about what you're doing and how you're doing it? What's your state of mind? Where do you want to go next?

My Guidance is always there, ready to listen, chat, offer pointers.

25

"Now, granted, you may feel a little silly at first, chatting out loud with a pretend person—or yourself—about the fantasy you're living, but that's a small price to pay for the walloping dividends."

We knew how to do this when we were children. A child who has an active fantasy life and lots of imaginary friends to talk things over with, to get new ideas from, and to help comfort him worries parents and other adults. They go to great lengths to remind the child that his friend isn't "real." Or that her extra place at the dinner table isn't really necessary. They imagine the child is unhappy. Maybe they're not doing a good enough job. Maybe the child will grow up not knowing the difference between fact and fiction. Maybe the child won't be able to make real friends. Or will end up unable to hold a job. Sheesh! Talk about borrowing trouble, as my grandma used to say.

I think the child experts are pretty clear on this—children should be allowed their imaginary friends. They learn things from them—about sharing, solving problems verbally, dealing with their fears, expressing their wishes. Talking out loud to a pretend person can be good for kids and good for adults, too.

So, make like a child. Get a cup of tea—or even two. Pick a time when you're not likely to be interrupted. Sit down in a cozy chair and tell the other person about your life. Go ahead and get creative. This is your time and place to explore your wants and dreams and build the future you never imagined you could have, starting in the right here and now.

You've always got a friend to talk things over with.

26

> "Intending is sort of a combination of 'I want' and 'I expect.' And a good place to start is to be intending for *small things* throughout the day."

The beauty of this new practice, this new idea of an open valve, is that you don't have to do it all at once. You only have to open that valve a tiny crack, to let the energy flow a little more, one thing at a time, to feel things starting to change.

The easiest way to do that is through daily practice. Daily intending for small, everyday ways does three things:

Gets you into the habit—every little bit you open your valve counts, and a moment of clear energy flow can reverse a week of cruddy blockage.

Opens your energetic pathways for bigger things—big wants need open channels to flow into your life, and by intending for little things throughout the day, you're opening up the causeways.

Provides some ready evidence—you'll be energized as you notice that intending works, and often works fast.

You can intend for things that don't matter much, or things that you care very deeply about. You can intend to have a productive meeting. You can intend to get where you're going on time and feeling good. You can intend for yourself or for someone else, or for even bigger things: the energy crisis solved, healthy children worldwide.

Because intending combines "I want" and "I expect," you can jump over some of the feeling of lack that can creep up when you start to think about something you want. "I expect" helps you remember that everything you need is here right now or on its way soon.

Intending throughout the day for small things will pave the way for bigger ones.

27

"Pat yourself on the back for every perceived obstacle you've created. Without them, you cannot know what you want."

We've all been there—when you work on something so hard for so long, you feel like you're at the top of your game, but the end result slips out of your grasp at the critical moment, again and again.

I've watched so many athletes get into this space. Maybe they've had a lot of early success and then it tapers off. They struggle to get the kind of results that once came easily, and they pour everything they have into getting those results. They are clearly at the top of the heap, in good shape, working hard, wanting it badly, and still not quite getting there. For someone who's been at the top and then faltered, the threat of failure is very real, and very scary. So, they've got a huge Want (continuing success, breaking through the barriers of their own and others' abilities) combined with some pretty major Don't Wants (never living up to their potential, getting injured, failing utterly). The Want may be huge, well articulated, invested in, but the Don't Wants are just as big, so things grind to a halt and all the practice and training in the world won't change a thing.

In contrast, a very little Want can get some incredible results because it often has very few Don't Wants attached to it—or none at all—and the result of just a little bit of action toward that tiny Want can yield a big surprise and some major success. You know this phenomenon better by the name Beginner's Luck: you pick up a bowling ball for the first time, you have a sense of the rules but know nothing about the possible pitfalls or mistakes, so once you get the hang of throwing the thing, you bowl strike after strike. You spent no time caring about the result, and that paid dividends. The next time you play, it's a miserable disaster, and it only gets worse as you frantically try to get back to the place of ease of that first time. Oh, well, you think, it was just beginner's luck. But, no—it was just a clear, clean path to a desire, and the energy swooshed right into the right place at the right time.

Harness the power of beginner's luck by letting go of the result and clearing a path for that wonderful swoosh.

28

"Use everything you know to flip-switch out of negative focus into any kind of warm fuzzy."

How many times a day do you catch yourself in the act of doing something you'd rather not be doing, and, while you're still in the middle of the act, you think to yourself, "I have to stop! I can't do this anymore! Stop!" Newsflash. You cannot stop smoking. You cannot stop overeating. You cannot stop gambling. Sure, you look around and there are all sorts of people who used to smoke, or gamble, or whatever it is, and now they don't. They just stopped doing whatever they were doing wrong, didn't they? They must have finally found the right tone to yell at themselves that made it impossible to go on. No, they didn't stop doing anything. They started.

The reason you can't stop anything: telling yourself to stop comes from a Don't Want. And thank you very much indeed for Don't Wants, because without them, we'd never be able to figure out what we do Want. Telling ourselves to stop and keeping our focus on that command sticks us in the mud of our Don't Wants, and then we never think to go on to the next stop—figuring out what we Want!

This is when we want to use something called "flip-switching." This is an automatic, easy-peasy, and preset topic that you can go to whenever you catch yourself thinking about a nasty problem, or trying to stop doing something. You can pick one for the day, the week, or the month. You must pick something about yourself that you love and appreciate. And then you have to really feel the gratitude and love pouring about that thing, whenever you flip the switch. You don't have to worry about putting the brakes on any other thoughts, because if you're really doing it, this will take quite a lot of your energy—to find a list of things you can really appreciate about yourself and really funnel your energy and love through those things.

Today is the first day of the rest of my starts.

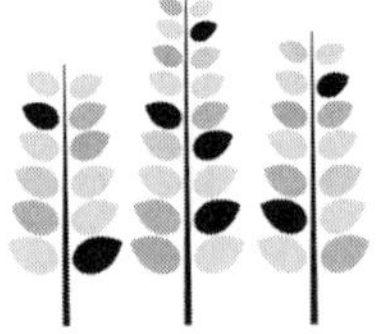

29

"Granted, we'll probably never stop having negative reactions, because contrast is what being physical is all about."

So, why do we even have the word STOP in all our languages if there's no such thing? If I can't stop doing anything, only work to start something else, what's the purpose?

There's a reason that stop signs are big and red. The word or the thought STOP can and should be a jolt of awakening, a warning of danger ahead, or a slap in the face when you're in hysterics. But that's it. Stop is just a momentary, powerful signal for change—it can never be the process of change itself.

Feel free to give yourself this signal. Do it physically if you have to. I made a commitment once that every time I thought about a particular problem, in this case, anxiety about a family relationship, I would jump up and down three times. I made a very strict rule for myself, and I had to make it physical 'cause I knew that my little brain would have to be jolted out of the habit. Believe me, it made for a couple of quite embarrassing moments as I jumped up and down on the train in the morning, or in line at the supermarket, or waiting to use the restroom (that was the worst). Jump, jump, jump was my signal that told me I needed to start down another path, to find the green light and get going.

Make a signal you can't ignore that says STOP! And then move on immediately to another topic, another thought, another task.

30

"Whenever you're feeling less than good, stop, regain your balance, and find a way to feel a little better, then a little better, then still a little better. Every Feel Better is a raise in vibration."

One of the reasons I get blocked after that initial "STOP" jolt is that I think that whatever I do or think about next has to be in equal proportion to the problem. That is, if my finances are a wreck and I just bounced a check, I have to come up with something to think about that will get me X number of dollars to cover that check and the fee right away. Not so.

You can take tiny, incremental steps to your new path—they can be totally out of proportion to the problem at hand; as long as you're doing *something,* the universe will respond. If you don't like where you're living and you want a new home, you might get in that feeling place and find yourself taking a walk in a neighborhood you love, just feeling great being there. And that is working toward your goal of a new place, even though a walk may seem to have little to do with the process of finding a new home, putting down deposits or down payments, and moving in.

Taking small, focused action on a Want will serve you better every time than action that is disorganized, overreaching, or messy. Even if it doesn't feel like you're "getting something done" about your problem, just breathe and know that you don't have to get anything done. The doing will come to you through the universe. And we are meant to be in a state of well-being—all of us; it is our true natural state. So, it's actually far easier to move toward that state than it is to move away from it, which is why the proportion doesn't matter so much. It takes a lot of pull and heft to get away from feeling good (we're just so used to it that it's become a comfortable habit).

If we stop discounting it, the incredible power of baby steps will chip away at even the biggest monster problems.

31

"Obviously, none of us are about to stop and scrutinize every thought we have to see if the fool thing is a Want or a Don't Want. We'd be loony in five minutes."

You know the feeling—after you've put your foot in your mouth at a party, or said something you regret that hurt a friend's feelings—the episode plays on repeat in your head for the next couple of hours. Then you think it's gone and go to sleep, only to have it resurface in your dreams. There are certain situations or problems that lend themselves to this kind of obsessive behavior, and, oddly, the simple action of becoming conscious of your everyday thoughts is one of those things, sometimes creating even more worry and obsession, even if the whole point of looking at your thoughts was to set you free from them in the first place.

I catch myself doing this all the time. I think of a problem I'm having and all sorts of little thoughts around it come bubbling to the surface, and I start trying to pop them, evaluating each thought on the merits of its truth and whether it comes from a place of lack or not. I pore over my negativity like a fortuneteller looking at tea leaves, my nose stuck so far down in that cup, I wouldn't know my answer if it were poured over my head, scalding me.

Then, I have to remember there are *two parts* to Lynn's instruction about Don't Wants: distinguish a Want from a Don't Want (and this can be an instinctual, momentary decision—you're usually right) and *then* the all important second part: flip your attention to something else. Do it however you can, and do it immediately. So, if you're having a problem, instead of trying to get to the root of it by focusing on it, try flipping to something totally different. It can be a preset topic for the day (something about yourself you're grateful for) or just a moment of flowing positive energy somewhere—anywhere.

No point in going loony when you can flip your attention to something else—anything else—and see results right away.

32

"Oh, sure, more times than not we're probably justified in our accusations, but so what! There's not an ounce of well-being that can squeak through the low, thick vibration of blame, whether it's justified or not."

Someone has slighted you, offended you, neglected you, or taken advantage of you. You tell them off and you do it well, adding a nice helping of blame on the other person and their feelings, thoughts, and choices.

Bravo! You win; you are right. You get the gold star. You feel so much better. You've made your case and you're absolutely correct, and justice and well-being ought to rain down from the heavens on your head. Things are going to change now that you've righted all the wrongs. Is that really what happens next after that kind of argument? Not so much. I can hear the whining now, and it doesn't become you. This is one of the absolutely hardest things to work on for ourselves, and it is one of the most essential: *drop the blame.*

Do you have to give in and let people walk all over you? No. Do you have to see the other guy's point of view? No. Do you have to lose sight of the truth? No. Do you have to make nice? No.

All you have to do is take your focus off whatever it is that you had to get so riled up about in the first place. You don't have to fix it, or change it, or prove that you are right. It feels good to be right, and then what? What is that rightness getting you besides a closed valve for everyone involved?

Righteous blame is happy to plunk down and spread out, blocking the solution to your problem (among other things).

33

"Even a little bit of forgiving at a time will work, then a little more, and a little more if that's the only way you can do it. But one thing's for sure: unless you want more of the same, forgiving ultimately means forgetting!"

Rome wasn't built in a day. Anything worth doing is worth doing well, and sometimes that takes time. The fable of the tortoise and the hare comes to mind—slow and steady wins the race. And maybe even more to the point, in a certain way, the grasshopper and the ants. The ants built up their store of food all through the summer, and when winter blew in they were snug and warm and fed. The grasshopper, of course, wasn't.

So, too, with forgiveness: we can build up to it—a bit at a time—starting with small things and moving on to large ones. Yet there's one thing that, as a child, when I first heard the stories of the tortoise and the hare and the grasshopper and the ants, offended me. I was way too young to think (or know or articulate) I was being told these stories so I'd conform to the rules. But I did think about what the hare saw on his deviations from the track—must have been interesting. And all the fun the grasshopper had while he wasn't storing away food for the winter. I think what I saw was that the hare and the grasshopper both showed flair and creativity. They seemed more fun. In my adulthood, I'm just contrary enough to say that the grasshopper was the hero—he lived in the moment, didn't try to control, and I'm pretty sure didn't hold on to blame.

What this has to do with accumulating forgiveness is exactly that. Yes, little by little, prudently doing something may be a good idea. But, at some point, we need to show some spunk, forget the rule of little by little, and just forget the whole blooming thing. The grasshopper would.

What am I ready to forget as if it never happened?

34

"Don't wait to feel good before you turn it on. Turn on all day long. Make it a habit. Buzz for no other reason than to keep your frequencies up, your valve open, and your resistance down to high-frequency energy."

"It's a long time to wait," is something my three-year-old son is fond of saying, about everything from how long it takes for an ice cream cone to be scooped to how long it will be before he sees his grandma for her next visit. Waiting is a disappointment and impatience is unavoidable. Waiting is a kind of resistance to what we are waiting for—because it is flowing energy into how long it will be before we are fulfilled, and reinforcing our current situation of *not having* whatever it is we're after.

Allowing our wants to happen goes far beyond sitting around and waiting. Allowing is a positive force. We make room in our lives for what is desired, we prepare ourselves with the knowledge that it is on its way, and we keep our energy flowing.

Allowing things to happen also takes the keen ability to sniff out what is inside us that might be setting up roadblocks to the desired outcome. Are we fearful? Nervous? Anxious? Those things are all speed bumps on the smooth delivery road that allowing can lay out for us.

Finally, allowing encourages the kind of active, restful expectation we've already talked about. We don't have to do anything *but* allow, and we will get strong signals about what action is needed, if any. And then that action can come from an inspired, free place, as opposed to something that is forced and rushed, which won't get us anywhere.

In all days, in all ways, I allow.

35

"Prepaving is simply sending your energy ahead of you, programmed with the frequency of your desire."

Imagine. Envision. Visualize. Say it out loud. Simply see. Close your eyes. Take a few deep breaths. Send energy to what the object of your desire is. Maybe it's finishing a project successfully. At the beginning of each work session, take one minute to do this. See if it makes a difference in the way things go together. Don't take my word for it, go ahead, try it.

Athletes know this works. They've been doing it for decades. There's a lot of new research in various fields—biology, physics, metaphysics, psychology—about why and how we can change our behaviors, how we can overcome addictions, how we can change our long-held beliefs about ourselves, how we can learn new skills, with the help of various techniques that incorporate our bodies, brains, and minds.

The people who created the Findhorn Community in Scotland famously sent energy to plants and grew huge luscious vegetables in a climate and under conditions in which they were not supposed to grow. (If you want to know more about how this works, you might look up a book by David Spangler, *The Laws of Manifestation.*) Programming desire doesn't mean anything fancy—you don't have to know any kind of technical language nor do you have to be esoterically adept.

All you have to do is take time to send energy to the place or person you want to be—and don't be surprised if the results aren't exactly as you imagine them. The universe often has a better idea.

36

"But in tense situations, you can prepave to create an atmosphere of trust and openness which will spawn congeniality."

My mom has a few stories that are pivotal to her business life. As a young woman, she worked in a small Midwestern outpost of a huge media conglomerate. Computers were just coming into usage, and they sent two guys out from New York to "help" my mom set up the system she needed for her marketing job. Problem is, these guys were there to tell her what she needed. When she tried to tell them what she thought she needed, they simply talked faster and louder, telling her what she really needed and why she couldn't have what she thought she wanted. The atmosphere was not one of trust and openness, as you can imagine.

As she tells the story, she hit on the technique that finally defused the situation, out of frustration. She couldn't out shout them, so she decided to talk more softly. The idea just popped into her head. One of the guys leaned forward, seeming to want to hear her. She saw that and talked more softly. Soon she was nearly whispering. And she had the attention of the room. The meeting proceeded. The techies learned something about marketing and my mom learned something about the kinds of reports computers could generate, and they got some work done. All for a little whispering.

My mom's prepaving was done on the fly and in the midst of an already tense situation. She remembered that dramatic turnaround, though, and eventually began to use the memory to send "whispers" ahead of her into tense meetings.

Prepaving works when we remember to do it.

37

"No matter how unyielding conditions appear to be, you can always flow Feel Good—even Feel *Better*—energy around them to change them. If you can know that in the deepest part of your being, the rest of this deliberate creation business will be a breeze."

If unyielding conditions never yielded, the word "miracle" would not be in our language. If impossible were the only choice, there would be no need to keep records or write history books, because time would be an uninterrupted repetition of sameness.

Keep this in mind as you try to look at a tough situation. I know how it goes, you call up all the information you have about an issue or a problem, you sift it through in your mind again and again, you hash it out in conversations with friends and adversaries. You turn the thing over in your mind some more, looking for the right mix of perspective and innovation that will break it open and bring about change.

Having gone through those motions once or a hundred times, you begin to lose faith. You begin to believe what others are telling you—that things are not going to change, that there may not be a solution, that you can't make lemonade out of lemons. And when you accept that, you start to die. You thought time was the only thing that made people get old? Loss of hope will do it faster than any hourglass.

No condition is set in stone, no situation is permanent, no problem is insurmountable.

38

"Sure, I will focus negatively, but only for a brief time—a few moments, a couple of hours, sometimes even a day or two if I really want to feel like old times."

Wallow. Okay, take the time you need. Woe is me, things are bad, they're getting worse, the country is going to hell in a handbasket. Did that make you feel any better?

I didn't think so. Yet we all do it, and maybe there is a hidden benefit in indulging ourselves in the feeling of all that's wrong.

It's almost as if our mind has a mind of its own. As soon as we've done any work on opening our valve and focusing on the positive, that's where our mind likes to be. It feels better, for heaven's sake. Yet sometimes we get complacent. We forget to focus on the positive. We forget to send and receive positive energy. And, when we're not consciously paying attention, we flip back to negative. But then, after a pretty short time, our mind says, "Wait a minute here. I like that other positive stuff better." See? It has a mind of its own.

Given the choice between positive and negative, I choose positive, again and again.

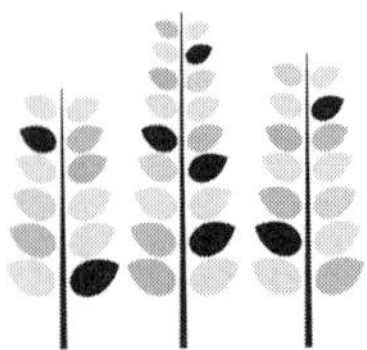

39

"[When something's bothering you] . . . if you'll take just three minutes a day to talk it out and talk it down, talk it out and talk it down, talk it out and talk it down, most of that fear will dissipate within thirty days, along with the unconscious resistance that's been blocking your Want."

Something's bugging you. You may not even be sure what it is, exactly. You don't feel right, your sleeping is off, your eating habits have changed. You think you're flowing energy to the right places, but you can't shake this feeling.

As you learn to direct your energy, there will be times that the very fact of the change in your thinking and feeling jostles things around in a way that brings some old belief or habit to the surface. Suddenly you can't shake that funny feeling, and it's dragging you down. Maybe it's something you thought you had dealt with long ago. Ask yourself *"What's bothering me?"* and talk about it, out loud, until you uncover the source.

Then it's time to reclaim the time it's taking in your life. The problem with a nagging feeling is that it saps your energy, cropping up throughout the day and sneaking up on you when you don't need or want the thought. So give it some rules, make a parameter. Tell that nagging old thing that it can have a few minutes every day, and, during those minutes, you can talk it out and talk it down, very gently reminding yourself that it's going to be okay and that everything is going to turn out well. When you give the fear that kind of structured focus, you release the power it has to sneak up on you, and, within a month, you'll find that thinking about it doesn't draw you in—that the feeling in the pit of your stomach is gone, and you can truly let it go.

Take the time it takes to brush your teeth every day to talk it out and talk it down.

40

"Pulling in a higher frequency is sort of like aiming a hose at a muddy old sidewalk. The heavy stream of water squirts away the mud to reveal some nasty cracks in the walkway. If you're not careful as you step on the sidewalk now, you might trip over one of those long-hidden cracks."

A friend and I were talking about her experience with trying to open up her energy to higher frequencies. She was initially inspired by the ideas she came across, immediately making some simple changes, and she noticed a difference right away. This encouraged her and she delved a bit deeper. Then she hit a wall, and hard. Out of nowhere, she said she felt shaky, had terrible bouts of paranoia that kept her inside her house, and generally fell apart. She got a chronic sinus infection that stayed with her for almost a year. She would come to my house and lie on the floor, asking, "What is wrong with me? Am I ever going to get better?"

All I could tell her was what I knew instinctually was true—this is a good thing. It feels like a bad thing but it's a really, really good thing. Or I'd try to be more specific and say I know you're going to get better because this is all stuff just working its way out of your system.

Nobody wants to live on that muddy sidewalk their whole life. The cracks underneath the mud are those old habits, the really strong ones we may be only barely conscious of: our feelings of inadequacy or a useless moral code. We've smoothed mud over them—which makes it feel like we're on pretty steady ground. Nothing can be too bad if it's an even surface, right? Then as we aim that powerful hose of fresh, clean water on some of the negative mud we've been slinging, the cracks come through big time, making our path bumpier and uglier than we'd led ourselves to believe it was. Then doubt sets in—what if this wasn't such a good idea? Before all this, I was miserable but at least I was functional. Now I'm not even sure I can do my daily routine without tripping over some old belief and falling flat on my face.

Hang in there and talk yourself down, a few minutes a day; remind yourself over and over that everything is turning out for the best.

41

"You are no longer hinging how you experience life on the actions of others."

Connections are the pith and plenty of our lives. Connections to family and friends, to nature, to the places and things we love, they all sustain and support us. A life lived in a vacuum is a pretty miserable one—even hermits have a profound connection to their tradition, and to history and learning. Many artists and writers who have divorced themselves from what we might think of as normal life are still connected to the universe through their own boundless imaginations.

It is possible to read into the law of attraction a kind of selfishness, or even narcissism. Or the notion that maybe we can hide out, avoiding the connections that can sometimes be as painful as they are nourishing. If we encounter this stuff in a moment when we're already leaning in that direction a bit—watch out. Oh, we can think, I am the only one in charge of my energy—everything comes back around to me, me, me. I mustn't pay attention to anyone else's energy, nobody else matters, so I can vamoose outta here and take care of myself by my lonesome. That sounds a lot like fear talking—fear of being rejected, fear of not getting what we want—and fear is the polar opposite of the freedom that the power of attraction can bring.

There are all sorts of wonderful ways we can strengthen the bonds that connect us to the world, even as we explore the idea that we don't have to hang around and wait for Thing X or Person Y to be in perfect position to claim our well-being. We can turn on and connect in any and every moment, and though we may feel like checking out from the people and things we love during hard times, if we can figure out even small ways to reinvest our energy from a positive, open place, we're going to reap the rewards (and, as a by-product, so will the people and things we're connected to).

Unhook your happiness gauge from things outside you, even as you pour your best energy into the things and people you love.

42

"Don't take score too soon. If your Wants haven't started to appear yet, relax. And keep your valve open."

How long does it take? As long as it takes. The universe does not own a Timex or even a much more expensive watch, at least, not one that arbitrarily divides time up into seconds, minutes, hours, days, so we can sit around counting the time until the next wonderful thing happens.

Relaxing is important because we don't know exactly when results will appear. So there's no point getting our knickers in a twist waiting. There's also no point in predetermining exactly what the results are going to look like.

If I'm focused on my exact picture, I may miss the real result—it came in the form of a job offer in a town where housing is plentiful when I thought all I was looking for was a place to live. So paying attention to everything—keeping your valve open and keeping positive—is important. Taking score focuses on zero-sum counting—and the score will probably never be high enough.

So what to do in the meantime? Write down fifty ways to relax. Then try each one of them. Or, if that feels too obsessive, take a walk today, and another one tomorrow.

Walking is good for my body, as well as good for taking my mind off the waiting and the score.

43

"So write your script, don't worry about the whens or hows, give up noticing it hasn't happened yet, get your eyes off the other guy's valve, and find ways to open yours."

Who's in charge here? There's only one right answer to that question, ever: "No one." If in charge means making sure of an outcome by force of will, by willful action, by trying to force others to our scenario of how things should be, we can't ever succeed at anything by being in charge.

We can't make things happen on our time schedule and in exactly the way we want them to, especially where other people are concerned, and since other people are always concerned, that means never. We can, however, be open to change and have faith that that change will bring about our desired changes and our well-being.

We can, in short, live open to the possibilities that we will get what we want and need.

44

"You don't have to be any more worthy, or deserving, or trustworthy, or upstanding than you are now. You only have to make one decision . . . just one . . . and that is to be happy."

A corollary to the law of attraction, the law of plenty states that you already have everything you need. No, I don't mean you're never going to have to go buy toothpaste again. I mean that the dynamic potentiality that surrounds you is not a commodity in short supply. Or, put another way—the power of feelings is right at your fingertips whenever you need or want it. It never goes away and it never runs out; in fact, the more you use this kind of power, the more you get. (What if electricity worked like that, wouldn't the power companies be sore?!)

Every time you connect to that feeeeeling place, you attract more of the same, and if you get more people involved, the effects are exponential. So, anything you need or want, since it comes to you directly through how you are energized, is never in short supply. Even if you don't have whatever it is you're magnetizing your way yet, you never have to feel the gnawing of scarcity again because you know that the law of plenty is at work.

Anything over and above your basic needs is sheer abundance, which is always close at hand. Abundance breeds gratitude, which in turn feeds more abundance. It's a win-win situation all around.

Abundance is a mindset, plenty is a constant, and the force enlivening it all is the feeling energy behind your Wants.

45

"Like any hidden talent that you've either consciously or unconsciously known was there but didn't feel comfortable bringing out, once you accept the fact that wanting is part of you, and that doing it is really okay, it becomes fun. Joy starts to flow."

I remember a conversation in high school—one of those first up-all-night talk fests with girls—and, somehow, we ended up struggling to talk about the most elemental thing about people—why humans do what we do. Why do we care for each other? Why do we work hard? Why do we love one another? And we all, more or less, came to the conclusion that we do all of this out of fear. We decided that love comes from fear of being alone, work comes from fear of starvation, life comes from fear of death.

There are certainly lots of people who would agree with this, or some more philosophical version of it, but really nothing could be further from the truth. The life force in us cannot be attributed to fear alone. Fear is not an elemental part of our humanity; it is a tool that we use to know when we're in immediate danger. Desire, on the other hand, is a part of us from the very beginning. We are hardwired to want, to reach out, to make connections, and I can't believe that life boils down to avoiding pain, hurt, loneliness, or death.

But fear is certainly a powerful motivator, and we've all been fed a steady diet of it. In the doctrine of fear, desire of any kind is dangerous because it might lead to a loss of control, which, in turn, might end up putting us in an unknown or painful situation. More importantly for the fear pushers, it might subvert a strict order of who controls and who is controlled. But true desire that is hooked into our deepest selves can only bring joy and growth, not only to ourselves but to everyone around us.

Wanting is an innate talent. When it's cursed, it will turn against us; when it's blessed, it thrives.

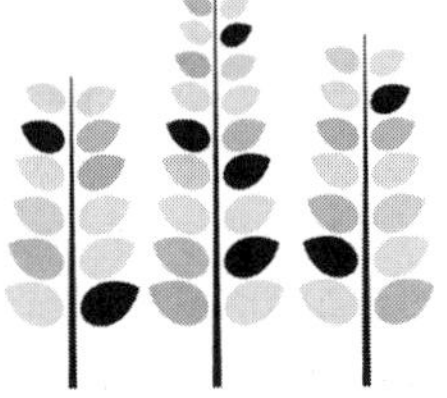

46

"We cannot live something that we are not vibrating."

I've been told that the divine actress Dame Judi Dench once said something like "you are only as good onstage as you are offstage." Meaning, you can't conjure up some feeling, or generosity of spirit, or courage, playing a part on a stage that you don't have access to in your offstage life. Most actors can fake it fairly well, but we know the difference when we see someone who is fearlessly willing to follow the story to any place it takes them, and we instinctively know whether they have the soul to pull it off. This is part of what draws us to truly great performers.

In turn, we cannot live something that we are not vibrating. We cannot make choices or take inspired action if we cannot truly bring the frequency of our feelings, hopes, and dreams in line with the vibrations of our current beliefs about ourselves and our situation. Any disconnect will result in failure, boredom, some grand attempt at faking it, or a combination of all those things.

But the good news is that vibrations cannot lie—and if there is a disconnect, they will point us right to it. So the failures are not really failures, they are simply guideposts leading us toward being as good in our everyday lives as we are in our fullest dreams.

In order to live the life you want to live, you must grant yourself the full range of your vibrations.

47

"Become aware of the feeling tones you roam around with all day long, from dawn to lights out. Stay awake. Become aware!"

What is it about genius artists, writers, scientists, composers, etc., that makes them tick? Is it passion? Obsession? Does it border on mental illness or even cross that line? Does it have to?

There is one idea that many great artists and thinkers share the ability (or disability, if you think of it another way) to see even commonplace things in a new light over and over again. That is, their brains don't shut out what they see, hear, taste, and smell just because they already know something about it. When most of us eat an apple, or cross a bridge on our way to work, we block out a whole bunch of information about the apple and the bridge because we don't need it—we're on task and on to the next thing. But these folks can't turn off that flow of information, and this can lead them to insightful new ways of looking at things, or lead them directly into madness, or both.

How much information about our inner state do we plug up, shut down, and cancel out all day long, every day? Maybe it's time to become a connoisseur of your own feelings, noticing the particulars in the way a great novelist would, capturing the details like a painter might. Turn things over and over in your mind, and talk about them out loud (people may think you're mad, so what?). Puzzle through your physical, mental, and emotional reactions as much as you can throughout the day, and be brutally honest with yourself. Every moment that you spend engaged in this kind of awareness is another chance for things to come together in a totally new and astonishing way.

Become an energy genius by simply expanding your awareness.

48

"Don't take this all so seriously; that just makes for closed valves. Lighten up, have fun with this, and it will happen faster."

"Humorless." The word echoed in my head for hours after I heard a friend use it to describe someone we both know. Humorless. It felt true—I'd never seen this person laugh at herself, or do something silly for the heck of it. Even her smile seemed somehow guarded, with a slight curl of her lip that made people wonder if she was sneering. Then it hit me. She's not humorless, she's scared. She's not restrained, she's panicked.

I can see it in myself. I turn away the goodhearted concern of others, I buckle down trying to make things better, I fret and fidget and give up in a huff. All because my inner monologue is listing off the things I should be doing, or haven't done right, or am about to get slammed with.

They say laughter is the best medicine, and it turns out that not only is it a great remedy for whatever ails you physically (and that's backed up by scientific fact), it can ease your journey in this life in so many other ways. It may take some practice, learning to lighten up. But there are so many ways to go about it, you're sure to find one that suits you pretty quickly, whether it's collecting dumb jokes, watching silly slapstick, or joining the circus. The rewards are immediate, and the first and maybe most important one is that you get to have fun. By grabbing hold of a few giggles, chuckles, and snorts along the way, even when something is difficult—*especially* when something is difficult—the ride will go a lot smoother.

Do something really silly, right this minute. Repeat hourly, or as necessary.

49

"When you play, you're in joy, pushing your frequencies way up off the charts."

It has become standard educational philosophy that play is a very real and necessary part of children's work. You can sit at a desk and do numbers and letters forever, but there are things that simply cannot be learned any other way. We start with peek-a-boo and the games get more complex and more physical as we get older. We learn to invent our own games, setting new rules and jumping into whole worlds we've created for the game.

Then at some point in growing up, we often just stop. Play becomes exercise—that weekly tennis match with your best friend—or a waste of time when you could be getting something done. But we forget that play gets something done, too—in fact, it gets a whole lot done while we're not even aware of it. To play any game that has a physical component, we have to be in the moment, reacting to what others are doing (and/or what a ball or Frisbee or rope is doing on top of that). It tunes our body in to a short-term goal devised by our brains. It takes us out of our heads and into a communal space with others. It releases our inhibitions and gets us breathing hard and laughing out loud. In short, it is a model we can use in the rest of our lives, in decision-making, follow-through, through competition, and with sportsmanship. Are you aware of how little you play? Do you think you could do it more?

Don't forget to play! Throw yourself into it, let it all hang out.

50

"All the positive thoughts in the world won't make any difference, not being a good person with a generous heart, nor praying, visualizing and meditating 'til dawn, nor even knocking our heads against countless stone walls in fervent attempts to capture lifelong dreams."

This is going to sound crazy, but a lot of what we think is "being good" or "doing right" is actually counterproductive, if not plain old wrong. We see it in our own lives—good people get steamrolled, hurt, abused, all the time. So then we think we must try to be good or appear to be good, but really spend a whole lot of time protecting ourselves from the same fate. Or else we just give up altogether on being good and chuck society's moral code but fail to replace it with one that comes from the truth of our own hearts, so we end up stomping all over everyone as we flail around trying to make ourselves feel better in a vacuum. Something's broken here.

Feeling like you're a good person is about lack. Why? Because you can only keep a tally of how good a person you are by tallying how bad you're afraid you could be, or how bad others are. So, striving to be good comes from a longing not to be bad, and that is pure lack.

Praying is often about lack (though it doesn't have to be). We often pray for ourselves or someone else when we think of them as incomplete in some way: unhealthy, needy, suffering. We can quite easily shift our prayers into a more productive space by seeing the people we are praying for (including ourselves) as being whole, and then feeling how we feel in relationship to their perfect health, their freedom, their hope (even if those things don't seem to be here yet).

Visualizing and meditating, like praying, are also often approached from a place of need. We feel we must meditate because something is not right, as a fix to a problem. And if we're trying to fix anything we're operating from lack.

Knocking our heads against walls certainly won't do the trick and will probably smart a bit. Trying to force ourselves into success through sheer willpower may take us part of the way, but it is a huge waste of energy, and we feel drained by the effort, instead of energized by it.

Does all this mean we should stop praying, meditating, being good? Does it mean we should throw care for others to the wind and just do what we want to do all the time? No way. It means we have to approach each of these tasks from the opposite direction of what we've been taught is right. Never pray out of fear, pray from pure joy. Never meditate to calm down or to solve a problem, meditate to offer thanks to the universe. Never slam your head into anything, it hurts.

Turn your motivation on its head and do everything you already do from a place of joy and abundance instead of fear and lack.

"We diligently watch our resistance to receiving."

Most of us, by the time we reach adulthood, have a pretty ingrained pattern that goes something like this: "I want it. I work to make it happen. Just when it looks like it's going to happen, I sabotage it in some way. It doesn't happen. I feel badly about myself." And then we start all over again.

Or we spend a lot of time and energy explaining to ourselves and others why we sabotage ourselves, why we don't deserve what we want. It has to do with our childhoods, or our parents' childhoods, or our religions, or the part of the country we're from, or the way the stars were aligned when we were born. It may, actually, have to do with that and a whole lot more. And it may be a good idea to know some of this. But, in the end, really, who cares why? What you really want is to want what you want and to let yourself have it.

In order to dissolve your resistance: Watch it. Don't judge it. Don't try to stop it by force. Befriend it. Talk to it. Tell it that it's served its purpose and send it on its way.

I am open to deserving what I want.

52

"Creation comes from feeling, not from thinking, and not from trying to pound things into place."

Creativity and rational thinking go together like square pegs and round holes. Or is it round pegs and square holes? In any case, pounding isn't going to do much good. That's not to say that creation doesn't involve hard work—there's a saying about invention that it's 1percent inspiration and 99 percent perspiration.

So whether it's creating a painting or designing a house or creating a new life—put your rational thoughts away for the time being. (You can trot them out later to make to-do lists and help solve problems as they come up.) Instead, let your body and your imagination be your guide. What do you see in your mind's eye and how does that make you feel?

If you're cool to an idea, try another. The hair follicles on the back of your neck or your arms might contract. Or you might find yourself grinning from ear to ear. Then you know you're on the right path. Keep on it. Put brush to canvas, pen to paper. The real work begins. The feelings continue.

Creation begins and continues in feelings.

53

"Like cutting a trail in the jungle, you swack here, and swack there, and pretty soon you have a nice clean path on which to trek back and forth. So you do. On the same subject! You think about it, and think about it, and think about it."

We're told that the power of the brain is almost totally untapped by conscious thought. So the true intensity of the thing must be out of this world, since even the tiny bit we're able to access is powerful beyond our imaginations. Yet the brain is so good at what it does that this can be its very handicap. We can learn and relearn and repeat over and over very quickly, and don't always seem to discern between a path, or habit, that does us good and one that doesn't.

The synapses in our brains fire with every thought, every emotion, every sensation, decision, or action. We're learning more and more about how that works, but the picture is at best theoretical of what actually happens. The path through the synapses is cut through repetition and, once it's there, most people believe it's there for life.

What?! I can hear you saying. You mean I literally can't wipe the slate clean? I can't go back and "fix" those rotten thought paths and addiction paths and whatever else paths that I've used to get myself into this mess? Nope. Besides, fixing sounds like it would need quite a bit of heave-ho, which won't get us where we want to be, in any case.

The best—and really only—thing to do is to make new paths. That same repetition of thought and decision and action can build a new path so clear and strong that the synapses fire away on that one again and again, and while the other one never quite disappears, it will overgrow through lack of attention.

Don't bother erasing old habits—you can't! Cut through new territory and claim it as your own.

54

"In asking comes the connection."

So often we feel we are screaming out into the void. "Heeeeelp! I have no idea! I'm lost! Somebody show me the way! Somebody give me a sign!" Our hearts and minds shout out an emergency message when we feel we're at the end of our rope, completely lost. We try our most plaintive cry for help as a last-ditch effort to save something that is all but lost.

But a cry for help, or a more calm version of it, which could be as simple as a question you ask out loud to nobody in particular, is not the end of a fruitless journey. In fact, it's the best beginning you could ask for. Because until you get to the place of being fed up and having had enough of whatever it is that's bugging you, you're not really connecting to the solution. There can be no answer if there is no question, right?

Don't hesitate to ask questions. Ask yourself, ask others. I had a teacher once who would explain a math problem up to three different ways, and, if you still didn't get it, he'd say, "Let's set that question aside for a moment while I think of another way to talk about it," and he'd come back to it later with yet another fresh take.

The universe offers an infinite number of ways to look at and solve any problem, but you have to ask the question first.

55

"Just like firing up a Want, until we learn that it's okay to *ask,* nothing is going to happen. It's a habit we need to get into and never, ever let go."

Ask early. Ask often. Ask your mother, father, brother, sister, teacher, boss, husband, wife, child. Ask yourself. Ask for what you want in the moment whenever you can. Practice at all opportunities. Ask the clerk in the store, "Could I see that necklace please?" (You don't have to intend to buy to ask. And you don't have to explain why you're not buying.)

A lot of people, especially people like mine of the Midwestern persuasion, feel uncomfortable asking for just about anything. They'd rather drink their coffee black than ask for milk and sugar—a simple enough request, one would think. But, somehow, to ask is to draw attention to one's self, to think that one is worth the time it takes someone else to bring the milk and sugar.

Ah, there's the rub. When we look at our comfort level about asking for what we want, we begin to see what we believe about ourselves—to wit, we're not really deserving of getting what we want. Well, of course, that's not true. We don't believe that, do we?

Asking for what I want helps me believe I am worth getting it.

56

"No one had told me—or any of us attempting to control our energies—about this rather unpleasant but apparently common occurrence that seems to happen when we start pulling more high-frequency energy into the body."

It feels like the world is going to end. It's terrible and ever so much sadder than if we'd never started this positive stuff in the first place. If you are near-sighted and don't have glasses, you think that all the leaves on the tree are meant to be a blur of green. Then if you look through a lens that corrects your vision, you see individual leaves and flowers and birds and much brighter colors. And, then, someone says—well, we're taking that lens away now. And we don't hear that they're taking it away only for long enough to make you a pair of glasses with a lens ground so you can see all those wonders.

It takes time—it's not an immediate process. And it's almost inevitable that there's that lag in there when we feel worse because we've seen the possibility, but we don't yet have all the tools or the resources. And we get slammed.

We're falling without all the old nets—the ones that caught us before we fell too far because things were never that great anyway. The ones above us that kept us from climbing or reaching for too much because we could never get it. So we climbed a bit higher and fell a bit farther and harder.

So now we know we can climb and we can fall and we can see different possibilities.

57

"There is no such thing as a victim, only those who choose to play victim roles."

"What?" I can hear myself scream. "The world is full of victims, there are wrongs and injustices and evil being perpetrated everywhere right this second." How can anyone say there is no such thing as a victim?

There are most definitely horrible things happening and there is huge suffering in this world. You'd have to be a complete idiot to deny that. But a victim is rarely created at the moment of a crime or a wrong—we create our own victimhood in our own hearts long before and/or long after any actual bad things happen. And then we tie our feelings of blame, fear, and self-hatred to the bad things that happen in an attempt to justify those feelings, to make them a part of the "reality" we feel we can't escape.

We feel very comfortable in this role of victim, and the more bad stuff we can think of to support us in this role, the more justified we feel (and the more miserable we feel). So we make ourselves into a big welcome mat for the very nasty stuff that we claim is making us miserable, and wallow in our helplessness.

Can you think of a role model—someone who has stepped away from the devastation of something terrible and is still the master of his own destiny? Can you become someone who refuses to be a victim?

58

"What are your smallest, your biggest, your oldest, your newest, your most deeply hidden desires, ambitions, aspirations . . . the ones that are so far out, so impossible, so unobtainable, that never have you so much as whispered them aloud . . . to anyone . . . not even to God? What are they? What have you stopped allowing yourself to want?"

Last week I found myself shopping for a friend's kid's birthday present. Looking for a gift for an eight-year-old girl who was starting to read comics, I got a brainstorm. A book about drawing. Not a fancy art book, just a book to learn about, practice, and enjoy basic doodling. I found a great book and wrapped it up, and she seemed to like it well enough, but, when I stopped by to visit a couple weeks later, I saw it lying empty on the table, untouched. I picked it up and started to flip through it, unconsciously grabbing a pen and some scrap paper to try out some of the techniques.

Then it hit me. I bought that book for myself. Sure, she might get a kick out of it in her own time, but I *really* wanted that book. I wanted to draw. So, I went out and bought the book for myself, or I should say for my trapped, eight-year-old self who really loved to draw and decided she was no good at it because of how the pictures came out.

We each have desires we repeat, in our minds or out loud, all day long. Some helpful, some not so much. Then there are those desires that would remain hidden forever were it not for a bit of creative sleuthing. They have to be dug out from under a heap of problems or issues that obscures them almost completely. Or maybe they're just so foreign that we have no idea where to begin, so we stash them away forever. Well, it's time to get to the bottom of this, because there's an awful lot of joy waiting for us.

Spend some time with a journal free associating, writing out some ideas of what you'd like to do as they come to you without worrying whether or not you can make a go of it.

59

"So here's yet another reason for giving more time to your Want, for the more time you spend on it, the more passionate you will become. And passion is creation."

I know a man who gave away his television set. He's an older man, who lives in a beautiful condo with a beautiful ocean view. He's a retired teacher. He tries to stay healthy, walks every day, and now reads voraciously for the sheer pleasure of it. He didn't give away his TV because he's intrinsically against watching TV. He doesn't think it causes brain cancer or anything like that.

He gave away his TV because he needed to make room for something else in his life. Living alone, it was too easy to turn the set on, and before he knew it, hours had elapsed. He'd watched some interesting shows, maybe a ball game, and maybe some not-so-interesting shows. What he hadn't done was write a poem or read a book or phone a friend.

He gave himself the gift of time, time to look out the window at his ocean view. Time to think about what he wanted to do in his retirement. To his delight, once he gave up the TV and gave himself some time, he found another Want, and a way to make it happen. He began with the germ of an idea to find a way to make the world a better place. And he started a foundation that will grant prizes to public school classes that start "green" projects. Who knew giving up a television set could give way to something with such a big ripple effect?

Give yourself some time to be passionate, a few minutes at a time.

60

"There's only one [word] which can lay claim to consistently winning the 'Top Negative Word Vibration' award. That word is 'money,' the most highly charged word in any language that uses the stuff."

I'm going to go out on a limb here and speculate that most of the people who say it's impolite to talk about money have enough to pay their rent. Then, again, maybe not, since we put such a high value on keeping up appearances. So there you have it—people who have a lot of money don't talk about money because they don't want to be asked for money or made to feel guilty or it's just not done. People who don't have enough money to take care of their daily needs, not to mention wants, don't talk about money because they don't want anyone feeling sorry for them, because they don't want to feel guilty because they haven't "made it" or it's just not done. People in the elusive and shifting middle ground don't talk about money for all of the above reasons. And more.

So how can we begin to take the negative charge away from money? That, as they say, is the $64,000 question. (Just kidding.) One way is to replace the negative energy with some positive energy. Step 1: count something besides your money. Health, talent, blessings, the ability to give thanks, the ability to set an intention. Step 2: forget what other people are counting. Yes, there is injustice—corporate CEOs making obscene salaries and bonuses, drug dealers, people making money off legal and illegal wars. They're there, and obsessing about them and the other supposed haves of the world is not going to dissipate the negative charge and replace it with a positive.

Money has no power to make me feel angry or envious.

61

"When no money was coming in, I had to do a lot more of what I call 'flip-switching,' the rapid altering of one's energy from negative to positive. I had to find ways to get me out of whatever worry-habit I'd been in, and open up that valve."

No one said the habit of worry is easy to give up. It's especially hard in periods where money or work is scarce. Maybe we don't have enough to pay the mortgage. We don't know where next week's groceries are coming from. Why wouldn't we worry? It's what we've been taught to do. A lot of people are even very sure that they don't work as well if they aren't under pressure, that they don't earn all they can if they're not afraid of the wolf at the door or nipping at their heels.

No one said it would be easy to switch to positive energy when the news is seemingly so bad—high unemployment, low sales, high foreclosure rates, no credit. Yet when things are grim is the very time we most need positive energy.

Now is the time to start paying very close attention to our energy. When we feel the negative coming on, we can do something concrete toward our goal. If it's looking for a job, we can make a phone call or send an email. If it's finishing a project and we're feeling too negative to actually do anything creative on it, we can clean up the office so we can work tomorrow.

When things are bad, I'm on the lookout for any positive gesture I can make.

62

"Forgiveness is forgetting the thing ever happened in the first damn place."

Forgive and forget. It's a proverb we learn in childhood—and rarely accomplish in adulthood. It slips off our tongue. "Forget about it," we say. Or, "It's already forgotten," usually when someone apologizes. But is it forgotten? And do we mean it—either literally or figuratively? It is difficult to forget things we might want to forgive—that a partner was unfaithful, that an employee stole money or resources, that a mother-in-law said a hurtful thing. So just what does it mean to forget the thing ever happened in the "first damn place."

I don't think it necessarily means we have no memory of the thing happening. I think it means that we have defused the negative energy around the memory. We know it happened. We no longer feel its sting. We no longer let the negative energy that was being generated by us and between us and the other person to dominate. We give up charging the memory—the anniversary of the day he left me or six months since my car was slammed into. We may, in the case of the former, remember the day and celebrate how good we feel. Or, in the case of the latter, feel grateful to be alive. But we're not marking the occasion by remembering primarily that another done us wrong.

Another way to "forget" is to practice a ritual forgetting. Again, there are some things we're not likely to forget. But writing them down on paper and tearing that paper up into little pieces before recycling it or burning it are symbolic ways to stop the negative energy. Finally, there are some things we can actually forget, and it's a good idea to practice doing so. If you don't rehearse over and over in your head everything that was said in your last fight with your partner, you are less likely to remember those words. In time, you may even—literally—forget them.

Try some creative forgetting.

63

"What unconditional love really means is: 'I will keep my valve open to well-being no matter what crazy thing you've done.' (Remember, you don't have to change it or even like it; you just have to stop focusing on it!)"

To love without putting conditions—on our partners, our kids, our friends, ourselves. How much trouble is caused in relationships when we focus not on the fact that we love someone, but on what they are doing that we don't like? Sending a message that "I'll love you if you stop doing something or change your ways" is sending a message that I don't love you now. And that goes for love of self as well as others.

It's a pretty simple thing to say we can't change someone else. But, oh, how hard we try. And we pray about it, and we make suggestions to them, and we admonish, and we nag, and we think if only, and nothing changes. Let's just say, "I stop putting all that energy to trying to change that person. What could I do with it instead?"

Today, I bring my focus to well-being, for myself and others.

64

"Stop focusing on, responding to, or worrying about how to control conditions that haven't changed yet. That's only getting you more of the same."

Every time you focus on, respond to, or worry about how to control anything, you become stiffer and tighter, shutting down the flow of energy. I can feel it physically when I do it—my spine crunches under the weight of my own efforts to control, and I find myself hunched or stooped over whatever I'm trying to muscle into being. If I can see and feel that much of a change in my body, I can only imagine what a mess my vibrations must be.

Rigidity and flexibility—energy responds to both. Think of a steel rod as a lightning bolt shoots through it straight into the ground. Then think of a lightning bolt striking a lake and branching out through the water's depth and width. In human beings, the energy flow through a rigid personality, or goal, or thought pattern, may indeed be powerful and effective. Many people have accomplished great things by High-Ho Silvering away at something until it happened. But the power of that initial burst of energy goes straight into the ground—powerful but short lived, and possibly dissatisfying.

In contrast, for someone who is flexible, who allows her thoughts and dreams to flow like water, the energetic jolt of a new idea or a burst of passion is free to travel on a much broader path, finding ways and means beyond what she could ever consciously imagine. These ways and means are all the more available in a flexible person because no path is shut down outright.

Getting into your feeling place is like doing vibrational stretches, limbering up in preparation for a burst of fresh energy.

65

"Try as we will, fix-it kits don't work. When we decide someone needs fixing, all we're doing is viewing them as 'wrong,' flooding them with negative energy."

Whatever energy we send out to others bounces off them and comes right back at us. So when we send out "I'm gonna fix your problem" energy to someone, letting them know we think there's something wrong with them, it comes right back at us, flooding us, too. We set ourselves up. Here's how it works: A decides to fix B's bad habit of, oh, say, smoking cigarettes. So, A harangues B and sits him down and lectures him on the detriments of smoking. And B feels stupid and powerless, and lashes out at A. Who feels better after this little exchange? No one.

In fact, "fix-it" kits don't work on ourselves, either. Imagine A and B above are just two different parts of the same person. Same result. Everyone is flooded with negative energy. No one benefits.

Imagine instead of fix-it kits, we each took responsibility for ourselves. And as a first, and ongoing, step, we take stock of ourselves, not as home improvement projects—plaster here, paint there, fix up the plumbing—but as the beautiful, spiritual, and physical beings that we are, without judging ourselves as good/bad, right/wrong. That opens up room for us to look at our behavior in any given moment and situation without sending that flood of negative energy. It opens up room for us to change that behavior if we choose to.

I watch the energy I send and receive, changing its charge from negative to neutral, so I can make choices that benefit me and the world.

66

"When we feel bad, or down, *or not much of anything,* we're disconnected and flowing the foreign vibrations of low frequency negativity throughout our bodies. In other words, if it's not about joy, it's always negative."

Never say no.

I used to teach a kids' theater class, and this is the first rule of improvisation in theater (and, I would argue, in life)—never say no. Never say no? I know you're probably rolling your eyes and thinking I'm off my rocker (and you're no preteen drama student), but hear me out.

You don't need no. No is a given: a negative, the contrast of the path you did not choose, the decision you veered away from, the failure to embrace what's really there in front of you. No exists without you having to reinforce it, or invite it to meddle in your affairs. But most importantly, no is a dead end. Going back to improvisation for a minute, I taught that instead of "No," you say, "Yes, and . . ." So, even if you don't want something, you can say, "Yes, and . . ." to redirect that energy to something you do want. That way the channel is open, and there is always something coming down the pipes.

So you're feeling down. On top of that, you're moping about how your low frequencies are drawing in more stuff to make you feel down, and the whole thing is shaping up to be a vicious circle. So you get stuck on the negative: I don't want to feel this way! Or the false positive: I want to feel better *now!* Both of those come from the lack of feeling good, so you try stuffing how you feel down your own throat as a last resort and force yourself into a smile, at which point, you fall practically to pieces with the wasted effort.

Try "Yes, and . . ." and open up the possibilities of an improvised moment, day, or life.

67

"Stop thinking the world has to change before you can be safe or happy. You create your own safety through your energy flow."

Regardless of all the wonderful attracting you are no doubt managing to do, you will most certainly find that there are still some unpleasant tasks in your life. At the very least, there will be some garbage to take out, some painful dentist appointments, some awful people with whom you have to interact on a daily basis. Is this a failing of your powers of attraction? Nah. But maybe you can turn even daily unpleasantness into fuel for the fire.

Or maybe it's far worse than the garbage—maybe you live in a dangerous neighborhood (sure, you're magnetizing your way out of there to a beautiful and safe home, but what about until then?). Maybe your financial situation is so bad that you're headed to the food stamp office, or a homeless shelter.

Think of any disagreeable task or situation, or even one that most people would think of as a real downer, as a tool. That's right—a hammer, a wrench, a nail gun. By directing your energy and changing your beliefs, any situation or action can be a part of the new life you're building, brick by brick. The great thing about tools is you pick them up, use 'em to get something done, and then *put them down.* Just so with an unpleasant task. Get into it, get it done, and then *let it go.* Lingering around it, or building up anger about it, or feeling shame or guilt about it just draws more of that same unpleasantness to you.

Do this and be amazed as unpleasant junk drenched in negativity transforms into just another tool for the job—all getting us where we need to be. We can feel gratitude even toward the crappy stuff in our lives, because it's all just bringing us closer to our goals. That's quite a turnaround.

Life's downers—small and large—can be picked up and put away in service of your grand scheme.

68

"No, not all at once; this thing is ongoing and will be for as long as I'm in this body."

Here's good news. Learning is a lifelong activity. We can, for as long as we are in our bodies, learn new things. Have new insights. Grow into our best selves. Not in a day, not in a week, not in a year, but for as long as we live.

We can focus on one thing at a time, opening in one area of our lives, knowing that we can continue opening; in fact, once we've started opening, nothing much can stop us. Once I say, "Yes, I want" . . . Once I say, "Yes, I will" . . . I have started on a path. I have opened to telling my own truth. And that is not an ending. It's a beginning.

Opening to my own truth is like riding a bicycle—once I know how to do it, my body's not going to forget. A week, a month, a year, five years can go by. And it's ongoing. If I ride regularly, I'll be able to ride farther, faster. If I open to the energy around me, I'll learn faster.

It is good to be alive in the moment.

69

"We send the magnetic feelings out, the universe obediently delivers. It doesn't react to our pleas; it only responds to our vibrations which come purely from how we're feeling."

But I can't help it. I feel horrible, miserable, sad, and lonely. And we can't control our feelings, can we? Say a car cuts you off in traffic. What's your first, automatic response? To shout a curse. To call the driver a name. To snarl at your passengers about the state of drivers today. Anger. Justified, right? That car cut you off. It's justified, and it's automatic, and you can't do anything about it. Right?

And you've just sent out a message that you're mad and you're not going to take it anymore. At the next corner somebody runs through a yellow light. There you were, chomping to go at the green—YOUR green light. That fool nearly killed you. Cuss, double cuss. Now you're mad and scared. So you slow down for a minute, but now you're worried that you're going to be late. So you send that vibe out. Lo and behold, a traffic jam.

Now you probably didn't cause the other driver to nearly run you down, and it's not likely that you're responsible for the overturned apple truck that stopped traffic for five miles in both directions. But, if your initial response had been to take a deep breath and then another and then another, and then the next thing that happened and the next thing that happened—well they might have all been different.

When you're ready to pitch a fit, take a breath and think about what you're throwing out into the world.

70

"It is so important for us to have a broad understanding of just what negative emotion is, how covertly it works, how to spot it, why we keep having it, and, oddly enough, how truly vital it is to the process of taking control."

Someone told me once that the crazier you are, the saner you have the chance to become. What I think she meant is that as you struggle with a whole host of difficulties, worries, obsessions, or neuroses, you actually have more opportunities to learn and grow as you go through those things than someone might who remains in a relatively balanced state.

This can be a great comfort, especially when you're feeling a little nuts or out of control in mind or body. All negative emotion can ultimately fuel our understanding. But those nasty feelings are tricky: they can catch us off guard, can play to our fears or insecurities, and worst of all, can masquerade as positive emotions. Think of how good it feels to an alcoholic to sink into temporary oblivion. Not *really* good in the sense of being tapped into a true life force, but certainly good enough in that moment. So the tricky part is diving in to discover a broader understanding of negativity and how it goes to work in your mind, and in your life.

What are your negative habits? Do you walk around judging yourself and others? Do you cower from making decisions? Do you shut down your creative impulses by deciding your ideas are frivolous or impossible? Do you choose temporary comfort over long-term growth? Take a magnifying glass to your neuroses and find out how they work. Be fascinated by them and ask them direct questions, aloud if you can. "Why do I believe in you? What purpose do you serve in my life?" Shine a bright light on them so that you can see them for what they really are.

Bless your negative emotions, as they enable you to understand, forgive (yourself and others), and move on.

71

"There's just no getting away from it; the overwhelming balance of power on this planet is on the side of well-being because that is the natural, omnipotent state of All That Is, including you and me!"

Sometimes I think the story isn't looking good for the side of the angels. Watching the news—hurricanes and earthquakes, not to mention war in places most of us have never heard of until there's a war there, not to mention . . . Well, the list is practically endless. Yet spending a lot of my time and energy listing it is not a productive task. I can succeed in making myself feel awful for a little bit if that's what I want to do.

What I cannot do is change the "natural and omnipotent state of All That Is." But what is that state? How do I know it exists, especially in my most despairing moments? I take a breath, and I consider the negative proof—if the balance weren't on the side of well-being, the forces of evil would have destroyed our race and our planet a long time ago. I take another breath and I consider the positive proofs—a baby's smile, a perfectly symmetrical leaf, a connection between the yous and the mes of this world.

I think about love songs. In so many of them, there's the inevitability factor—the person falling in love just can't help herself. So she gives in to it. There is no getting away from it. So, what if I think about the balance of power being for well-being and just give in to it—with every breath I take, in every waking moment, and my sleeping moments, too? Imagine what a life I'll live. Imagine how much I'll affect the balance of power.

May I remember with every breath that well-being breeds well-being.

"Stop being a wimpy wanter. Want big in quality, as well as quantity! And don't ever stop creating new Wants. The ultra high energy You are needs outlets to flow. Create them!"

Reach for the stars. Let yourself dream. Think big. What have we got to lose? This is not the easiest advice in the world for many of us to follow, especially those of us who grew up in cultures, families, or parts of the country where it's not exactly polite to say out loud what we want. We get the message very early and very loud that it's also probably not all right to want what we want.

Corollaries of the "it's not all right to want" law are if you want one thing, then you have to give up another. If you want something, then your sibling/parent/friend/partner/colleague is going to have to give up something. You can't tell me this isn't reinforced at work. Who among us hasn't asked for a raise and been told the pool for raises is just too small? What would happen if everyone asked for that size raise? Well, the pool might have to get bigger. Or the staff smaller. Or some of you might have to (and want to, I might add) find different jobs. In any of those events, me wanting is not the problem.

As we create our wants and let them grow, we also learn flexibility—if one thing doesn't come through in the way we desire it to, we might shift our energies slightly and see it come through in a different way, maybe even bigger. As we open up, we find more things open to us. We increase our wants and our gets by leaps and bounds. All this happens when we stop being a wimpy wanter.

The next time I catch myself being a wimpy wanter, I'll ask myself what would happen if I asked for twice as much. Three times? Ten times?

73

"The moment you become aware that you're feeling a little shaky or off case, ask yourself *What's bothering me?* and keep at it until an answer comes. It will."

Many of us were raised with a "just suck it up" mentality. One favorite saying in that vein is, "When the going gets tough, the tough get going." So, does stopping to take time to figure out why the going got tough mean you're not going where you set out to go?

No. Unequivocally and without a doubt.

When you're feeling shaky, not sure of your path, there's really no point barreling ahead on that path. Indeed, it might still be the right path for you. And, until you stop to figure it out, you won't know if it's the wrong path, the wrong approach, the wrong time.

Asking ourselves what's bothering us requires time and honesty—time to let the answer well up from our hearts and the honesty to admit we've found the answer even if we don't like it. Even if it means taking a turn away from some of the people in our lives, or quitting a "good" job.

May I ask the question with courage and be receptive to the answer.

74

"They're just the garden variety type of feelings we have all day long. But once you learn to keep track of which ones feel good and which ones feel less than good, you're home free."

I have a ready excuse for my own tendency to resist change in my life: it's too hard to move forward because it would mean changing everything all at once, and then I'd be lost, without a leg to stand on. As if my bad habits were my sum total, and to make a positive leap in my life I would have to solve every past or present problem I've ever had. As if in order to feel good today, I'd have to revisit every moment of feeling badly I've ever had and pick it apart to figure out motivations, illusions, and reality.

If we had to do all that before making a change, there would be no person on this earth ever capable of changing his life. And it's easy enough to see there are plenty of people who have changed in all sorts of ways. We may not feel like we can join their ranks, but that very feeling is the single and only thing preventing us. Don't get me wrong, that roadblock is very real. But it's not real because it is inherently true, it's real because we endow it with a heck of a lot of power to control us.

As it turns out, all you have to do to make sweeping, positive changes in your life is to figure out how you're feeling right now. Period. Because most of us are so focused on the scope of our entire life, we spend quite a bit of time evaluating the whole kibosh and looking for big, sweeping emotions that will come in and clear out all the old dusty stuff. We're trying to muster passion by thinking about how great our lives would be if we sat around being passionate all day, and then judging ourselves harshly if that doesn't materialize. So scale back to the garden variety level of your feelings. Notice what you notice for five minutes at a time. Make a habit of watching yourself think and feel, instead of just blindly going along for the ride.

Everyday feelings hold the keys to your future, and only by seeing them clearly can you learn to flow energy to the feel good places and pull it back from the feel bad ones.

75

"When we can look at ourselves in the mirror in full approval and say, 'You are who you are, kid, and I'm learning to love every funny little thing about you just the way you are,' we're on our way!"

Figuring out how to love ourselves unconditionally is one of the hardest things most of us will ever do. There is an endless list of reasons why we don't like ourselves, let alone love ourselves. We are constantly nitpicking, judging, tearing down, punishing, shaming, and belittling ourselves. How about cutting it out, already? It's going to take some time, and some discipline. Every time you catch yourself in a negative thought pattern about yourself, flip your focus immediately to something that you love about yourself. You can pick one thing for the day or for the week so that you don't have to waste time thinking, "Oh, I can't remember anything I love about myself."

Never mind if you deserve that love (you do) or you've earned it (no need) or if you're capable of giving it (you are).

Eventually, you'll start to hear a new voice in your head. It's your voice, but if it helps, you can imagine it sounding like one of your parents if you had a supportive one or an older sister or brother—someone who admires the heck out of you and loves you with all your faults, not in spite of them.

You're on your way, kid, and I love ya so much, I can't even say.

76

"When storms come, you know what created them and what to do."

It is still tough for me to embrace the idea that any and every problem in my life is self-created. In fact, sometimes it's easier to look at it as a kind of metaphor, or a viewpoint; I don't have to parse out or justify the logic or illogic of it to make use of this idea when I've got a problem. When I can hold this seemingly crazy idea close to me and really take it in, I can stop worrying about blame and negativity and feeling like a victim. Whether I'm a victim by anyone else's standards becomes irrelevant, and I'm suddenly free from the weight that that term carries with it (justified or not).

It's a scary thought that we might have created our own misery, but it can be a comforting one, as well. Often, the worst part of a difficult situation is the feeling of helplessness. We are frozen because we can't imagine how this happened to us. If we can say, even for a minute a day (and believe it), "I made this! And I can make something different," we are on our way to leaving behind the feeling of being alone and vulnerable in our situation. Again, whether it is right to feel that way or not in the particular situation doesn't matter as much as we think it does. You can be right in your misery 'til the cows come home, but you're still going to be miserable.

When we manage to override that feeling of powerlessness, even for just a little while every day, we can face our problems from a new angle, take them by surprise, and conquer them. We can claim them, own them, and only then can we talk them out and talk them down, little by little chipping away until we tip the scales toward feeling better.

Our fear of the storm adds immeasurably to its force. When we reclaim the fear, the wind dies down and the hail turns to rain.

77

"How do we get rid of those beliefs we now see as destructive? One way is to play 'let's pretend' to generate the emotion *opposite* the one that comes from the belief you want to change."

Start a program of one-a-day belief busting: every day pick a new (old) belief and conjure up the absolute opposite feeling to the one it gives you. For example, if you know that on the outside you are a people pleaser and are always trying to make everyone around you happy as a thin veil over your own insecurities and judgments, then you want to get into the opposite feeling. That is, you want to feel perfectly comfortable letting people be happy or unhappy on their own terms, and to do that from an inner place that is judgment- and insecurity-free. Do some pretending and imagine yourself in those shoes.

When you get in a good feeling opposite place, make it physical—do something concrete to solidify it in your body—this could be as simple as saying "no" to yourself or others when you feel your motivation is trying to please. Or it could be as easy as smiling, or putting some money in your wallet and walking around deciding what to spend it on.

You can also pick one thing to bust for the whole week—playing with turning the same old belief on its head every day for a week might actually break it open in a new way.

Play the opposites game and see how easy it can be to turn rock solid beliefs upside down.

78

"It's so important I feel good that I'm going to behave differently more of the time!"

I've talked to people who've quit smoking. Some of them after long years. And it's supposed to be one of the most difficult habits/addictions to kick. One woman I know used a statement very nearly like this quote on her path to quitting. It had gotten to be that she felt bad in a bunch of different ways—she was having trouble breathing, she had about six colds per winter, she felt embarrassed to have people she was just meeting know she was a smoker (since smart people don't smoke and she, rightly, sees herself as a smart person), and she was always edgy—protecting her supply—where and when could she have her next smoke?

She quit because she imagined she'd feel better once she did. And it became important for her to feel good about herself, both physically and emotionally. So, after a particularly bad cold, she made the daily choice to feel better. She behaved differently more of the time—smoking less, consciously choosing, noticing her feelings particularly around the where and when she could smoke, reminding herself how much better she felt. And it worked.

What behavior do you want to choose to do differently in order to feel better? Make a simple plan. Try it out. See what happens.

Feeling better is a choice I make.

79

"We've been taught that we gain only as we labor, that action is the magic word. Do, do, do; work, work, work, strive, sweat, toil, and then if our luck holds, we just might come out ahead."

Let me set something straight—labor in itself isn't the enemy, here. No one's saying that we should all grind to a halt and see how the world hands us everything we want on a silver platter. The fact of the matter is that finding the silver platter is in how we think about work: how we approach it, plan it, and carry it out. Then the fact of our work will feel incidental, breezy, and marvelous. The work will feel like it's doing itself.

Think of work as a lump of clay, or even the tools used to sculpt that clay. You can handle those tools, polish them, organize them, fiddle with them, and knead that clay for a lifetime without ever producing something that's appealing to anyone, least of all, you. You can put a lot of time and energy, a lot of brain and willpower into the sweating, striving, and toiling with zero result, or close to it. Even worse is if you do all this thinking that the final touch that will bring everything to fruition is some kind of wild stroke of luck. Might as well put your eggs in a basket and throw the basket in the back of an open pickup truck on a country road.

It's time to transform what we've been taught about work, and to realize that we are capable of accomplishing any work we need to do to really get what we want, and it is possible that any work we need to do, we can accomplish easily and freely. In fact, it will not feel like work at all. The value of work is not increased by how hard it feels to accomplish, or how much you sweat and stress as you do it. The really valuable work is inspired, and, while it may be taxing, it is not exhausting—in fact, it can be, and should be, exhilarating.

Rediscover the magic of inspired work.

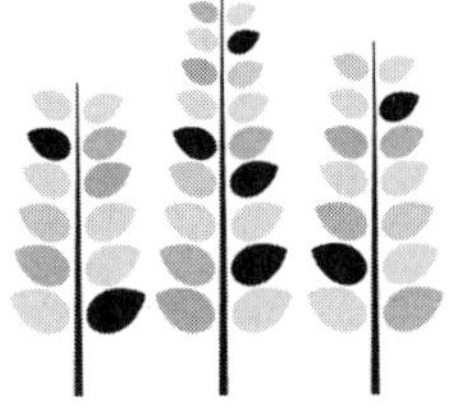

80

"Learn to turn on at will, no matter how you choose to do it. When you turn on, you open your valve, you lower your resistance, you vibrate positively, you attract positively."

Smile—at yourself in the mirror when you first wake up. At the clerk behind the counter when you pay for your gas or pick up your coffee. At your colleagues as you greet them. Smiling is perhaps the simplest way of opening ourselves up, of saying, "Here I am, Universe. Ready and willing."

Repeat some simple words that help you remember to open yourself up for all the good the world has to send your way. Say them out loud. Say them under your breath. Sing them in the shower.

Count your blessings. Marking all the good things in life—health, enough food, friends, family, the sun warm on your face, the shimmer of blowing leaves. Small blessings, big blessings, count them all. See if you can get to a hundred. Keep a notebook. Write down five a day or ten a day. Repeat them. And invite more into your life.

I make a practice of attracting positively.

81

"So crank up your passion and put your fears to rest. Sure, you're going to have some bumps in the road ahead, but who cares? You'll know what to do with them, why they came to you in the first place, and how to turn them into breathtaking rewards."

Wow! It sounds like a pretty cool ride. When I was a child, my family moved to California. One day we went to Santa Cruz, where there's a wonderful old wooden roller coaster. My dad loved roller coasters, and he and I got an unlimited ticket and got on and rode and went back around and got on and rode. I stopped counting at twelve and lost track of the number of times. It was a magical and breathtaking day. And I can and do vividly call it up.

To have a passion for riding roller coasters is to have a leg up when it comes to understanding the up-and-down ride that following a dream or a passion brings. I know when the coaster car falls, it's going to go up again. Up and down is part of the process. I really "get" that. And when I remember that I get it, I use that knowledge to push me up the next hill because I know that without going up the hill, I won't have that wonderful and breathtaking ride down to the goal I've set.

Find your own getting-over-the-bumps metaphor and memory.

82

"We're like toddlers on training wheels just learning to maneuver in our new world. Everything in that toddler says 'get up and go.' So it does, again, and again, and again, no matter how many times the tumbles may come. That's called passion . . . and practice."

Kids have an undeniable passion to grow up. They're fascinated by even the most mundane adult tasks (talking on the phone, going to the post office), and they hurl themselves headfirst into figuring out their own abilities and the world around them. Once we grow up to fill out the shape of our adult bodies, we forget that passion. The urgency of repetition and learning tapers off, replaced by the feeling that we've been there, done that. We lose the need to constantly explore, discover, and push the limits of ourselves and our surroundings. For some, this is such a devastating loss that they push themselves into thrill seeking, or addiction, just to feel that rush of the new again.

But so few of us are real grown-ups (by which I mean, fully realized mature human beings). The few who do seem more grown up than most also seem to be more childlike in a way than their adult peers, because they know that we all thrive best when we're engrossed in our passions and knee deep in exploration, no matter how old we are.

We could all stand to stir up a little passion through practice. Or, better yet, a little practice through passion. Then the practice won't even feel like work.

83

"But now that deep feeling of aloneness, and our frustration of now knowing who we truly are, is pushing us to wake up and remember, a push that is coming directly from our soul, the divine record-keeper of our being."

There is a song at the end of the musical *Into the Woods* by Stephen Sondheim with the line "You are not alone. Believe me, no one is alone." It is a huge struggle in many of our lives to understand that we are not—in-fact we cannot be—alone.

Our sense of abandonment and the fear that comes with it can motivate us to do crazy things: to make choices we hate or live our lives in a way we might otherwise run away from. What if we were able to fully comprehend, whenever we called up the feeling, our oneness with everyone on the planet? Not only them, but with everyone who has been and everyone who's coming. It's the biggest crowd there is, and you cannot be alone in it—even when you feel your most lonely and terrified, you are still not alone.

Interestingly enough, that dreaded feeling is a major gift from the universe. Because we are here to experience contrast, and our very sense of aloneness can be a divining rod that points us in the direction of finding our place in the whole.

You are not alone. How does that knowledge affect today's outlook?

84

"Got hurt feelings? What someone said has nothing to do with us, only what they are attracting into *their experience,* and we happened to walk into it."

Most of us can think back to a moment when someone said something hurtful to us. Just recalling the memory can bring back a mini-version of the physical sensation we felt at the time—blood flowing in our ears, a tightness in the chest, tears welling up. That memory is in our cells and we give it power and credence if we can't look at it, really feel those feelings, and then dismantle the whole thing.

To take apart an old feeling, we have to find a way to create a new belief about it. One of the ways to do this is to understand that what felt like a lightning bolt of anger coming out of the blue to slam into us was really just the discharge of a surge of negativity in and around the person who dealt the blow, and we happened to be in the same airspace. If we threw some energy back at them at the time, even our "hurt" energy, we were willing participants and multiplied the pain involved.

Can you make a new belief about how the universe gifted you that moment for a particular reason? If an insult stays with you viscerally, it may be because there's some kind of truth to it—if not on the surface, then maybe underneath. Or maybe the gift was just to discover more about your negative feelings—to encourage you to become a better observer of how you are flowing.

Old feelings + new belief = letting it go.

85

"You'll have up days, down days, fantastic days, cruddy days, deeply emotional days, and days when you'll be ready to throw in the towel. Yet I'd be willing to bet you won't, not now, not knowing what you know."

Would you be embarrassed if I asked how many books on your shelf promised to "change your life"? Would you blanch if I asked you to describe how many programs you had started out on but never completely found what you needed to stay the course?

The new is so foreign to us that it almost never feels comfortable, and we associate our comfortable place with our identity. So we try a new plan or a new way of thinking and it energizes us at first; then we hit some stumbling blocks as our resistance builds to something that might take us far out of our comfort zone. And then we stop, making the excuse that "It's just not me. I'm not like that." We slide back into our old worn-out beliefs and we feel a little better because, at the very least, those beliefs fit like good old slippers, and even if we're miserable in them, at least we know that particular misery, and we've acclimated ourselves to it. We even think that misery is a part of who we are.

You were not put on this earth to get used to being miserable. I know that for sure. It's a waste of your time, your talents, and your beautiful soul. Period. The law of attraction draws on what you are at your deepest core. It certainly may not be comfortable at first to spend much time with that deep part of you. But it is not someone else's plan, or thought, or outline. It's just you—it can only be you. You are the creator of your destiny and as you find your foothold in that knowledge and learn that nothing can stop you but yourself, it will be very hard to go backward.

Start on this path to a deeper, truer you, and never look back.

86

"If we are verbally or mentally accusing, berating, or disapproving in any way, we are attracting negatively."

There's that old saying, "If you can't say something nice, don't say anything at all." A corollary could be: If you can't think something nice, try thinking something else. Sometimes (especially when I'm feeling a bit smug about how well I'm doing being positive, attracting what I need into my life, like I'm winning some kind of attraction contest, as if), sometimes, I hear what I'm thinking about the other drivers on my morning commute. These are words most people don't use in polite company.

So I start out feeling good. I curse out drivers doing what I consider to be stupid things, and then? Then I become cranky and annoyed and impatient. It's like an immediate demonstration of attracting negatively. I'm guessing we all have our own example of this.

The trick here is "try thinking something else." In the case of the drivers, maybe I think, "Wow, I'd better drop back from that guy." And I take my time and I arrive at the office relaxed.

Make a list of situations or people you've thought of accusing or blaming. How can you turn it around?

87

"If you want to help someone out of their immediate suffering, sending a simple 'It's going to be all right' will usually quiet them down and give them an opportunity for a moment of Feel Good."

We don't, of course, know the future. So, it's not the future we're predicting when we say, "It's going to be all right." What we're doing is creating a moment of calm. Other words work, sometimes, too. "There, there." Or "Hush, hush." A hand on a person's shoulder also conveys, "Stay here, stay in the moment, it will be okay. It is okay."

The fourteenth-century mystic Julian of Norwich is often quoted as saying, "All will be well, and all will be well, and every kind of thing will be well." More of the story is that she heard these words in a vision, at a time when she was mortally ill, perhaps with the plague. And her suffering was relieved.

Saying the words or hearing them. Saying them to ourselves or to others. These acts—saying and hearing—create a space for positive energy to flow in. Sometimes, it's a small space; yet, often, it's a big enough moment to engender more like it. And, then, we know we've come through the worst of the suffering.

Create one moment of "feel good" and enjoy the one that follows on its heels.

88

"Don't justify your feelings with an 'I'm right and you're wrong,' even though that may be the case. That closes your valve and plugs up the flow of higher energies to all other areas of your life. Remember, you plug up one, you plug up all."

There's a sad little joke that goes something like: what does the little girl who's right all the time get to do at her birthday party? Celebrate it by herself. It really doesn't make any difference who's right and who's wrong about what Aunt Sadie said to Uncle Lester forty years ago. Or, for that matter, about who forgot to turn the dishwasher on. Or who forgot to balance the checkbook. Whatever disaster—and was it really a disaster?—that happened because of that thing has already happened. Now we get to deal with it.

You read that right—get to. Get to find the lesson in it. Get to let the energy of love and forgiveness flow between you and whomever you're wanting to blame for being wrong—even, or especially if, that's yourself.

Getting stuck in a right/wrong tug-of-war wastes time and uses up energy. That's pretty obvious. The trick is to recognize it in the moment. Stop, take a breath. Chew those words. Don't let them come out of your mouth. Now, swallow them. Open to: we have a problem and we can figure out how to solve it.

Open to the solutions flowing, and they will.

89

"Usually when we forgive, we are acknowledging that whomever we're forgiving has done a wrong, which is probably true. Then, even though we say we forgive, we secretly hold on to the dastardliness of the wrong. Yet true forgiveness is about no longer holding on to or stewing over (focusing on) the thing that got us all riled up to begin with."

Let's think of things we don't hold on to: the too-hot handle of a pan, a cold metal stair railing in winter, a rope slipping through our hands, a heavy box that makes our arms quiver. You get the idea. Holding on to all those things hurts.

We put them down.

Of course, we don't just drop them. We put them down in a way that is safe for us and those around us. We don't just drop the pan of boiling water, letting it splash all over. We don't let go of the railing if it means slipping down a flight of icy stairs. Dropping a box of books when our arms are quivering could result in a broken toe. Forgiveness is like that. People say, "Oh, just let it go." And we do need to let it go, because holding on to it hurts us.

The real question is how to safely and effectively let it go, making sure our letting go doesn't fall heavily on our own head or someone else's. Forgiving a friend for being late doesn't work if your forgiveness is conditional on her never being late again. That's a small hurt. To forgive a bigger hurt takes a bit of thought and work—how to lay the burden down where it won't come back to hurt you or someone else. Each of us needs to figure that out and practice doing it.

I practice shifting my focus away from what hurt me in the first place.

90

"When your joy no longer depends on what anybody else thinks of you, or what anyone else does, then you've 'got it.'"

Never underestimate the power of peer pressure. It holds more sway over some of us than others. Part of that may be how we're raised—always to consider what the neighbors might think. And part of that might be our temperaments—some people seem innately less timid about expressing themselves than others. But, sooner or later, we all learn that doing the same things the same way as others in our family, group, town, or country is not what makes us happy. That is to say pretty much that other people can't make us happy—either by what they do or by their attitude toward what we do.

No matter how comfortable we are living in a situation in which we do things the way "our people" have always done them, sooner or later, we're probably going to bump into a situation in which we're not comfortable. And given that peer pressure is strong and self-motivation and pleasing ourselves need often to be learned, it's really probably better that this happen sooner. We can all use the practice.

My joy resides in me, and while I hope others in my life will share it, I won't try to force that.

91

"Habits of a lifetime—and eons of inherited genes—die hard."

Your energy is flowing; the conflicts around you are shrinking; the blocks to your success, health, and happiness are evaporating. Even as you get the hang of this power of attraction stuff and some wonderful things are flowing into and through your life, I can pretty much guarantee you that you will have at least one ongoing battle. It won't be with your circumstances, because now you understand that those are changeable and you don't have to tie your worth as a person or your happiness to those circumstances. It won't be with your thoughts, because now you know how to sift out which are useful and which you can get rid of. The battle won't be with your family, friends, or any social or political structure around you, because you will realize that the way to live in harmony with all of those things is to claim the power that each individual has to create his own happiness.

The battle will be with your own habits, and the instincts you inherited from your ancestors. No matter how off base we now realize our old thought processes are, they still feel like home, like a good, old, worn-in pair of shoes, and we can walk for miles in them before we even notice the difference. Staying vigilant to those old habits can be a real draw on our energies, and old feelings of guilt can pile on top of them as we think, "I know this is wrong—why am I still living out these old patterns?"

Forgive yourself, and forgive yourself at the drop of a hat. Welcome the old habits as you would that crazy old uncle. Familiar, yes, but nobody really wants to spend much time in his company. Watch yourself go through the motions without judgment, and then switch tactics, energies, or perspectives to jump to a new track.

Forgive yourself, and do it at the drop of a hat—easily and without judgment.

92

"As long as we're reacting to conditions, something will always be wrong."

If you ask my friend Candace how the party was last night, she'll start with a litany of things she didn't like, food that tasted a little funny, awkward moments, and people who were acting strangely. And then, after five minutes of griping, at the end of it all, she might very well say how it was really great and she had quite a nice time!

Are you one of those people who finds fault wherever they look? Who thinks they are pretty well off, or fairly satisfied, or even moderately happy, but can't stop noticing how much there is that is just plain *wrong?* I'm with you—it's not hard for me to look around and see problems, failures, inadequacies everywhere. (It's a bad habit, I know, but never mind me; I'll just sit here and judge myself for my habit of being judgmental!)

Why are we like this? Why do we think that nothing can be really right without an equal and opposing force of wrongness? We are like this because we are giving too much credit to conditions.

Your situation, or the conditions surrounding an event or a project or a task, will never be the sum total of things. Never. So stop acting like they are. Stop loading your pockets with those stones—you don't need 'em.

Remember that you get to choose how you are going to feel no matter what is happening. When you remember that, you don't have to worry what goes wrong and what doesn't—it'll all just be part of the bigger, better whole picture.

93

"The more feeling we flow to prepare the way for our actions, the smoother and more fruitful the results will be."

I have a friend who does a lot of presentations for his job. They're not all directly selling things to people, although the idea is that they ultimately lead to that. He always tries to find a way to connect to people with a story that's memorable and engaging. And to do that, he dreams his presentation. He thinks about it a little bit. He imagines himself doing the presentation, feels the exhilaration of it going well, and then he goes to bed and dreams the presentation he will give the next day. I've never thought to ask him how he stumbled on this method, but it's practically failure-proof. I once watched him do a presentation, get turned down for a product he thought was a shoe-in, never miss a beat, present two more things, and come away with big sales for them. It was a pretty astonishing performance.

The only time I saw him rattled was when a presentation fell apart in the middle because the client changed all the ground rules. Even so, the only way I could tell he was upset was that his face was a bit flushed. I asked him afterward what he thought happened. "I didn't dream about it." That's all he said. And, in that case, although it took a bit longer, the client came around, as well.

A little bit of thinking goes a long way. Salespeople know this. Actors do, too. Find your feelings, your emotion, around a project, and let the feelings flow. Imagine what a successful completion will feel like. What will your face feel like? Your belly? Your feet?

Ready, set, feel. Let the feelings flow before the action begins.

94

"Any action taken from a place of lack is always counterproductive."

It's easy enough to understand this metaphysical principle in our heads. Things go better if we're in a better mood, have a better attitude. It's even pretty easy to live by it when we're not feeling some kind of lack in our lives. But trying to remind ourselves of it when we're short of cash, or feeling unloved, maybe during the holiday season, or feeling like our projects never come to fruition—well, that's a whole other proposition.

So, if we know that action taken from lack is counterproductive, one way we could handle that is not take any action on days we're experiencing that feeling. The problem with that is the feeling of lack feeds itself. If I don't take an action to attract more money, for example, because I'm feeling the negative pull of lack, I compound that pull. I drag myself further down into the pit.

The alternative is to address the lack head on. Look at the feeling. Don't judge. Don't tell yourself you shouldn't feel lack. But talk to the feeling. And yourself. Let yourself know what it would take to feel differently.

Flip the feeling and you flip from counterproduction to production.

95

"Open to receive! Put those signs all over your house, 'OPEN TO RECEIVE!'"

This is advice to take to heart. Three-by-five index cards, a bit of tape, and some markers in lovely colors work well. It can be an act of opening just to go out and buy these. Or, you can use whatever paper and pen you have in hand. Three words: "open to receive." The very act of writing them opens us up.

Once you've posted them, please remember to look at them. And when you look at them, please remember to take a minute to close your eyes and envision your heart opening. What does that mean to you? Is it a warm feeling? Is it a feeling of accepting whatever this day brings? Is it envisioning the object—person, job, feeling, state of mind?

Finally, a little bit of gratitude goes a long way. Gratitude is a miracle worker. It's a change catalyst for experience, attitude, and circumstances. I've found a great way to end my "Open to receive" meditation is with a simple, "Thank you for all that is."

Today I take a minute to make myself open to receiving what I ask for.

96

"Learn to look at contrast without having to cross the line into negative resistance."

When you get the hang of using the law of attraction, will you stop having occasional angry and nasty thoughts? Will you stop seeing red when someone cuts you off in traffic? Will you stop being annoyed, crabby, or frustrated? Probably not. This stuff, or stuff like it, is a natural reflection of the necessary contrast all around us, and for a while after you dive into this energy business, it may pop up a little stronger even than usual. The "bad" stuff will seem to be everywhere, but not to worry—it's just providing some nice contrast to the good stuff going on all around you.

Let negative events, thoughts, and feelings be there. The worst possible thing you could do would be to deny their existence and cram them down. Remember that bad stuff does not mean you're a bad person—it just doesn't. I like to try and look at bad stuff like the narrator of a nature show about the habits and conditions of a newly discovered species that has never been studied. Of course, I'm talking about myself and my own life, but that little bit of distance lets me say, "Oh, it's amazing to see the quick defensive reactions at work. Wow, look at that anger and aggression—how splendid!" Validating all the bad stuff from this outside point of view somehow lets me release it faster so that I don't hold on to it and let it grow into something that could block my energy flow.

Yes, you may still have miserable days, and you're most definitely going to be thinking some negative, jealous, angry, selfish, terrified thoughts.

But the new you is not going to take a gamble by giving those thoughts and feelings free rein to create your existence. Your new outlook is too precious, the possibilities are too extraordinary to let go.

Let the bad stuff be real enough so that you can acknowledge it, feel it, understand what's going on, and finally show it the door.

97

"Everybody knows what they want in life, right? Wrong! Wants are about the most frightening, misunderstood, neglected element in the entire human race, and I'd lay odds that, for most people, just thinking about them is more terrifying than a dentist's chair without painkillers."

I'd wager that when people think about what they want, they're thinking one of two things: (1) thinking about what I want is just setting myself up for disappointment because I'll never get it. That's scary. Or (2) okay, I don't like how things are, so I'll just sit here and think about what's wrong with my life and what I want to make it better. And I'll think and I'll think, and I can't think of anything. That's even scarier. Yeah, way more scary than a dentist's chair.

If we say out loud, even quietly, that we want something, we seem to think we're standing up in the woods during deer-hunting season with a target on our backs. Someone is going to shoot us down. And the world not being an any more evolved place than it is, yeah, someone—even someone we love—is likely to tell us all the reasons we can't have what we want.

So how do we lay aside this fear—the first step in figuring out what we want? We need to be gentle with ourselves. We don't tell a child who's leery of going to the dentist for the first time to just shape up and stop being a baby. As long as it took to develop our fears of stating what we want, that may be how long it will take us to begin to ask and answer honestly the question.

So take a breath, take the time, and pick one thing you want to do or say or hear today.

98

"The ultimate goal, of course, is to stop see-sawing with open valves, shut valves, open valves, shut valves. That's like calling a dog and telling him to stay at the same time. Everything jams to a halt. How, then, does one retain passion for something that hasn't shown up or happened?"

I always thought "if at first you don't succeed, try, try again" to be one of the most annoying adages ever dreamed up by anyone. I know, I know, the stories abound—hours, days, years of practice, trial and error, and then *voilà!* Victory—the gold medal won, the money earned to buy a house, the goal achieved. And then what? One odd thing about a passion that shows up or a goal that gets accomplished—we find the appetite was in the anticipation. Not always, but often enough to make it worth taking a look at what it is we really want. And what we'll do when we get it.

Jonas Salk didn't give up when his first attempts at finding a polio vaccine didn't work out. And what's even more telling is he didn't stop with a polio vaccine—he went on trying to discover preventative vaccines until the end of his long life.

I am inspired by Dr. Salk's answer to an interview question about who owned the patent to the vaccine he invented that pretty much eradicated polio. Salk was asked: "Who owns the patent on this vaccine?" He responded: "There is no patent. Could you patent the sun?" So, if our passion is predicated on the success of ownership, maybe it won't happen. If it doesn't show up the way we think we want it, maybe we'll get clearer on what we really want and why we want it.

If what I think I'm waiting for doesn't show up, may I pay close attention to what does.

99

"Like everything else, when we stop getting lost in the conditions and start dealing with our own valve, life takes on a new glow. If we would look for ways to appreciate and praise, rather than to criticize and blame, we can be the essential catalyst that helps tip the scales up to positive attracting for everybody, including ourselves."

Ever seen one of those dot pattern pictures—it's a visual trick and doesn't look like much of anything until you get your eyes focused the right way, and then all of a sudden a clear, 3D image snaps into view. Think of your life like one of those pictures. Each moment, every decision, every twist of fate is a dot, a little cluster of information, memory, and inspiration. And none of it makes much sense when you're looking at the dots by themselves. But take a step back and refocus; let go of what you think you see (a bunch of dots, a string of bad luck) and allow yourself to piece together the real picture.

When you do, the sum of the parts is astounding, a real punch in the gut, the *aha!* moment you've been waiting for. Just as when you look at the unfocused picture, the effort may be a strain—the muscles in your eyes and brain resist looking at the information in a new way, and you might even feel a little woozy. A perspective shift in your life can similarly feel disorienting and unnatural, but when the real picture springs up in front of you, the relief and ease it brings are well worth the discomfort. Once you see it, you can start to see the negative cycles in your life for what they are: victim mentality, addiction, fear, low self-esteem. Your mind will start racing as you reevaluate your circumstances and choices with renewed meaning and vision. It will take some practice to return to that momentary uncomfortable but ultimately divine space of clarity.

Take a look at a familiar situation in a new way and see what you attract.

100

"Go for material things, of course, but also stake your claim for universal or intangible things."

So you're feeling pretty confident that you can magnetize what you want into your life. And maybe what brought you to all of this law of attraction stuff in the first place was some basic, material, everyday wants and desires. No judgments here—go whole hog and get that Ferrari, if that's what makes you all buzzy.

Hey, while you're at it, why not throw in a few more desires? Remember, nothing is impossible. Let's vibrate for our whole family to feel joy, for a greater sense of freedom for ourselves and our loved ones, for climate stabilization, for healthy oceans, for children everywhere having plenty of good food to eat, for cooperation among people and nations. Why not? *Nothing is impossible.*

The greatest work we do as human beings is to serve each other. I don't mean servitude, I mean service. This is the thing that ultimately gives us the most personal gratification we'll ever know in our lives: spreading our energy and other precious resources around to help others.

Wanting is taking charge. Wanting is creating. Fulfill your reason for being—that's the true richness of life.

101

"Anything you try to push away, you automatically include into your vibration for attraction."

When a crime is committed in our society and the perpetrator is convicted, we take action by locking him away—to punish him, to separate him from society, and, theoretically, to reduce the risk to everyone. But in many indigenous and aboriginal cultures, the thought of separating a victimizer from society is crazy. There is a fundamental knowledge in these alternative legal systems that when you push away any undesired element, you give it more destructive power, and the balance of the whole society shifts. The goal of these legal systems is aimed more at reintegrating the perpetrator and the victim back into the social and moral fabric of the community, to restore the equality to both sides that was disrupted by a criminal act.

The same goes for unwanted elements in your life or your own community. Anything you try to keep away through fear or by force will redouble through the attention it gets. It is much more difficult to find positive ways to reintegrate the energy that you don't want and change it through the force of your positive vibrations. But, in the end, that's the only choice we can make to bring in balance and happiness.

Push it away, and you lose control and give it power at the same time. Draw it closer, accept it, and you have the chance to change it.

102

"Now you've entered the uncanny world of synchronicity, you're plugged in, connected to your Source energy, going with the flow. But you'll never see it, or learn to trust it, if you're not watching for it."

There's such a thing as being blindsided by good luck. A bolt out of the blue—an offer of a new job, an inheritance from a great-aunt you only met once, a new friend who offers you a vacation house, an old friend who offers you love. Any and all "positive" events can disconcert us if we didn't see them coming.

They're disconcerting because we're not trusting that we can go with the flow, that anything good might happen to us. They're disconcerting, sometimes, because they're not "exactly what we expected." Say you've been plugging in to your source energy, asking for a life partner, and an old friend reappears in your life and well. . . . But, wait, this isn't what you ordered up—you wanted a *new* partner, not an old friend. You didn't think the partner would look like this, come into your life this way. What were you watching for? And what did you get?

Some skeptics say that people find synchronicity only because they look for it. Their point is that it doesn't exist and the people who are looking for it are reading too much into events. I don't know about reading too much into events, but I do know they're right about one thing—synchronicity doesn't exist—or at least you won't see it if you aren't looking for it. And when we do look for it, we see so many more rich possibilities for our lives. It's that simple.

Today I'm going to look for what I want with the sure knowledge that that will help me get it.

103

"Think only about what you want, instead of the lack of it."

There is a saying among actors that the best way to get a job is to book a plane ticket. Meaning that as soon as you commit to going away to see family or on a vacation and become unavailable for work, the universe sends you the perfect job on a platter. The saying is often intoned in a kind of mock-misery—you want nothing more than to land a great role in a wonderful project, but there's always a catch; in this case, that you're out a big chunk of cash for plane fare.

When you book that job in conflict with your other plan, what's really happening is twofold. First, the expectation that you are going away takes the pressure off whatever possibilities are in the works. If you know you're not going to work while on vacation, you stop thinking nonstop about what will happen if you can't get work (a big Don't Want). So, by booking those tickets, you're taking the Don't Want down a notch, and the underlying Want of getting to work doing what you love can come through a little stronger—so in comes the work. Second, the simple act of planning a vacation or going to see friends or family is about committing to doing something you want, and because you're acting on one Want, it paves the way for others to come through, as well.

You can trick your energy into doing this for you again and again, and you don't have to spend a bunch of money on a plane ticket you can't use. If you've lost your keys, stop looking for them—every moment of frenzied "I can't find them!" tucks them away deeper into wherever they are. Do something around the house that you really want to do and that takes some solid mental energy. You can even make the trick better by saying out loud, "I'm never going to find my keys, so I'm going to hang this painting just where I want it instead." Most likely by the time you're done, the location of the keys will have popped into your head.

When faced with a Don't Want, throw yourself into a Want—even if it's totally unrelated—and clear the way.

104

"Stop processing; start living! Stop dissecting; start experiencing."

To stop processing is not to deny or stuff your past. It's not to lie to ourselves or others. We don't reach adulthood without having some emotional hurts, some psychic knocks on the head. That's the nature of living in this material universe. And, sometimes, somewhere along the process, maybe with the aid of a well-intentioned but wrong-minded counselor or friend or self-help book, we stop denying and we start grinding. We perseverate—I am like I am because this happened and then that happened. And if my mother/father/first love/teacher/boss hadn't, then I wouldn't. And then, and then, and then . . .

There is a third way. We can go ahead and look at our past—recent and remote—but without judgment. That is without judging ourselves or others. Look at it, express it, admit it, acknowledge it, accept it, and move on. Express it and let it go.

And how, pray tell, do we let it go? Well, we won't if we're not engaged in the present. So the best way to let the past go is to jump into the present with both feet, experiencing all there is to experience. And, remember, no judgment.

The best way to let go of the past is to live in the present.

105

"Empowerment is the willingness to forge ahead, no matter the unknown."

Empowerment is the ability to be in the moment. If we're actively engaged in our work, open to the feelings and atmosphere in the present moment we're in, doing what we have to do now, we have far more power to deal with the unknown future. And, let's face it, the future is always unknown.

In fact, if it weren't unknown, if we knew every obstacle, bump, twist, turn, curve ball, and blessing the future has in store for us, we might never start a new project. We might never create a Want and pursue it.

So empowerment is the gift of forging ahead in the moment, working on the part that's right in front of us, trusting the universe will give us the grace, insight, inspiration, and stamina for dealing with the unknown. To be empowered is to be open to our own powerful center, to be in touch with our own guidance, and to act from that place of strength. Empowerment is not bestowed by the Emperor of Empowerment sitting in a chair on high. Nor is it stolen by the Wicked Witch of Weakness.

Empowerment begins and ends at home.

106

"I was learning to live without worry. It was astonishing. I seemed to have found a means to live in a state completely counter to what I believed to be normal."

We worry that if we stop fretting about all the ways we are in danger every day that something is going to sneak up from behind and take us off guard. Of course, we know by now that this kind of thinking is laying down the welcome mat for just such an occurrence (and if it does happen in some form, we feel even more justified in our initial worry). But let's take a look at the alternative.

We've all heard the stories of near misses—the woman whose daughter keeps her home from work at the World Trade Center on 9/11, the man who gets off a plane before it takes off and the plane later crashes. The premonitions in these stories come to people who are open to receiving them for some reason or another. We are all psychic, connected to the universal energy around us through our minds and bodies, but most of us can't sift through the information, so we either tune it all out and miss valuable clues or we try to focus in all directions at once, which rarely does anyone much good.

When we release ourselves from the litany of worries that plays on repeat throughout the day, when we finally figure out that it is most certainly possible to live a life free from the weight of fear around our necks, then we are primed to pay attention to the gut feelings that help keep us safe and happy. In fact, when you're plugged into your Guidance, the messages come in their true form—positive feelings signaling opportunities for change and growth, and negative ones warning us about some danger or trouble. (Of course, some negative feelings from old issues will probably be hanging around and will have to be sorted out.) There is nothing more thrilling than going from the static of unintelligible, constant worry coming from a jumble of sources to a state of open calm connection to your Guidance, which leads you into and out of all the right situations at just the right moments.

Turning off your fear turns up the volume of your instincts.

"Always flow your energy first, then engage from inspiration."

When you watch tennis on television, you might hear the commentators use the phrase "dialing in," which refers to someone who is in the zone, going for big shots and bringing their energy and their game to the table to make their shots and win rallies. The opposite phrase is "clamping down," and that one's pretty obvious—the player is going through the same motions, trying to make the same shots, but their energy and movements are confined in some way, and often as a player pushes to get out of that state, the vise simply tightens further against their will.

I love the phrase "dialing in" because there's a focus on the preparation, the inner life. It's not about going after something, or pushing past limits, or even freeing or flowing energy. It's very simply about making small adjustments inside yourself before you engage, or whack the ball, or burst across the court. It's also about zeroing in, narrowing focus on the task at hand and letting the other tasks and voices drop away completely as you pick up the line of desired action.

You can't take inspired action by repeating a mantra of "inspired action. Inspired action! INSPIRED ACTION!!!" The result would surely be a major clamping down. The best way to take inspired action is to very simply and honestly explore the task at hand, and call up whatever resources to be at the ready when you need them.

I will dial in and tune up my focus, and the actions will take care of themselves.

108

"You begin to take inspired action versus grinding action—the difference between success or a flop."

Do you ever feel like you couldn't possibly be doing more, and yet you still aren't doing enough? It's like you're riding a bike up a grueling path, steadily plugging away—your muscles aching and out of breath. And suddenly someone whizzes by on a motor scooter, waving as their dust cloud envelops you. It doesn't feel fair. How come some people work themselves to the bone for little reward and others just coast?

Yes, there are certainly inequities in our resources to begin with—but I'm talking more about the action itself, the force and the work it takes to push you up that hill, no matter where your journey starts.

When you allow yourself to play around with your Wants and desires before you set one physical thing in motion, you will be shocked at the difference when you do start to act. The longer you play, the easier it will go (and the faster and richer the reward). Getting your energy in order and your thinking in a helpful place before you go replaces a lot of the physical strain of a task. The universe responds to energy—and it is only a social custom that we have come to believe that the physical energy of work is more appropriate or effective at getting things done than the mental and spiritual energy of playing and dreaming.

Let the dreaming inspire the action, not the other way around.

109

"Actually, the majority of the world is quite well off."

How do we measure well off? Think of the difference in weight we give to one feeling of lack, or to a setback—say a business deal not working out—compared to appreciating the things we do have, the things that work right.

Consciously putting our attention on the positive is not something we're taught or expected to do. And the more we bemoan the things or resources we don't have, the stronger we feel the lack. We might get to the point where one negative thing outweighs a thousand positive things.

One way to remember what we do have is to take the time to appreciate them. Out loud. Go ahead, count your blessings, count what you do have rather than what you don't. And, if at first you can't think of any, please persist.

The more I count my blessings, the more blessings I have to count.

110

"A freedom of life is waiting for you that is beyond any capacity I have to describe, a freedom so unnaturally extraordinary that one can only know it through the joy of living it."

Suffering is a given—part of the human condition. If we think that mastering our energies means that we'll never be in hurtful situations or have ugly thoughts again, we're in for some disappointment. Contrast—good and bad, light and dark—is one of the defining characteristics of our time on this planet, so we might as well have a way to manage it.

The problem is that we've inflated this idea of suffering through feeding it a steady diet of worry, anticipation, and fear. So, even though most of us suffer relatively little in our lifetimes, we spend so much time expecting to feel bad or remembering feeling bad, that we draw out the pain to an unbelievable degree, and, in the process, we usher in more of the same.

We've created our own captivity. Experiencing that unnatural, extraordinary freedom through the joy of living is our birthright. Pain is powerful stuff, but our fear of it is even more powerful, making us deny ourselves the freedom to live. So, the idea is to take away that power, even by reclaiming just a few minutes here and there from the grip of fear by flowing positive energy. You don't have to do it all at once, just get the snowball going and then work on it a little every day, and chip away at the captivity you've created.

I cannot promise you that you will never suffer again. I can promise you, however, that you will never again be imprisoned by your suffering.

111

"See her [Earth] in peace, and you will help to bring it about."

Envision peace, starting at home. Come to peace with yourself. Accept the things you cannot change, change the things you can, as the Serenity Prayer suggests. And then consider the ways you—and I—tens, hundreds, thousands, millions of people can make changes through the power of prayer.

See the Earth with water restored to pristine condition, so that all the children of the world have enough to drink. See rich, thick topsoil, so all the people on the planet have enough to eat. See the world as a hospitable, habitable, loving mother. See the peoples of the world not fighting over who "owns" Mother Earth's resources.

It won't happen all at once. It may not look like much at first. Yet as we make small, incremental steps, in growing numbers, seeing the Earth at peace, the Earth will, over time, come to a balance of energy that we no longer disrupt and disturb.

My thoughts, my actions, my vision multiplied by the many children of the earth—we can make a difference.

112

"The point is to get off autopilot and pay attention. Listen! Stay alert for that little push, watch for signs, tune in to hunches. If it feels good, it's Guidance."

We think we're listening all the time. Our ears are open, and information is filtering into them in the form of sound waves, so end of story, right? Wrong. We rarely listen. Or, maybe it's that we rarely hear what we are listening to.

Listening is about a broadened awareness. Listening happens basically through your ears, but, if we think of listening in a metaphorical sense, we can carry it into the realm of listening to our hearts, or listening to the quiet voice inside us.

Expanded, the idea that you are listening means that you can place yourself on the receiving end of any information the world has to offer. Listening is often about filtering out what we do and don't want to hear. It is our habit to only hear what we expect to hear in any given moment, and this includes messages from the universe about our Wants.

If we could plan out how, when, and where our next desire was coming down the pike, we'd be wonderfully suited to living in a bubble of our own making. While there are certain things about that bubble that might be comforting, it is ultimately a prison cell in which you can't *hear* anything. Take yourself out of that bubble and you can notice the fact that what you want might be coming from any direction at any time, and all you have to do is open up your awareness to see the myriad possibilities.

I practice staying in the moment and listening with my whole self.

113

"How many times have you said to yourself, 'I just got a hit (or a hunch, or a gut feeling) to go there,' and so you did; you went there, and then found out it was a good thing you did. You were following your Guidance."

Spouses met. Jobs found. Guidance isn't all burning bushes in the Bible. Or voices from angels in another dimension. Guidance is sometimes quiet, sometimes persistent, and there's really no way of proving it right or wrong. But stories of "coincidences" abound. Frequently, it's the small things—picking up the phone at the end of the office day without checking caller ID. Foolish? Maybe if you don't trust the instinct that said, "You're outta here." You might find yourself roped into a long discussion and agreeing to a project you don't want to take on just to get the other person off the line. Or, if that little voice says pick up the phone and you do, well you might find yourself on your way out to dinner with an old college friend who just happens to be coming through your city on business.

Guidance is internal. If we're looking for outside validation—my teacher, mother, brother, boss says I should do this or that or the other thing—well, that might be good advice, and it might even be guidance if we're looking for ideas that we can internalize and check out with a feel test.

It helps to develop our own feel tests, and one way to do that is to pay attention to the accidents or coincidences that happen. How did I feel—besides relieved to be alive—when I didn't go at the green light and therefore didn't get hit by the truck barreling through the red. How did I feel right before I picked up the phone because I knew it would be good news—maybe small news like my dry cleaning was done?

Pay attention to stomach flutters, the ends of your fingers, the back of your neck—the more you do, the more you'll learn.

114

"If we race in to please, rescue, or placate, we are attracting negatively."

This piece of wisdom about attracting negatively is not a case of opposites attract. Nor is it akin to the saying, "damning with faint praise." It's a bit closer to "killing with kindness." Yet that's not quite it, either—because the truth is that "when we race to please, rescue, or placate, we attract negatively" is not ironic, sarcastic, or metaphorical. It simply is—the truth.

What happens when we tell a simple little white lie—trying to please Mom or help a friend out with an excuse? Maybe there aren't immediate dire consequences, but I can feel it in my body, a sort of tensing in my gut. As human beings, we're meant to pay attention to that tension in the gut. If we don't, over time, we risk losing our ability to discern our own truth, and, truthfully, we put our physical health in jeopardy. The negative energy we're attracting can make us sick. Not to mention the negative energy a relationship based on falsehoods attracts.

The opposite of pleasing or placating is not acting out or condemning. Nor is the opposite of rescuing, abandoning. Yet, when we act from any of these stances, we attract victim energy to ourselves. And, we end up screaming at the person we were trying to please. Or walking away from the person we were trying to help (including ourselves). When we are slower to react, we are more likely to talk—and act—from our truth. Slow truth and positive attraction trump fast reaction and negative attraction any day of the week.

Make a list of ten slow actions to take the place of your usual reactions.

"The energy of money needs outlets; no outlets, no money."

There is a tried and true business adage that you have to spend money to earn money. So a statement like "the energy of money needs outlets" is no airy-fairy concept dreamed up by someone who thinks she can live on air and chanting. (Just wanted to make that point, because many people think this energy thing is fine for relationships and maybe feeling better, but certainly not for something as "real" as money. Uh huh.)

Think of Ebenezer Scrooge, a man so famous for holding on to his money, for not letting it do its good work, that his very name has become a common pejorative word—a hoarder, not only tightfisted, but mean-spirited. Of course, in *A Christmas Carol,* Scrooge is given—and takes—the opportunity to create outlets for his money. And all's well that ends well.

So create an outlet for your money—when you have a little, maybe give a little of that little away. Or splurge on a bouquet of flowers. Celebrate the good fortune that is coming.

Money, keep it moving.

116

"Even feeling moderately concerned (sort of our life story) shuts the door to abundance and well-being, which is our God-given birthright."

Let's call a spade a spade and concern what it really is—a time suck also known as worry. Worry takes up way too much room in any room, and it just won't stay neatly folded away in the closet. Moderate concern leads to major concern. The minute we open that door in our minds, out it pops and demands that we pay attention to the "what ifs" and the "so whats."

What if I felt good? Would someone else feel bad? How do I know that? And what makes us think that abundance—material or spiritual—is a zero-sum game. If I have more, my neighbor has less. That's what our materialistic culture teaches us. But is that really true? Or is there enough of what matters to go around?

The real question is what I do with that moderate concern when it arises. I knew a woman who grew up on a farm in a part of the Midwest where the growing season was short and the soil was rocky. Her mother wouldn't let her board in town to go to high school because she'd already lost one child to influenza, and when the daughter was sixteen their family house burned down. But during my friend's long life, even though many things happened to her that she could have worried about, she refused to, in her words, "borrow trouble."

What can you (I?) do to shut the door on worry and open the door to abundance and well-being?

117

"Since energy can't die, and all of us are most assuredly energy-based, fearing death is nothing but a monumental waste of time that evokes nothing but more negative energy. The sad thing is, we've been so cleverly taught to fear death, we've totally forgotten how to live."

Change. Energy changes. It moves, it changes character. Positive energy attracts positive energy. And the converse is true, too. Life is change. Death is a different kind of change. None of this is to be feared.

Take a breath, then another. Three times. Your body is different than it was four breaths ago. If you bring in peace and light with these breaths, you are living. If, over time and gradually, you take these breaths and let yourself think of a time when your energy will exist without a body that needs to take breaths, you can begin to let go of the fear we are taught about death.

Take another breath. Then another. Three times more. Your body is different than it was four breaths ago, and you have let go of some fear. You are living. You are remembering how to live.

May I use my energy to live fully and die happy.

118

"It's not about money; it's about how you're flowing your energy. The money will come when you stop looking at how much of it you don't have. You can't look at 'not enough money' and feel anything but negative emotions, which disallows the flow. So find more ways to open your valve."

Money is probably the single most difficult thing to open our valves around, especially when we don't have enough of it. How easy is it to stop thinking about where the rent is coming from? How silly does it seem to say out loud to ourselves, "I have everything I need," when, clearly, I don't have the money to pay the utility bill. Yet, dwelling on how hard this is, how much of a stuck valve, brick wall, sunk ship feeling not having the money is, only creates more stuck.

If I can't get to the place where I can give up worrying about money, the only thing that works for me is to focus entirely on something else. This might be a task I know how to do but don't do often enough to do on automatic pilot. For me, that can be threading the sewing machine, even if I don't have a mending project. I always have to think about the order and the eye-hand coordination to get the thread through those passages, and it's just enough to take my mind out of worry mode. Sometimes taking a brisk walk will do the trick. The longer I can take my attention away from the "money problem," the more I can open up.

It's not that opening up means having specific ideas about how to get money. Nor does it mean that I can stay open without keeping my attention on staying open. Opening up does mean that there is a possibility that solutions I have not thought of or worked toward will present themselves, and I'll be awake and paying attention to see them.

In a time when your negative emotions about money are NOT present, take time to think of at least two ways to turn the negative around for those days when "lack" threatens to take over.

119

"You're not only connected to the force of well-being, you *are* that force. That force is Life. That force is passion. And passion is creation."

Well-being, even when we recognize it, can seem fleeting. We trip on it. We convince ourselves it's accidental. The sunshine, the cool breeze, the child's smile, the lover's kiss—that's what connects us to our feeling of well-being. Well, maybe. But surely there are days that the sun shines, the leaves rustle, a child grins, and a lover hugs us good-bye that we feel something entirely different. So what is the source of the force? It can't be totally due to the conditions we find ourselves in.

Hint: there is a right and obvious answer. Me, myself, and I. Sunshine comes and goes, and everybody knows we couldn't exist without the rain. Children smile, laugh, and cry—letting us and themselves know how they feel and what they need. Even on literal or metaphorical rainy days in our lives, we can connect to the force of well-being by letting ourselves know what our passions are, by choosing them and expressing that choice.

An expression of well-being and, therefore, passion and creation, can be small. Some days maybe all I can muster is a fleeting appreciation for the fact that I am grateful I can express my sorrow by crying. Other days will be different. And if I nourish my well-being by noticing what I do to create it, it grows bigger and stronger. Sometimes inch by inch and sometimes by leaps and bounds.

I will make one gesture toward creating well-being today.

120

"Those cracks are our resistance, our inner critic or naysayer, our old ideas of social rights and wrongs, our old low-frequency security blankets being laid bare by the higher frequencies."

When I was a small child, I was fascinated by dog whistles. The idea was that dogs, who can hear at higher frequencies than humans, if they were trained to, would come running at the sound of a whistle. I'm pretty sure they didn't catch on widely because dogs will also respond to verbal commands and humans whistling.

Thinking of those dog whistles, though, makes me wish I had a kind of high-frequency tool—one that would help me let go of my old ideas and ways and listen to the truth of my heart. And, as it turns out I do have such a tool. It, too, is within me. And when I call on it, I can hear my resistance breaking up. I (mentally, at least) sputter, "Yes, but . . ." or "I can't because . . ." And then I switch to the higher-frequency "Why not?" Why not live the life you want to live? Why not tell your inner critic to take a hike and take Ms. Naysayer along just for fun? Why not give up old ideas of tit for tat? Speaking only when spoken to? And then only mouthing polite inanities? Why not tell the truth—to myself and to others?

I give up lying and covering up in the name of politeness and welcome the truth of my life.

121

"Don't think that finding something about yourself to appreciate is namby-pamby. Believe me, it's tough. No matter what our position in life may be, most of us hold such great distaste in acknowledging our own attributes or talents that the thought of having to dig up a new one each day for thirty days can be really irksome."

We live in a culture that prizes individual effort and achievement, and that's often how we measure worth. So, if we can find anything to appreciate about ourselves, it's usually that we did a good job, landed the contract, got the part, made a million bucks. Now, all those things are good and maybe they're even what we appreciate about ourselves—that we can take care of ourselves, that we can use our talents—oh, no, wait, it's just luck, you say? Well, see, that's the problem.

We do have talents. We come into these bodies with them. We cultivate them. It may be a talent for cultivating friendships, for making other people feel at ease. It may be a knack for making other people laugh. It may be a talent for seeing successful business strategies and making money. We have qualities. We tell other people our appreciations. Why is it so hard to appreciate our own selves?

A thirty-day exercise to write down one different thing I appreciate about myself every day is not for the faint of heart. Go ahead, try it, I dare you.

Thirty appreciations in thirty days will change your life.

122

"Expect your Wants. Expect them!"

If you're obsessing about a Don't Want in the form of suffering or a tragedy you'd like to avoid, and you obsess about that Don't Want day after day, you're pouring your valuable energy into some ugly stuff. And, more importantly, you're blocking your valve big time, and you need to figure out how to get beyond it.

You are a powerful magnet, and you live in the world with other powerful magnets. The frequencies are going to interact in ways that you could never predict, for better or for worse. This world is all about contrast, and, yes, you may be attracting a lot of the negativity as well as the positivity, but dwelling on the thoughts or the feelings that brought about whatever crap has befallen you is a pretty sure-fire way to clamp down on that valve and bring on more of the same.

Dwelling on the positive, on the other hand, is a pretty sure way to attract some of what you want into your life. Don't take my word for it, though; try it. Start with something simple, maybe a lovely cup of tea or fifteen minutes to read. Work your way up to your heart's true desire.

Name, out loud, one Want you expect today.

123

"What dreams have you put aside? Your ambitions, your forgotten goals, even your littlest desires—what are they? *WHAT ARE THEY?*"

If you're like me, you have a "someday" list—a list of things you've set aside and hope to do one day when you have enough time, enough money, enough energy. Living in a foreign country, working on a ranch, model trains, whatever it is. This is the list that hangs around in your psyche, pretty near the surface. Well, near enough to yearn for and fantasize about and then beat up on yourself that those things aren't happening any time soon, and maybe never will.

At what age do we stop asking children what they want to be when they grow up? Maybe when we think they're old enough to know better than to want to be Batman or, as one friend's kid recently told me, "a princess farmer." Well, I'm here to say it's time to be a kid again—and pretend for a moment that the whole world is your toy store. It's time to go beyond our "someday" list and dig up all those hidden desires, even the ones we've never dared acknowledge to ourselves. There is no work in this toy store, only play, and the aisles are infinite, with new things popping up every minute, every time you have a thought or a feeling.

Give yourself permission to want whatever it is that you want. Give yourself permission to remember long-dead desires, and to make chances for new desires to pop into your life every day. No restrictions, no holding back. After all, this wanting can stay totally in your head, your journal, or it can be spoken out loud, even hollered to the hills—whatever you like. This is unfettered dreaming, and there is nothing better.

Ask yourself to remember the long-buried dreams of your childhood, and invite yourself to build new ones.

124

"Still, I was always worried—about everything. With a grin on my face and a good word on my lips, my constant focus was on lack—in either myself or others. Just like everybody else I knew."

We can smile and smile and smile and say everything's just fine until the cows come home. But if we don't believe the cows are going to come home and provide good rich milk and cream that can be made into butter and cheese, then, we have a problem.

Lack is a funny thing—we can't seem to get enough of it. It pops up everywhere. Things can be going fine at home, at work, even in the news—but suddenly I feel like no one is going to love me. Or like I might not have enough money for next week or next month.

The tricky part is talking to the part of ourselves that's feeling the lack without measuring. Reason doesn't take our focus off lack. Sending ourselves loving and reassuring messages can help us take the focus off lack. Reaching out to others can help us take the focus off lack. And, practicing a smiling good word and finding out how to really mean it—"I'm fine"—helps us take the focus off lack, too.

I'm going to practice looking for luck, not lack.

125

"I'm talking about total personal freedom: freedom from boredom or monotony, from needing to prove or justify, from needing to need, from anxiety, and from all the imprisoning Shoulds of life we have so staunchly placed upon ourselves."

Have you ever tried to live a day or even an hour without saying the word "should" to yourself? It's an insidious word—should. We put a lot on our shoulders. Right now, I should keep working on this project. I should also go downstairs and finish my laundry. I should, I should, I should. Oh boy! If we're not careful, "should" takes over and then, next thing we know, we're tied up in one kind of knot or another.

In fact, the work I need to do is getting done. In fact, the laundry is not going to get up and run out the door if it's not attended to this minute. In fact, there is really no reason for me to be anxious at all. And so I set the timer and set myself the task to practice living without a "should" in the world for just an hour.

And it's a wonderful feeling to live without a "should." When we do, we may choose to take a walk, bake a pie, read a book, spend an hour with a friend. Mostly, we choose to put ourselves into an attitude that allows us to choose our best life all the time, a minute, an hour, a day at a time.

I'm giving up "shoulding" for what I want to do.

126

"Never mind how you're going to do it. Never mind you can't do it right now. Where you're going has nothing to do with where you are now. Nothing! You've got to remember that."

I have a friend who is in the beginning stages of a big project that she's been dreaming about for a long time. She started out very enthusiastic, excited about the project and attracting great people on board to help her out. She took a couple of steps forward and invested a lot of time and energy, and then faltered. Self-consciousness set in. "Who am I to think I could ever do this?" she moaned to me one day on the phone. "I could maybe pull off one aspect of this huge project, but here I am undertaking to do it all at once, and I'm not really qualified for any of it."

I know the feeling. In that first moment of inspiration, we are all experts in any field because we are connected to the authority of our higher self, which knows all about literally anything we'll need, or has the means to easily find out. As soon as we click over to our planning, organizing, getting-it-done (or as Lynn says, "High-Ho Silvering") self, negativity begins to seep in.

You can't know what the future will be. Period. But this won't stop that brain of yours from working overtime to try and generate a million and one possible outcomes (wanted or unwanted), and map your path of action to each of them. You'll stay up nights thinking, obsessing, and digging a hole for yourself. Whenever you feel this kind of energy starting to take over, *take a step back.* Remind yourself that you can't articulate *how* it's going to happen until you've done it, and the only way to do it is from a centered, loving, positive place that is born of the strong connection to your original passion—being in touch with the feelings generated by the pure gold of inspiration. Go back to that feeling again and again, however you can get there, and the plans will make and implement themselves.

You cannot know how to get from point A to point B except by making the journey.

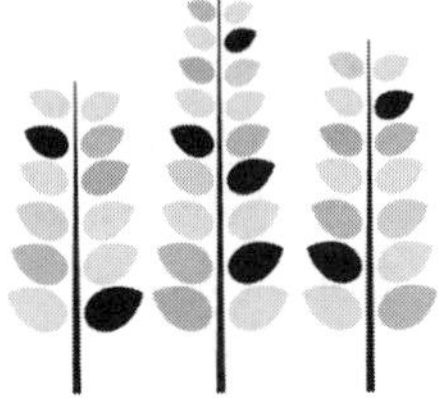

127

"Mainly, just lighten up. Be natural. Get off your case for not being perfect. Pat yourself on the back for effort. Give yourself credit for wanting to take control of your life. You will, sooner than you think!"

"I think I can," the little train chugged up the hill—until it got to the top, when it knew it could. Acting "as if"—it's not just for children's stories anymore. So if you want to quit smoking, lose weight, get rid of the excess emotional baggage that seems to hold you back, one thing to do is to adopt the "I think I can" attitude.

"I think I can" doesn't mean I already did it But I do get credit for thinking I can. And I get an E for effort for trying—for not eating sugar for one day. Or cutting down the smokes to seven. And like the quote says, I also get credit for wanting to make changes.

I got a phone bill in the mail today, and I was puzzled because I'd just paid a phone bill in full—after I let it go for two months and they were threatening to turn off my service. So I see the envelope and I go into panic mode, and then I open it and I see that it's not a bill at all. It's a twelve dollar credit. I'm not sure why I have this credit, but I know one thing. Seeing that credit lightened up my mood considerably. Credit is like that. Giving it, taking it, getting it in the mail.

What are you giving yourself credit for today?

128

"Don't live for the end result, saying, 'I can't feel better until it happens.'"

It sure seems obvious that if we wait to feel better until some one thing happens, we're really never going to feel better. As the very brilliant Gilda Radner used to say in her character as Rosanne Roseannadanna, "It's always something." There will always be some other "it" waiting in the wings. It's like mathematics—you can only approach infinity, you can't ever quite get there.

And don't we know by now that the end result is frequently not what it's cracked up to be? Could that be because nothing outside ourselves can really make us feel better? Can that be because we're in charge of our own feelings—sad, mad, up, down, happy—all of them?

So, if we really want to live life to the fullest, fuller than any hair products commercial, smoother than any luxury car ride, happier than any day at the beach, there's really only one thing we need to do—and that's live each moment as fully present in that moment as we can be—not blaming ourselves or others, not complaining, not waiting for something else to happen. And there will be moments that are less fun than other moments, and there will be moments that are way more fun than we ever expected.

Today I won't wait for perfection while I live my life.

129

"Practice is what this new way of thinking and being is all about. It has to be; it's too new, too foreign. Right now, this concept is just so many words on paper that may sound enticing, but the proof is in the pudding. And that means practice!"

"Practice makes perfect," we've been told again and again. Well, let's leave aside perfection for a moment since I'm not sure it exists, and, if it does, I'm pretty sure we've already attained it, for whatever that's worth. Let's just say, "Practice makes." A nice, short sentence. Practice is the single best way we can make anything new happen in our lives. Remember, we've already been practicing for quite a while by repeating the same old unwanted thought patterns and resulting actions again and again. Practice makes ugly habits as easily as nice ones.

Making new paths in the brain happens moment by moment, decision by decision, feeling by feeling, action by action, and repeating those takes practice. The initial idea or inspiration is the springboard, the catalyst, the refocus you need to get started, and then you'll need practice to really get the job going.

I've heard it takes twenty-one days of repetition to make a new habit you're likely to keep. However, if you're anything like me, you might set up your twenty-one-day plan like this: "Okay, I'll force myself to do this thing for twenty-one days in a row, and then it'll all be over and locked in. So, on day twenty-two, I can stop trying; I've crossed the finish line, so I can relax." Of course, relax in my story means give up. Then I wonder why the fool thing didn't stick, when I did it for twenty-one days straight just like I'd planned.

The commitment to practicing might in itself take some practice to master, but if the practice comes from a real desire to change, there's no way it'll stop at twenty-one days.

130

"Start your day with the intent to look for positive aspects about everything and everybody. Then intend to find them."

There's an old truism about the three most important things to consider when opening a retail business: location, location, location. If you want customers to buy from you, they have to be able to find you and get to you easily and conveniently. And, if the location is good, the store will attract more and more people to it. If you want your best life to find you, the truism is: intention, intention, intention.

Times of economic downfall can be especially trying to our intention to find positive aspects in our everyday encounters. No one knows what the future will bring, but in our society, somehow we think we're secure if we have money in the bank. And so, when our money is threatened, it becomes nearly impossible to intend to find the positive aspects. And it is at just such times that we need most to remind ourselves of our own good intentions.

Intention is the key ingredient in this finding-what-we-look-for game. If we're looking for a downer, we'll find it. If we're looking for thunderclouds, we'll find those. And if we're looking for the silver lining in those clouds, well, yes, then that's what we generally find.

Today intend to find the silver linings.

131

"Never, ever start a new project, business, venture, undertaking, activity, relationship, or *anything* before scripting it and flowing some excited, passionate energy to it *for a good long time.*"

When I was fifteen and just starting to think about where I might go to college, I had a big talk with my dad. I had known from a very young age that I wanted to be an actor and work in the theater, but I told him that I thought I ought to go get a liberal arts education, to have a solid foundation in life beyond just an acting conservatory. He knew enough to see that part of that desire was born from fear of trying and failing at the thing that I loved doing most. And he gave me some advice that was the opposite of what most parents would say to their teenage kids setting out for a life in the arts. He said, "If you have something to fall back on, you will."

As a culture right now, we seem to have embraced the idea that when heading into something new, it's best to just dip your feet in the water. Then, you can check it out while you stay aloof and detached, and, if things look like they might not pan out, you can beat a hasty retreat at any moment. Well, this is as good a recipe for failure as any I've seen.

As it turns out, I wasn't invested enough in my passion at that point in life to go for it fully, and I did get a wonderful liberal arts education on my way to being a theater artist. Then I added writer to the bill, which is as it should be. I sometimes wish that I had taken my father's advice and had the courage to jump without a net, and trust that I would never, ever need one.

Spend some time getting fully invested and passionate before you even begin and watch the thing blossom as soon as you get in there and get your hands dirty!

132

"How can we turn our backs as if we didn't care? This may smart a bit, but the answer is that we're all here to have the experiences necessary to learn our various lessons, whether we're playing the role of good guy or bad guy. An injustice of any kind is always—*always*—a lesson for both sides."

I could not live if I did not turn my back on injustice. We all do it every day—it may be an injustice an ocean away. It may be an injustice next door. I cannot single-handedly feed all the children of the world, or stop poverty, or war, or insults to people who are different. By turning my back, I learn, among other things, that I am incapable of injustice and justice.

There are many ways in which I also contribute to the role of justice—from picking up trash, to contributing money to my causes, to my spiritual practice. I learn from these, both that I and others are capable of justice and injustice. I learn that I am capable of despair and of choosing not to despair.

The ebb and flow of power, the exchange of energy, the choices we all make—consciously or unconsciously, the circumstances in which we find ourselves and the choices we make under those circumstances—all of that exists for us to learn our various lessons, chief among them being that none of us is perfect. What we can all do is to learn from our situations—in which we are the victims of injustice and in which we are the victimizers: own up to which we are, look at how we got into that place, choose to move forward. What my mother said is true, "The world is not fair." Injustice is a constant teacher.

Today I resolve to keep my eyes open to the lessons I see around me.

133

"Make more statements every day about what you want, and why: big things, little things, nonsensical things. The more Wants you have, and the more you get excited about them, the more dramatically your energy will flow."

So, first there was a little trickle of a stream, flowing over rocks. On it went, meandering slowly down a water course. And then a stream joined it, and another. It became a pretty good-sized river in its own right. Then one fairly large river flowed into it, and it was a bigger river, and it flowed on until another large river rushing down from the mountains joined it, and it became the mighty Mississippi. Lots of energy in that flowing water. Lots of moving molecules—transporting goods and people north and south, generating power for a good share of the middle of the United States. Of course, I'm not comparing you to a river. I'm just talking about how things start small—in Itasca State Park in Minnesota, you can walk across the Mississippi on rocks without getting your feet wet. And then the river gets larger—in parts of Missouri, you can barely see across it.

So, if you're not getting what you want or you don't even know what you want, make like a river. Gain momentum and add water (or Wants) every day. Start small if you like. Maybe you want an apple for lunch. (And maybe, lo and behold, your co-worker turns up with an extra.)

What else do you want? A solution to a problem that's been bugging you? Say that: "I want to know what the resolution to my dilemma with X is." The beauty is you don't need to know exactly *what* it is you want to ask for or what you want in a given situation. And if what you want seems frivolous—a bouquet of flowers, a half day off, a call from an old friend—say it anyway. Because wanting that beauty, relaxation, and connection is going to create more beauty, relaxation, and connection in the world. Trust it.

I give myself permission to say ten things I want today.

134

"Make a decision to be a lover rather than one wanting to be loved. If you are flowing loving appreciation TO someone, then you are flooding yourself with that frequency of light, and you will never notice that their river is not currently flowing to you."

One of the easiest ways to understand that love doesn't have to be, isn't, and really can't be an equal back and forth all the time is to think about a mother's love for a child. From the minute she wakes up in the morning, the mother of an infant is flowing love to that baby. That baby cannot live if a mother, or someone, isn't flowing food and water and shelter and love toward her. And a mother will do that. She will give up sleep. She will go out of her way. And she will keep doing that for her children.

At some point, the children start to consciously flow love back—a pat on the cheek, a big hug. And the energy of light and love is flowing both ways.

When we reach out in love to a friend or a partner with no expectations of exactly what we'll get back, we are showing our love. We are also getting the feeling of loving, which opens us up, with that person or perhaps another, to receive the flow back of being loved.

We say love flows, but love is really more like a warm, clear lake we bask in than a river flowing in one direction or the other.

To give love is to get love—sometimes from unexpected sources.

135

"The single greatest cause of emotional pain on this planet is separation. As we accept our oneness, pain vanishes."

If I can't sleep at night—and I admit there are times I wake up at three in the morning wondering what's going to come of the world, my family, me—I have begun a little counting practice. (There's something to that old adage about counting sheep.) What I count are my connections. This is a kissing cousin of counting my blessings, and I don't worry about the overlap or whether they're really two subcategories or anything like that. I just start counting.

How close I am to my family, even though some of them have died. That's one. I name each of them and think a connected thought. Two, three, four, five, six, seven. I think of a grade school teacher. Eight. Of people I've worked with in the theater, worked with on other projects, people I'm grateful to for their contributions to society, people from history, the arts, science, who are connected to me by their work. Now I'm up in the hundreds.

Or I'm soundly and blissfully back to sleep. I don't mean, by this fairly lighthearted meditation, to minimize the emotional pain of feeling alone. What I am suggesting is that each of us can find ways and times and small concrete thoughts or actions to feel our connection to the greater world around us.

Go ahead, smile at someone on the street.

136

"Allow your body to be what it is, then, if you want to change it start scripting."

How do I feeeeel myself thinner, healthier, stronger? I can't tell you how many times I've heard this, and how many times I've caught myself thinking it. This is almost always a big, old Don't Want making a lame attempt to hide out in the disguise of a Want. I really, really want to feel skinny, sexy, fit into all my old clothes. But, really, I don't want to be undesirable, I don't want to love my body for what it is, I don't want to take responsibility for neglecting my health.

You can change your body through flowing your attention to a Want—it can even be a superficial one about getting into that bikini you wore in college, if you like. But tread carefully. Our body issues are so heavily inlaid with negative thoughts and emotions that you'll have to keep a sharp eye on what you're really thinking about and doing. If you want to lose weight and find you are judging yourself for not being what you think you ought to be, your valve is closed. Open it by imagining some of the perks of being lighter in a way that takes your focus off the dreaded pounds. Imagine the feel of the fabric of your clothes brushing against your skin in a certain way. Feel how much easier it is to do a pushup or a lunge.

I will love the gift of my amazing body before I even try to change it with a Want.

"We cannot deny ourselves without denying others. If we deny ourselves some deep desire in order to please others, we're imposing our own guilt on those persons by claiming we are doing it for them."

The stereotype of someone who denies herself for others is the mother—who gives up her career, her hobbies, her life for her children. And, while she might not harp on it, might not even mention it, the children are sure to feel vaguely guilty because they know how much their mother is giving up for them.

There is a way we can love and care for others, even please them some of the time, without giving up our own centers. And it's up to each of us to find that way. I can take care of my family and pursue my career. I need to make choices, but when I make those choices from a place of "can't," I demean both myself and the family I'm trying to take care of.

Whether we're mothers or fathers or teachers or doctors—no matter who we are—when we deny ourselves because we think we need to care for or protect someone else, that's going to come back to haunt us. We're going to suffer not only what we denied ourselves but also the ire of those on whom we tried to place the guilt. Sooner or later, they're going to realize they don't want it and give it back to us.

Denying myself in the guise of doing something for someone else will come back to haunt me.

138

"We have a right to our desires, no matter what our religions may say to the contrary, or our parents, or friends, or co-workers."

Why is it that we teach children they don't have a right to their desires? Oh, there are lots of "good reasons." They should learn to care about others. They should learn that they don't always come first. They should learn that what they want isn't always in accord with what the other (most often the "other" in question is the parent, teacher, or other authority figure) who's teaching them wants.

So maybe we all need to learn that we can't always get what we want. But maybe there's a way to learn it so we don't feel ashamed of or bad about the wanting itself. Maybe we could begin to teach ourselves (and our children) to examine what it is we desire in light of our lives. To use our own free will to determine whether filling that desire is something we want to do or something we want to defer or re-channel.

In journalism school they used to teach the 5Ws and an H—who, what, why, where, when, and how? It's a quick way to make sure you have all the salient details when reporting a story. And it's not a bad list of questions to have to hold up against our wants. Examining our desire for who it will affect, what it really is, why we might have it, where and how we might achieve it—that's a rational thing to do. Feeling bad or ashamed because we have no right to a desire, well that's another "W"—simply wrong.

Try telling yourself you're worthy of getting what you want, but even if you don't get it, you're not a bad person.

"When we are talking about what we don't want, we are disconnected from our core energy."

Conversely, when we talk about what we do want—when we dream, fantasize, describe, revel in—we are not only connected to our core energy, we are increasing the potency of that energy as we speak.

Think about someone you love. When you envision that person's face, do you think, "He doesn't have brown eyes. She doesn't have blonde hair." No, you think, "He has blue eyes. She has brown hair." And so on and so forth. That's where the energy is, that's where the juice and the truth are—in what these people are, not what they're not.

The power of positive thinking for what we want works pretty much the same way. So when I find myself talking about what I don't want, all I need to do is flip the switch. "I don't want chicken for dinner." Don't even need to say it. Say instead, "I want pasta for dinner tonight." What other Don't Wants can I flip—negative to positive?

When I find myself talking about what I don't want, I know I need to stop and flip the switch. What I do want is in there somewhere.

140

"We have no idea how great is the strength we carry within us, the power of the infinite."

There are documented accounts of mothers who have single-handedly lifted cars off their children. To me that act is the true meaning of miracle, an act of love, accessing a power the mom didn't know she had to save a child. In cases like this, it's physical power the women accessed. And they likely did it without thinking, almost without consciously deciding, just as a person might run into a burning building if they heard someone crying for help, and carry out a little old lady who weighs more than they do.

These physical acts of strength are inspirational, not only because they involve selfless acts and generally have some kind of happy ending. I think they can and do inspire us to access other kinds of strength within ourselves. There are some times when we don't need that spurt, we need strength every day to get through a bad time. We need the power of the infinite to guide our thoughts and our actions. And the good news is that we have it.

So how do we convince ourselves of that? By paying attention, every day, to big ways and small, the ways in which we use our strength. By getting to know, love, appreciate, and not judge our strengths *and* our weaknesses. By opening ourselves up to the connections we have to the universe, and letting our strength grow.

I am grateful to be aware of my immense strength.

141

"We came [to Planet Earth] in search of diversity and differences. We came, strangely enough, for the *contrast*."

Since I was a child, I have had a habit of picking up information through snippets of people's actions and conversations, even taking on a mode of talking or thinking as if it were a costume in a play, trying it on for size. When I see movies, I occasionally catch myself, hours after I leave the theater, having a thought pattern or putting a sentence together in the way one of the characters might. It can be a fun, momentary thing, but I've learned I have to be a bit careful—I am just more likely than others to slip into a persona like mine, but not quite, and that can be confusing (for me, and especially for friends and family).

I love the differences in people, and yet I have always been driven to be enough like other people to feel I always fit in. I'm not comfortable being the fierce rebel in the room, sticking to my guns no matter what—I'd rather quietly hold on to my own beliefs and sink into the wallpaper. But I admire and love so many people who are those thinkers and doers at the edge of things, and sometimes I get caught up trying to imitate them and end up feeling pretty silly.

There is no prescription for the actions, words, thoughts, or feelings that will make you happy and turn your life around. There is no "good" or "right" or "better" way to do things, only ideas, sketches, exercises to get you closer to your *own* way of doing things, which is the ultimate way. If there were some one true path, the trek to enlightenment would be a journey toward sameness—with everyone slowly crawling into the monotony of looking, acting, and feeling the same. Oh no, no. We came here to experience all that we can in this body—and the universe will throw us plenty of experiences that we consider good and bad, and our reactions to those experiences will run the gamut. And that's how it's meant to be. We need the dark to see the light, and vice versa.

Next time the universe throws a hailstorm your way, give thanks for the lesson about sunshine.

142

"Learn to observe through feelings, not your head."

We all have various levels of literacy—that is, we are all comfortable with different kinds of languages to different degrees. Much of this is taken for granted or even unconscious. If you've never been much of a reader but you can easily navigate your way around a car engine, you have a higher mechanical literacy. If you can pick up new dance steps immediately but are lost when it comes to anything beyond the most basic math, you have a higher physical literacy.

Most of us have almost no emotional literacy. It is not taught in school or at home. Those who have high emotional literacy are often said to be psychic or have a sixth sense. And even those people often learned it by accident out of necessity (e.g., growing up in an abusive home) or out of methodical determination (e.g., a police detective). There is almost no casual, regular study of our emotional lives.

So what do we do? We rely on what we have learned and developed—our brains, thought processes, and problem-solving skills. These are all great tools, but they are the least of what we need to truly evaluate most life situations.

When we develop our ability to observe based on feelings, we expand our skill set in unimaginable ways.

143

"Don't try to find the ugly, dark, nasty causes of whatever it is you think is wrong with you. Stop it! All you're doing is giving more attention to what you don't want."

The question is, do I need to know why I always cry when I see blue flowers in a white vase? Or do I simply need to acknowledge that and let the emotions flow through me? Therapy to help us move beyond disabling trauma, the kind that doesn't let us get out the door or make friends or do a job, is all well and good. There is nothing wrong with it.

I know a man who's a retired psychologist. I don't know if he originated this phrase or not, but whenever he hears someone say something such as, "I can't make a commitment because my father left me," or "I can't learn to be positive," or "I've always been afraid of failure," his response is "Until now." Try it. When the voice inside your brain won't shut up about how sad, lonely, frightened, stupid you are because of all that was done unto you, simply say "Until now." That simple little phrase sidesteps any searching for causes, and I begin to give myself the message that no matter what made me cry when I saw blue flowers in a white vase—my mother died that day, or my dad hit my brother over the head with them scaring me and making me never want to live in the house with a man—or whatever thing it is—I simply respond, "Until now."

When I give up looking for root causes, I can give up the behavior they supposedly caused.

144

"Always remember that what has been has nothing whatsoever to do with what can be! If you've had a tough time all your life, you have the tools now to turn that around."

I have read countless biographies of actors, athletes, industry leaders, you name it, in which the person was told again and again, "You just don't have it in you—you aren't that talented and you might as well find something else to do." I personally would find those kinds of statements crushing to the point of defeat—I'd immediately consider myself a total failure. And yet, so many people are able to bounce back from that—in fact, for many very successful people, this kind of criticism is a huge motivator. How can this be?

The genius in these people is that they are able to see that those statements have nothing to do with their value as a person (even if they are personal insults!). They wouldn't even consider the fact that they might actually be a failure because of someone else's opinion—they've got to figure out what they can do for themselves. They can look at the feedback as a learning tool, taking what's useful and discarding what's not. They can apply what they learn in a spirit of perseverance. Maybe even more importantly they can put the feedback into the context of an overreaching goal or dream that goes way beyond the scope of small critiques. They can envision, feel, taste, and smell where they want to be. It may be the far side of the moon as far as anyone around them is concerned—completely impossible. But these folks know that nothing is impossible, and that every setback, or mistake, or failure just puts more tools in the toolbox that will get them where they want to be.

Setbacks and tough times help fill up your toolbox, and that toolbox can build anything you can dream up.

145

"The sneakiest way we shoot ourselves in the foot with our Wants is by making statements of blatant contradiction, forever canceling out the positive flow with negative flow."

Get out your gun! Here are some examples. See if any of them are familiar to you. "I want more money. I'm tired of struggling to pay the rent." Or, "I so want to feel spiritually connected; but sometimes I think it's just in my imagination."

Lynn Grabhorn's suggestion for dealing with our tendency to invite the negative in to overtake the positive, thereby undoing all our work, is simple and elegant. Look at the negative half of the statement and play with rephrasing it so that we feel good about it in some way. Eventually we can get to the struggle inspiring me to get really creative about earning money. Or to honoring my imagination, letting my doubts help me embrace a sense of whimsy and spontaneity. Just saying it isn't enough, though; you have to find words that you really feel great about.

So instead of shooting yourself in the foot, maybe the image is that you're shooting off beautiful multicolored sparkling energy, kind of your own private fireworks. And you're getting sparks of ideas about how to get more money using efforts that won't feel like struggle. Or maybe changing to more healthy eating habits without thinking of how, every time you lost weight in the past, you've gained back more.

Rephrase, rephrase, rephrase. I can do that.

146

"[There are] hugely different outcomes that occur between *inspired action* and *fear-based* action."

This is a story I don't think my mom would mind me telling. Many years ago, she left a job she wanted to love, had worked more than sixty hours a week to love, and couldn't love, but she left under less than ideal conditions, with a not-very-good opinion of herself and a lot of fear about her prospects for doing good work in the world, not to mention making a living. I was just a kid, but even I knew she was pretty much a mess.

One of the things she did was to join a class, the kind that helps you build your resume and your confidence at the same time. Now, you'd have to know my mom and know how much she really doesn't like these kinds of groups and then you'd know that she was probably pretty desperate. And she was afraid, being an arty type, that she wouldn't fit in with all these business people. So she acted smug and aloof. She certainly didn't let her amazing ability to create multiple and sometimes unconventional solutions to problems shine.

Until one night. The group game was to trade fake currency for ten minutes, trying to get certain numbers of each denomination. The person with the most money at the end won. The leader said that no one had ever won this game without getting all the high denominations. Well my mom immediately had the solution. And she went around selling the coveted, scarcer high denominations for lots and lots and lots of the lower ones. She drove a hard bargain. And she won, but the problem was no one ever knew about it because she was afraid to put her hand up before she'd counted all those bills. And by then the leader had gone on to something else. So inspired became fearful again—and a lesson.

Practice recognizing your fear so you don't have to act from its base.

147

"Our expanded self vibrates in a frequency we would call—if we could feel it—pure, unadulterated ecstasy (must be nice!)."

How will I recognize my expanded self when I meet her? Will she look the same, feel the same, seem the same to others? Yes and no. But mostly no. I recently met a woman, Jan Frazier, who wrote a book called *When Fear Falls Away.* In the book, she tells the story of asking the universe that her fear of a medical procedure be taken away. It took her a few weeks to realize that fear had left her life entirely. She had gotten more than she asked for. She felt different and people she knew recognized a change, although they couldn't quite put their fingers on it.

But unadulterated ecstasy is probably not going around with a huge grin on our faces. It's not a constant state of excitement. Or giddiness. Or the happiness that sometimes comes with anticipating a wonderful event or remembering a special time.

I think of ecstasy as contentment seen through a magnifying glass. I think most of us have had glimpses of it in our lives.

The key to feeling ecstasy is to invite it in and then notice when it arrives.

148

"When our valve is open and we are allowing our primary energy to flood through us . . . ***there is not one blessed thing in this whole wide world that can harm us."***

Some days it's a real battle to get to an open valve. The closed-valve cycle has you in its grip: the alarm clock doesn't go off, a gust of wind rips apart your umbrella in the middle of a downpour, and your boss singles you out for a verbal beat down. Sure, you probably created this through your own vibrational pull, but dwelling on that fact in this state certainly won't get you up and buzzing again. And your brain won't stop clicking off the *what ifs* and the *shouldas* and the *why mes.* You're having a hard time putting the brakes on the ick you're throwing out into the world (even if you know all about the law of attraction—that only makes it worse by adding a layer of self-hatred and blame to this garbage heap of a day because you know it must be your fault!).

You can't always turn off the negativity like a spigot—so why not try using it to your advantage? That's right, you can funnel all your nastiness into some trash talking at your own closed valve. Look at things from a purely selfish standpoint, and even try letting yourself get a little silly about it.

"What have you done for me lately, closed valve? Seriously, I'm clamping down with all my might to shut off my own life force and it's hard work, and you're just sending me all kinds of garbage in return."

"Hello?! I have devoted my every waking moment to the wonder twins of Fear and Worry, and yet Fear and Worry are not swooping in to save the day as they promised me they would when the going gets tough. Forget it."

"These boots are made for walking, and here they go. See ya later *why me!* Arrivederci, *shoulda coulda woulda!*"

Make fun of your closed valve, and yourself, and jostle things into action again.

149

"Unconditional love does not mean loving in spite of conditions; it means recognizing that loving is the only condition."

Loving is the only condition. And, like charity, love starts at home. To give unconditional love to others, to receive it from others, we also (and maybe first) need to unconditionally love ourselves.

So what does that mean? I don't love myself with the caveat that I'll love myself more when there's less of me to love—such as, I lose the weight I want to lose. I don't love myself when I am living with my valve wide open and then stop loving myself when I shut down for some reason.

By the time we reach adulthood, most of us need to repattern ourselves for unconditional love. Giving ourselves presents. Treating ourselves to food that is good and good for us. Taking ourselves for walks. Taking playtime for ourselves. Taking quiet time for ourselves. Each and every one of those things will help us build our love and affection for ourselves. We get to the unconditional part by going down these paths. And by practicing flipping a switch from judgment to love every time we catch ourselves making conditions.

Unconditional love takes practice.

150

"Don't ever, ever, take uninspired action while your valve is closed, or while you're in the middle of a problem. Get your valve open first, then listen for your Guidance before acting."

Lucille Ball was an inspired actor and comedienne. And some of her most inspired comedy, to my mind, illustrates exactly the problem of acting when you're in the middle of the problem. The bit that comes most readily to mind of the consequences of acting in the middle of a problem is Lucy working in a chocolate candy factory, and, as I remember it, the problem is she can't keep up, so she tries increasingly desperate (and hilarious) actions to keep up.

My grandma had one of those kitchen plaques that said: "Don't just do something, sit there." Now that's a novel idea. I could be wasting time and energy—precious resources—running after a solution to a problem. Or I could be sitting. And here's a little secret—sitting there is not doing nothing (as in the opposite and more conventional cliché—don't just sit there, do something).

Sitting is—no surprise here—a good way to get in touch with the little voice that will become, if we listen, the Voice or Guidance that shows us a way out of our difficulties. Sometimes we get inspired and find a solution to a problem. Sometimes we see that the problem is the solution—like creating one of the world's all-time funniest comedy sketches out of a problem. Sometimes we see there is not a problem.

Take a minute for clarity today.

151

"The only thing you have to do is say *YYYEEESSS!!!* to it all, and to Life, and wake up to how good it feels to feel good."

Wake up to how good it feels to feel good. Find out how feeling good multiplies at least as fast as feeling bad does. Have you ever watched a two-year-old have a total meltdown? It can (and usually does) start with something small—not wanting to have her shoe tied. Not wanting to leave his friends behind at the playground. "No, I don't want to" escalates in seconds to a sobbing, grieving surety that everything is wrong and never can be right again—until the storm passes and the little one's internal sun comes out faster than you could ever imagine is possible.

Most of us have been socialized out of expressing our feelings as openly as a toddler does. And I don't know if that's a good thing or a bad thing. Surely, we couldn't have everyone lying on the floor, kicking their heels. But maybe if we did that, at least figuratively, for a little bit, we'd know what it feels like to wake up to our feelings. And once we've woken to our feelings, we could take the next step.

That would be the step that allows us to say "yes" to all that is, without judging it good or bad. That would be the step that allows us to stay in the present moment without going ballistic with anger or mad with sorrow, without projecting ourselves into the past or the future—what happened before will happen again, and I'll feel terrible. That would be the step that allows us to say this isn't so bad, in fact it's good to feel sad when I'm sad and happy when I'm happy. That would be the step that allows us to say "Yes!" to life and to acknowledge that what is, *is.*

Whatever today brings, I say "yes" to it in my heart.

152

"Don't take score too soon. You can't write a script today and say 'where is it?' tomorrow."

Not all of the old clichés about how we might live our lives are negative. Two come to mind: A thing worth doing is worth doing well. And: Good things are worth waiting for. The second, perhaps, relates more obviously to not deciding too quickly that what you've asked for is not coming into your life.

Now, about that thing worth doing well. Yes, you've laid the groundwork. You've opened your heart, your mind, your life to what you desire. Well done! And what else might you do? To put aside our daily lives in anticipation of what will be is neither living in the present nor is it doing something well.

As you wait, live each day to the fullest, not simply in anticipation, but savoring each thing that is in your life. Look at your script. Make adjustments as need be. And, whatever you do, remember to look for the signs and synchronicities, because the fulfillment of a script is by nature not always as we exactly imagine it.

Instead of taking score, may I take right action.

153

"I'm not going to pull any punches; this is tricky. Staring at—and responding to—what's in our face is what we do. To change that means we would have to give up our cherished right to have—and agonize over—our precious problems."

Trick or Treat! When are we going to wake up and see that we play a trick on ourselves all day long, every day, when we could be having unlimited treats? Put it like that, I hear you saying, how can I refuse?

Here's the catch: you have to give up your problems. You have to give up even thinking that problems are problems. We all trick ourselves into thinking that the only way to get rid of our problems is to solve them: we have to puzzle it out, muscle into it, and get the job done. And are we surprised when this process heaps more problems on the existing ones? Well, yes, we are often surprised. If we can't work out our problems, the next best thing is winning the lottery, or some other life-changing stroke of luck. Ever seen one of those documentaries about the miserable lives of most of the poor fools who do win the lottery? Scratch that one.

But problems are a part of life, and we have two options: hem and haw about them, commiserate, propagate and spread the word and energy, agonize and fertilize. OR, let it go. Let it go. LET IT GO!

Easier said than done, but the only treats we're ever going to get from our problems will come from letting them go. Or, at the very least, letting go of the idea that they are problems, letting go of their vampire power, which is to suck positive energy by breeding negative energy.

Treat yourself by lightening the load of your heavy problems.

154

"If you're just having a passing thought about a Don't Want, no problem. But if you're giving some passionate attention to something you truly do not want—even when you think it's a Want—it will eventually grow up to smack you."

I am a master at fooling myself. "That's not bothering me."

"I don't get worked up about stuff like that."

"I'm not going to let my feelings get the better of me."

I say all of these things, over and over, again and again. I am just beginning to realize that though they might be well-intentioned, they are steadily ruining my life.

Passing thoughts about Don't Wants really are no problem. In fact, they are a great tool—warning me that something might not be quite right, or reminding me that I am not the master of the universe. I'm here to go along for a wild ride of ups and downs, and that's a good thing. Lingering Don't Wants are the real issue, because they pull your focus and draw your energy in the opposite direction from where it ought to be.

So in my haste to be sure I'm not lingering on anything, I valiantly try to stamp out negative thoughts or feelings and move on. I passionately want to be rid of the aching negativity that sometimes descends, and so I stuff my feelings, which is pure fertilizer for the damn negativity.

If you take a quick moment to deal with negativity—rather than denying it—it can't grow up to take a whack at you later.

155

"The point is, the energy of blame always makes a bad situation worse. Always!"

Picture a chain reaction of events—sitting down with a child (maybe yourself as a child) to lunch with a lovely sandwich and a glass of milk. You've been told not to wave your arms around when you talk. But, you're excited to tell the story, and, then, oops, the glass tips over onto the plate. The sandwich is ruined, and milk is dripping onto the floor.

In some households, this is not a big deal. Mom wipes up the milk, makes a new sandwich, smiles, and says, "It's okay, don't cry." In some households, mom gives the child a look, flounces to the kitchen to get a paper towel, angrily wipes up the milk, puts the whole mess on the plate, looks at the crying child, and says, "Well, no use crying over spilt milk." And that second child knows, not by words, but by attitude and actions, that he is being blamed, and he cries more and feels worse. Or, escalates the situation by "accidentally" sweeping the messy plate off the edge of the table. Bad situation, worse. (And even worse is the family in which the child gets blamed by words *and* actions for spilling the milk.)

Blaming—ourselves or others—makes us feel worse and drains energy away from our ability to make a bad situation better. Not only that, blaming lives on—insidiously—in our hearts and minds. So, the next time a similar bad situation arises in our lives, we start from a position of remembered negativity.

I give up my need to find out who's to blame.

156

"I no longer charge in like the Lone Ranger against unwanted conditions to fix them, fix them. Indeed, old dogs most assuredly *can* learn new tricks."

The song lyric tells us that fools rush in where angels fear to tread. And there's no fool like an old fool who keeps doing the same thing over and over, expecting a different outcome. Rushing in to solve a problem rarely works. Cooler heads will prevail. And trying to fix other people's lives (or even our own) by trying willful action is a fool's errand.

So, whether you're an old dog of twenty, thirty, sixty, or eighty, you can learn the new trick of minding your own beeswax. Of sitting still and waiting for the right time to bring some energy or insight to a problem. Of being open to the good that will come when we're open to it.

Riding around on a white horse, wearing a mask, saving the good guys and putting the bad ones behind bars, and leaving town in a swirl of dust, leaving only a silver bullet behind, and never hanging around long enough to see what happens next—really, is that any way for an adult to act?

Here's a relief tonic: make a list of the things you don't have to do.

157

"The first thing to do is to get into a good feeling place and get your own valve open before you do any thinking about the person. Then you can inspire—not ensure, just inspire—that same valve openness in the person you're thinking about. You're no longer attempting to paint on their canvas, but you're genuinely offering them paints and brushes."

Sending energy to someone, praying for them, can be an exercise in inspiration or an exercise in control, just as giving them advice can be. And, unless a person asks for specific advice or direction about how to do something or solve a problem, it's most often an exercise in frustration. Big time. For both you (the sender of energy) and the receiver of energy. No one feels any better. No one has any creative inspiration. And no one solves any problems.

Getting your own valve open before you think about the other person is asking for a more general kind of inspiration: that you may want to send opening thoughts and energy to the other. May that person be in a receptive mode. May they feel the love that is around them. May they write a script that creates an abundance of what they want and need (not, please remember, what I think they need).

Rarely, very rarely, when I'm in that open state, it may come to me that what so-and-so really might love doing is, say, for example, a new writing project. And, if I know that person very well, and know that she may be open to hearing my suggestion and that she will either make it her own or let it go, I may mention it to her. Then all I need to do is to remember that once mentioned it's gone from me. It's her picture to paint.

When you want to help someone, say this aloud, "I'm open to sending clear and open energy to __________________."

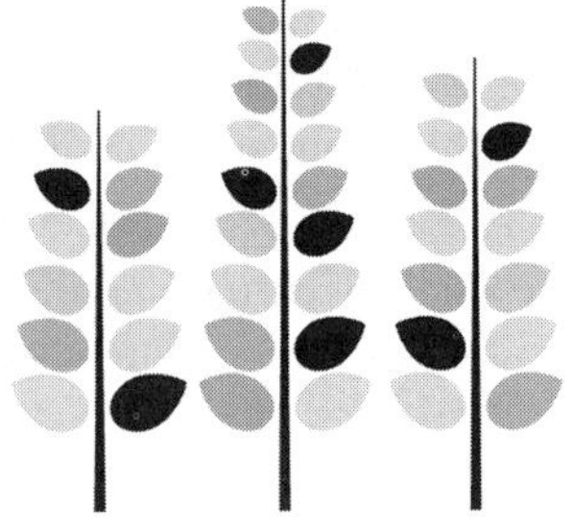

158

"It's not right versus wrong or good versus evil. It's closed valve versus open valve, connected versus disconnected, happy versus unhappy."

We talk about loneliness being the human condition. Epidemic. More people live alone now in this country than at any other time. We're disconnected, from our families, our friends, our selves. It doesn't matter if we live alone or with others; we feel lonely. We feel unhappy. Does loneliness create unhappiness? Or does unhappiness create loneliness? It doesn't matter! Really, it doesn't.

We probably can't feel connected and happy all the time. And we're not wrong or evil when we feel discouraged or disconnected or lonely. We can't force ourselves to happiness.

What we can do, though, even in our bleakest moments, is to remind ourselves that we can be open. I let the universe know I am open to feeling just a little bit better, just a little. And, pretty soon, my heart is open. Nothing has changed, yet I feel more connected and happier.

Open up and remember—I can't drink water with a closed mouth.

159

"A continuum of days that are extraordinarily happy comes by my design."

Continuum is a mathematical term for a series or a whole, according to its dictionary definition. It is a "whole, no part of which can be distinguished from neighboring parts except by arbitrary division." Now, I'm sure anyone with a pretty rudimentary understanding of mathematics might shoot this down—but, speaking metaphorically, if a continuum is a whole and no parts of it can be distinguished one from another, a continuum of happy days is a series—a weekend, a week, a month, a year—in which basically no one day can be distinguished from another.

That is not to say there aren't high points and low points—such as, days that mark anniversaries of birth and days that mark anniversaries of death. What it says, instead, is that if I pay attention to when and how I am happy, then I can choose happiness every day as a sort of baseline. And that happiness does not necessarily change from day to day.

We can't say what will happen to us on any given day. We can choose the frame of mind with which we greet our days. A design is a repeated pattern. As we repeat the pattern of choosing happiness, it becomes fuller and richer over time.

Today I take a step back from life to begin to see the design of my happiness.

160

"If we are feeling trapped, ignored or neglected, unsafe, misunderstood, or shortchanged, we are attracting negatively."

Feeling passionate, thrilled, keen, energized? Then it's coming down the pike, whether or not you deserve to feel this way by anyone else's standards (or your own). You can be on the lowest rung and still feel those things on a daily basis, and sure enough they will be on their way. Feeling downtrodden, taken advantage of, humiliated, stuck? Then, sure enough, that's what will be coming right up for you. You can be in a great position in your life by anyone else's standards and still feel like you're under a boulder.

What I'm trying to say is it doesn't make a difference if you're feeling the wrong things for the right reasons, or the right things for the wrong reasons. Once you're in the feeling place, in either a positive or a negative direction, the energy couldn't give a hoot if the bad feelings are justified or not. The universe doesn't read the back story; it has no interest in the moral value of this or that—it only dials in to what you are feeling and sends more of the same.

I would never pretend to discount the reality of neglect, abuse, or lesser evils—they are, of course, poisonous, but our negative reactions to them are not the antidote to the poison we might wish them to be. No one should have to live in fear or pain, and yet we all do at some point or another, and a reaction to the fear and pain that reflects it back, instead of somehow turning it around, will only sink us deeper. We may not have had control over the original misfortune, but we are in charge of the fallout.

More of the same. More of the same. More of the same.

161

"It's hard for us to swallow the concept that what has been in life has absolutely nothing to do with what can be. That's diametrically opposed to how we think things work."

Here we are, highly evolved and highly involved. Observing, watching, predicting outcomes, making decisions. And because we are fairly logical beings, we assume that things will go as they have gone so far. Babies test the laws of nature—after twenty times of that food falling on the floor, they know for sure that's where things go when they're lobbed off the high-chair. (Then it's on to testing how mad their parents get when the food gets chucked.)

We're programmed to expect more of the same—that things will go more or less as they always have. But what about when things aren't going as they should? How do we assess and work to change our lives, from the inside out? How do we address prejudice, injustice, or plain old personal unhappiness when we're stuck in old beliefs that tie us to the same old, same old?

Incredible change, in ourselves or in our environments, is often a chaotic affair, and, whether it comes in fits and starts or all at once, it can be a wild ride. Of course we'd be nuts to discard all the knowledge we've gathered over the course of a lifetime, but sometimes we'd be better off if we remembered that more of the same ain't necessarily so. Or at least it doesn't have to be.

If we can harness the power of attraction, we can use this moldy old belief—with a slight twist—as an asset. If we are working on magnetizing our wants in the present or even past tense (e.g., "it felt so great to finally get that raise") and we can really feeeeel being there in the moment fulfilling the change we hope for, then our tendency to draw in more of the same will actually start to draw in more of what we expect, because we're already feeling it as a part of our lives (even if it hasn't arrived quite yet).

When we harness the latent power of "more of the same" we can make the change we long for.

162

"The whole process of deliberate creating is really quite simple, but not always easy. At least, not at first. In fact, I'd be inclined to say it's a bitch."

Just when you feel you're swinging along, really getting the hang of this attraction stuff, it smacks you in the face. Something you've been working for falls apart, or a shift in circumstance has left your energies seemingly wasted on a lost cause. Frustration sets in. Then anger. Then hopelessness as you second-guess the inner voice that led you here in the first place. The idea is simple, but the practice isn't always easy: keeping on your toes, being honest with yourself and others, directing and redirecting your energy, staying one step ahead of your own negative reactions.

Old habits die hard, and the habit of negative thinking probably dies hardest of all. It seems hardwired into our personalities, and when we go on the attack with a new way of being, that old habit is going to hold on like hell and drag us down in the process.

If you can believe it, it's actually a great sign when your negativity flares up, even if it threatens to take over worse than ever before. It means you're making progress, because the old habit in you feels threatened enough to try and make a stand. Negativity thrives on the attention you give it, and it grows fast and furious with just a little help. But the secret is that when it loses your attention, it shrivels to the root almost instantly. Talk out loud to your own negative thoughts, and let them know they're on the way out whether they like it or not.

If it feels like you're taking fifteen steps back for every one forward, you're probably at the brink of a real breakthrough.

"When thinking about a regret, find a feeling that feels better."

This is a very simple instruction. It is also very profound. Perhaps the greatest thing about it is that it can be done and repeated anytime, anywhere, whether you're alone or with others. Regrets are kind of like crabgrass. They pop up frequently, no matter how well we're taking care of our lawns; they're tough to get rid of and they spread.

We don't really have to use toxic measures to rid ourselves of them, though. For instance, trying to replace a regret (I didn't get the job) with a revenge (woe to him who didn't hire me) isn't going to be very effective in getting rid of the regret. Nor is it going to open us up to the universe.

We can't think away regrets. Pure reason won't work. I shouldn't feel badly that I didn't marry my college sweetheart—it was so long ago—and I can't do anything about it now. That is *not* going to replace the regret with a positive feeling. Having a positive feeling take the regret's place is really the only way to get rid of it.

My feeling memories trump my regrets any day of the week.

164

"Make more decisions in every day, about your mood, your safety, your work, your relationships, your parking places, your shopping. As with Wants, decisions summon the energy and provide outlets."

I was at a dinner table with three other women the other day, and we all sat and looked at our menus, chatting away. The waitress came to take our order and every one of us looked around to the others to start—oh, no, no, you go ahead; I'll just go last and figure it out while you all order. Then we realized none of us had any idea what we wanted, and we asked for a few more minutes, laughing at ourselves a bit.

I've been at many tables where the women (sometimes the men but more often the women) don't or won't decide what they want. I'm not talking about what they want out of life or their deepest desires; they can't even figure out if chicken sounds better than fish! Some guys do it, too, but I think women are more likely to rely on indecisiveness to mask the fear of putting their desires out there and making their wants known.

I think part of the logic goes that if you don't know or don't decide what you want, you theoretically can't be disappointed with any outcome that happens, as long as it's sort of okay. There are a few obvious problems here: (1) "sort of okay" is pretty cruddy as a long-term goal; (2) if you're not making decisions, you may be avoiding some disappointments, but, more likely, you're just going to be masking some bitterness that's going to grow like a mushroom in that dank moodiness; and (3) you're missing out on making the decisions that will summon the energy you need to get what you really want.

Make as many decisions as you can, big and small—and then relax. Let the universe go to work.

165

"The more civilized man became, the more separate he felt. The more separate he felt, the more fearful he became. The more fearful he became, the more alone he felt. The more alone he felt, the more he struggled. The more he struggled, the more he blamed. The more he blamed, the more he lived life as a victim."

It's a long and winding path that got us here. It's in our DNA and behavioral patterns handed down over thousands of years. It's in our culture. And it's got to stop. We've nearly civilized ourselves right out of existence, doing bad things unto others before they do unto us. Or because they've done unto us, or our fathers, or theirs.

It is time to stop the descent into separation and start the spiral path back to our center and to the connection we need to discover. Recently, I read about a hormone that women seem to have more of than men. But the really interesting thing is that in perceived danger situations, in many women, instead of, or in addition to, adrenaline kicking in, this "tend and befriend" hormone, oxytocin, kicks in, as well.

So we do have an innate impulse to reach out and connect, to take care of others (and ourselves). We don't have to respond to the fear-incited response our bodies may have to hit or shoot or push people away with a verbal tongue-lashing. Each of us, each day, can take small steps away from victimhood, through fear, back to connection.

I make an effort to take a step toward true civilization by connecting with a fellow human being today.

166

> "So see and then feel things to be the way you'd like them to be. It would take only a few of us doing this on a regular basis to initiate desired changes. A noble goal, perhaps, but it beats making things any worse than they are by 'ain't it awful-ing' the situations you want to change."

Mahatma Gandhi said, "You must be the change you want to see in the world." Most of us grew up with some idea of who Gandhi was. The specific changes he wanted to see in the world stemmed from his early experiences in South Africa, of being beaten and thrown off the front of a train for being an Indian. That discrimination and personal humiliation led him to take on the task of nonviolently wresting control of India from the British, a task that took tens of years and thousands of people to achieve. The end result was not only Indian independence. His influence reached far and wide, including to the civil-rights movement in this country in the 1950s and 1960s.

The beautiful thing is that his influence, as well as that of the millions of people who have set their minds to change the world, continues and lives on as each and every one of us see and feel things the way we'd like things to be.

Another quote from Gandhi speaks to that idea: "Always aim at complete harmony of thought and word and deed. Always aim at purifying your thoughts and everything will be well." What we think affects what we do, make no mistake. So, it doesn't behoove any of us to even think any of those clichés about where the world is going. It certainly doesn't help to say it out loud. Sure, we have to pay attention and be aware of what's not the way it ought to be in our lives and in our society. But we don't have to moan about it.

Today I take the first step of seeing a change I'd like to make happen. It can be small because it will grow.

167

"You are not separate from the power of infinite well-being. You are not separate from the power of creative Life force. You are not separate from the universal power of All That Is. That power is your power, because that power is You. And your power, like the divine laws by which it is governed, is absolute."

How to feel part of that power rather than apart from it, as if we're an island, as if no one else has ever felt like we do, as if we don't belong to the human race and all of creation. To my mind, the sort of despair feeling isolated brings on is one of the worst feelings, ever. And that feeling itself creates a cage that's hard to escape from.

Most of us were not, as children, taught to really believe (1) that we're connected to a great power of creative life force and (2) that we have that power inside us. In fact, I can feel myself cringing as I write. My power is absolute—I don't think so. If so, why am I not richer, thinner, happier?

Maybe because I haven't claimed my power. Maybe because I haven't breathed in the well-being the universe offers to all of us. Maybe because I haven't noticed the dry earth and then bemoaned the rainy day that softened it. Maybe I haven't stopped to see the tiny blades of grass pushing through the newly watered soil. That is power. And it is outside us and inside us.

May I notice my connection and my power.

168

"There is absolutely nothing wrong with being so-so about anything, or frustrated, or even angry. Anger and frustration can be grand motivators. But if you stay in that energy, flowing out those low vibrations about your Wants, all you're doing is making sure you never get them—not to mention how you're negatively affecting every other area of your life!"

When our three-year-old son gets tired and hungry, he goes into a state of extremes (more so even than usual). He loses what little filter he has, whatever allows him to keep his emotions in check somewhat throughout the day. These are the times of day when we see the biggest fits, on both ends of the spectrum: frothing anger with tears and pounding fists on the floor on the one hand, or laughing so hard he can't even stand up on the other.

If you can manage to step outside of the situation for a moment, it's a really beautiful thing to watch a child's tantrum. It's pure in some way because it is immediate—it has nothing to do with old grudges, or guilt, or self-esteem issues. It's just a good, old-fashioned crash landing of feelings, completely alive and in the moment. He fully experiences whatever he's feeling in that state, and when it's gone, he drops into bed or into our arms, released and relieved.

This is the best model for anger and frustration that I know—getting it out in a fast and real way, not blowing it out of proportion into some prolonged resentment, never allowing it to take root and hang around to affect the rest of your day or to drag down your Wants.

Throw yourself a good tantrum, let the anger wash through you completely, and then say goodbye to it until the next time.

169

"We are beings who possess the sacred ability to implement any outlandish desire our limitless minds can concoct, for we possess unregulated, unrestricted, uncontested freedom of choice, no matter what those choices may be."

It all comes down to realizing you have complete freedom of choice, no matter what your circumstances. You get to choose your own destiny—how great is that?

But what happens if choice itself becomes a pitfall for you? It can be uncomfortable to make choices—it certainly is for me. I have a natural inclination to passivity, reinforced by my circumstances, that makes me feel comfortable. Maybe it's because the prospect of freedom of choice comes with the responsibility to own the choices you make as yours. So making choices can seem laced with fear and self-doubt, the very precipice of regret.

Comfort can be helpful, or comfort can be a security blanket, which is why I have to remind myself occasionally that what feels good is not always the same as being in a feeeeling place. Oblivion can feel sort of good. Addiction can feel pretty good a lot of the time. We can get tied to our hurts as our security blankets, refusing to forgive ourselves or anyone else and keeping our valve firmly shut in the process.

Freedom is the only thing that can set the stage for a continual feeeeeling place. And the best kind of freedom, ironically, is that which is tied in service to people and things you love.

170

"Yearning for, wishing for, longing for, even hoping for are not activities of focusing on what we want."

"If only . . ." If you ask me, those are two of the most insidiously nasty words in the English language. If only I had a better job, a bigger house, more money—oh yeah, everybody wants more money—a more loving partner, better kids. Then I'd have everything I want in life. In the meantime, I'll watch TV, shop 'til I drop, and wish I were happier.

"If only . . ." Those two words can kick us out of the present moment faster than a speeding bullet. They can shoot us to a "possible" future we're pretty sure can never be ours—with the aforementioned house, kids, job, money. They can sink us back into a past where "if only" we'd made different decisions then we'd have what we want now. When we let "if only" take over, we are essentially saying we don't like what we have, and even though we're reciting a list of how we want things to change, we're pretty sure they're not going to.

One way to stop yearning is to start counting. By the simple act of counting what I do have rather than listing what I long for, I move into a more optimistic state of mind and heart. I begin to see possibilities that simply can't coexist with negative thoughts. I also begin to see that I have choices—and that I can make choices a step at a time to move me toward what I want.

I picture "if only" flying away into the sky.

171

"Stop thinking about anything that closes your valve: any thing, any body, any situations, any event, any circumstance, any place, any movie, any food, any driver, any boss, any scene, no matter what, *NO MATTER WHAT!*"

These are strong words. And I'm a betting woman—and I bet that your first reaction, like mine, is, "I can't do that." I wrangled with the "easy enough for her to says" for a while. And the "yes, buts—I have to see my cousin Sarah no matter how much she shuts me down."

Next, I got to the what ifs. What if I just did this—just for a day. Does it really mean I should see my family or my boss? What does it really mean? Ah, now I felt like I was getting somewhere. I have to see my cousin Sarah, but I don't have to get into her shut-down space. I don't have to commiserate and listen to her about things that happened in the family before we were even born that made our mothers like they are and us as we are. I just don't have to listen. I can, in fact, tell her I'm not going to listen to that and suggest she try the chocolate cookies. They're scrumptious. And let her know that chocolate is good for her soul.

The real point here is not to spend time thinking about or worrying about these shut-down things and people when we're not in their presence. It is, further, to learn to make choices, when we're in their presence and when we're not, that lead to our opening up, not shutting down further.

No matter what happens, I commit myself to staying open.

"By day three [of my first ten days] I was finding that probably 97 percent of my days were given over to worry, concern, anxiety, and fear. That awareness depressed me thoroughly, then made me furious, which surely didn't help. I had no idea I had been worrying so routinely, so unknowingly."

Just trying to change our focus can sometimes bring up some surprising results. Do you know that old psychology trick—trying not to think of something, anything? It's practically impossible and it's maddening.

So telling ourselves not to dwell on worry, concern, anxiety, and fear is *not* enough. We are trying to shift habits of a lifetime. We have been encouraged to be anxious and afraid—after all, it will help us choose the right thing. In fact, we've been encouraged to worry since we were small children, probably pre-verbal; the scarcity model has been enforced and reinforced over and over again. Mom leaves. She might not come back. Did anyone ever think to teach us how to recognize that she will? And then we're told to look out—we might fall on our bikes. We might get our hearts broken by that first boyfriend. We might even get hit by a meteorite. There's a lot to worry about. (I write that with the written equivalent of tongue-in-cheek.)

The only thing to do when we can't change our focus is, well, to change our focus. Getting mad and getting depressed might bring our inability to concentrate on the positive to the fore. It's not going to change it. Paying attention will.

Paying attention with loving-kindness and no judgment. It's a skill that can be learned.

173

"What we need to see is how easily and effortlessly we keep our happiness away from ourselves. We also need to see the excuses we usually chalk up to 'reality.'"

Yeah, sure, whatever. Nevertheless, the reality is that we can't get what we want in this life. We have responsibilities. We have limitations. There are things preventing us from doing what we want. Does that line of thinkng sound familiar to you? What excuses do we chalk up to reality?

Most of us do this almost without thinking about it. We probably learned it at the family dinner table—it's reality that you shouldn't eat dessert before the main course. Says who? Or we learned it in the schoolyard. It's reality that the biggest kid in the class is a bully and you have to give him what he wants. Says who? It's a reality that I'm stuck in this dreary day-to-day existence because I'm not well-educated, or not dynamic enough, or I'm naturally depressed—fill in your own blank here.

Or, better yet, begin to see if, bit by bit, you can erase these realities. Are there alternate realities in which you can eat dessert first, you can befriend the terrified bully (on the playground or inside you), you can imagine smiling at each day?

Spend fifteen minutes a day creating an alternate reality. Start small. Imagine big.

174

"So guess who's creating the shortages!? We are! It's that very concern we all have over not having enough that's diminishing our supplies."

How much time do parents spend on the playground teaching kids to share? And why is it so hard for adults to share? We allow people in other countries, or other cities, or other neighborhoods to go hungry, to go without adequate shelter, to freeze because we think there aren't enough resources to go around. It's good business not to have food and grain surpluses, or so someone said, so we no longer do. We're so afraid that we won't have ours that we forget any lesson we ever learned as children about the importance of sharing.

How can we, as individuals and as communities and countries, convince ourselves that there is enough to go around? A start would be to consider more carefully what we need. Surely, many of us have way more than we absolutely need to keep from starving.

If we panic that there won't be enough—money or food or resources or love—for us as individuals, we can be pretty sure there won't be. What's more, if many individuals hoard, we're creating a situation in which there's even less for everyone else.

Giving up the idea that there won't be enough to go around goes a long way toward assuring that there will be.

175

"This is not just simple 'wanting' to be thin or well. You can't just want and expect it to happen. It's refocusing and refeeling, refocusing and refeeling, refocusing and refeeling. Your body will always respond to the image you give it, provided it's accompanied with the appropriate feeling; fat or thin, sick or well."

I just read an article on obesity, describing a movie called *Fat*. According to the studies documented in the article and the movie, doctors and our current medical field know very little about obesity. And what they do know could be seen as pretty discouraging. Something like 95 percent of people who lose weight gain it back, plus gain some more. Maybe our bodies have a primitive leftover "starvation" gene. Or maybe it's something else.

Whether we're talking about obesity or some other kind of "condition" we see ourselves suffering, what kind of subconscious message are we sending our bodies? And, more importantly, how can we change that message?

The answer to that is in Lynn Grabhorn's words about "refocus and refeel," and repeat and repeat. Go easy on yourself. Stay light and positive. Give yourself time.

Try it for thirty days. Refocus and refeel.

"Yet money, like everything else, is nothing but energy. And attracting it, like anything else, is nothing more than an energy-flowing process."

In 1925, Florence Scovel Shinn published a book called *The Game of Life and How to Play It.* She was not the first to write about the metaphysical law of attraction and prosperity, and she wrote about it in an understandable, practical, and playful way. Life is, after all, a game. So, the first "rule" is to lighten up. The second rule is to act "as if."

If we act as if we are loved, a little bit at first and then more and more, it feels as if suddenly we are lovable and loved. If we act as if we are smart, we become smarter. If we act as if we have money for what we need it for, lo and behold, we have the money we need.

We don't necessarily have the same amount of money we "think" we need. We don't have the money we want for some kind of nonspecific purpose. In order to attract, we need to act as if. Shinn recommends making what she calls a "demonstration." She tells the story of a woman who needed $3,000—a specific amount—to pay off specific bills by a specific date. The woman made the demonstration, meeting the author for an expensive lunch—acting as if she had the money. And she was able to get the money from a wealthy cousin. So, she asked the universe, she acted as if, she sought out her cousin, she asked, she created a flow, and she got what she needed.

May I have the wisdom and the discernment to recognize what I need and create an energy flow to bring it into my life.

177

"One of the best ways to uncover some of those long-hidden wants is to pretend."

The greatest triumph of humanity is evidenced in children more often than adults—and it's the ability to pretend (for real).

There's nothing better than watching a group of five-year-olds set the ground rules for a game of pretending, announcing in their loudest voices who they are (the bad guy, the dog) and what they intend to do (find the treasure, build a house). Once the ground rules are set, quickly and forcefully, the playing begins and the rules are for real, with everyone living up to their given conditions in the best way they can. Then, if it turns out something doesn't work, the rules can be changed and be restated with just as much authority as in the beginning; a quick aside of, "Okay—the dog can talk now and tell the people what to do," and it's back into the world of the game.

Among the many things we forget somewhere in the throes of adolescence and early adulthood is how important (and real) it is to pretend. Is it that we think because we never actually turned into a dog as a result of our game that there is really no useful skill being developed? We might as well say that because we never became an astronaut that we should stop stargazing. The truth is that pretending is a powerful key that can unlock our deepest desires. This is why we love movies, novels, even video games.

Giving some serious time to unfettered pretending each day can unlock the biggest secret of all—what you are here to do, the very meaning of your life.

178

"Naturally, you wouldn't be wanting something if you had it but if your only focus is on the fact that you don't have it, it will never come. It can't, for your focus is on its absence."

I'm hungry. The few things loitering in the fridge could never combine into anything edible, and there's no time and never enough money to fill the cupboards to bursting. I'm budgeted to within an inch of my life, scared to death. And did I mention I'm hungry? So hungry, I can't decide what to eat.

Gratefully, for most of us in the developed world, "nothing in the fridge" usually means two options instead of ten, and what we throw away in old food could feed whole families in faraway places.

It falls to us to remember that *being hungry* is not the same as *going hungry.*

Said another way, *wanting* something is not the same as *wanting for* something.

It's the same story with our emotions, our basic needs and desires. Equating *want* with *lack* is fundamental, a basic part of our language: the verb *want* means desire, while the noun *want* means lack.

Is it possible to look at being hungry (not going hungry) as a gift? Hunger is a signal that your body is ready for food, and, if you never get to the point of hunger, you're overriding the cravings that are linked to the nutrients your body needs at any given moment—sodium, potassium, fats.

If you're too worried about going hungry, you're never going to enjoy being full.

179

"So the first step in forgiving (and you're probably not going to like this) is releasing the resistance that caused the blame in the first place, meaning the ability to say . . . and mean, 'Who cares!?'"

When a situation arises in which forgiveness is called for—of ourselves or others—there are really only two choices: let go of the blame and forgive. Or don't. In forgiving others, we can't say, "I forgive you," and then proceed to tell everyone we know what a terrible thing the person in question did. We have to let it go. My third-grade teacher can't be blamed for my inability to do long division. Not anymore. The statute of blame ran out long ago. And I could have learned how to do it on my own long since. In fact, I probably could even have learned to solve quadratic equations if I spent as much time on them as I have explaining that my third-grade teacher is to blame.

So, hey, okay, I forgive you, Ms. Smith. I don't care, and I mean it. Now that I've forgiven an old hurt, I guess it's time to turn my attention to how I learn to do this before decades have passed. Step one: stop telling other people what X did to you. Step two: say it out loud. Go ahead. Practice, "I don't blame BLANK for BLANK." (Fill in your own.) Say it until you can say it with conviction.

Still feeling some resistance? Do a little math. The equations go like this: blame equals wasted energy. Resistance equals wasted energy. Forgiveness equals feeling lighter and having more energy.

What are you going to do with all that extra energy?

180

"Ferret out that beautiful sweetness deep within you. Find it, feel it, allow it, and fan it. Male or female, we all have it."

Does it feel silly to think about ferreting out sweetness in your heart? Okay, think of how you feel when you see a smiling baby nestled in its mother's arms. Remember that feeling. Think of how you feel when you smell the first cut grass of the summer. Remember that smell. Think of the great feeling of pleasure and anticipation for the first sip of coffee in the morning, or a bite of chocolate, or whatever your favorite is.

To allow ourselves the memory of a past pleasure is practice for allowing ourselves to feel the sweetness in our hearts. There are other ways to ferret out that sweetness. One is, of course, to take a minute—or a second—to recognize and savor a little sweetness every day as you experience it. A pretty cloud, a wiggly puppy, a friend's smile—even on the saddest, bleakest days, there's something. And that something is easy to miss if we don't make an effort—to notice and to appreciate.

The more we notice the beauty around us, the more we notice the beauty within us.

181

"If the two of you are fighting over money, open your valve and write your new script. Start talking with your partner about what you want and why, not what you don't want and why."

Okay, that sounds easy. Talking about what I want. Yet, especially in tense money times, it's rarely as easy as it sounds. Most of us need some remedial work about "I want . . ." statements. A classic goes something like this: "I want you to stop spending money on frivolous things." That, I submit, is NOT an "I want" statement. It might start with the right words, but the sentiment is pure control and close down. A less loaded, but still negative statement, is "I want you (or even us) to stop spending money so we can pay our rent." The loaded negative connotation of "frivolous" is gone, but the statement says nothing about why the person wants to pay the rent on time. He loves the apartment? She feels secure only with bills paid? "Why" statements that are honest about your feelings allow both you and your partner to take a look at those feelings, each of you owning your own, and co-write a brand new script.

In writing scripts about money, it seems as if the more, the merrier applies. You can't have too many talks when you first start. And certainly practice, practice, practice, but there is no perfect. See if you can set aside just a few minutes. See if you can start with what you want. Then move to the whys. When we are accustomed to blame and scarcity, it can take some time to open to resource allocation and abundance.

Take the time to rewrite and claim your money scripts together.

182

"Then get over the guilty victim mode that says you're only a good person when you're giving; that's dogmatic hogwash!"

Where does this come from? For some of us, it seems to be the religion we were raised with. Add that to the expectations of family—whether it's the women always make the meals and make sure everyone else has enough to eat or the men always make sure everyone is provided for. Or that the eldest, youngest, middle kid—whichever you are—can only get attention by visiting grandma, taking out the trash, doing, doing, doing.

We all, every last one of us, have a story with slightly different details that boils down to us trying to get other people to love us (by doing for them) and, ergo (faulty logic to follow, folks), when other people love us, we will be good people. Not only is it dogmatic and keeping us in the guilty victim jail, it is stupid and wrong reasoning. The question is how to give it up.

Well, we could give up giving other people our time, attention, money, gifts, whatever, altogether. My bet is that, in and of itself, wouldn't make us feel good. When we love others we want to give to them. So a better way might be to go to the core. Take that guilt out into the light of day. Look at it. Sit with it. Talk to it. Ask where it comes from and why it's here. Find out all you can about it. And then, gently and firmly, tell it to go away. That's all.

I am not a good person depending on what I do or don't give. I simply *am* a good person.

183

"If you've got a bunch of negative people in your life right now who are strongly into lack, that's a pretty fair indication of what station you're still tuned into."

There's an old Gospel song that tells us to "turn our radios on to Jesus." We can tune in to just about any message we want to hear. In the case of having a lot of negative people in our lives, we may just need to be listening to only part of their rap and tuning the rest out. Or we may need to tell them, gently, kindly, firmly, that we're no longer in the negativity biz. And while we love them because they're part of our family or some of our oldest friends, we will be pointing it out and then tuning them out when they turn up the negatron volume. Maybe there's even a catch phrase to use, "la, la, la." Or something equally silly.

In the most extreme cases, it may be necessary to stop seeing certain people for a while. But, since positive attracts positive, and many (not all, but many) people prefer to feel positive rather than negative, the folks in your life—seeing the change in what you're tuned in to—will start to tune in to the positive themselves. Wouldn't that be lovely?

The real benefit, or lesson if you will, about those negative people in my life is that it's an opportunity for me to look at me. What am I doing or saying? What am I feeling about myself? What image am I projecting that I'm attracting all those negative people? And how can I change that?

Turn your radio to a new channel—sing in the sunshine—and count your blessings, among them what the people in your life can teach you.

184

"So we came bouncing into the world like Don Quixote with the cockeyed inborn programming that says the greatest adversary we shall ever confront in life will be this thing we call money, the dragon against which we must war to the death. And most of us do!"

Whenever I see the words "money" and "war" in the same sentence, I think about how many wars have been fought throughout history supposedly about principles—which really turned out to be about money—and control of it or the resources that will bring the victors more of it. The answer, looked at from one point of view, is pretty nearly all of them.

What if we look at money as if it were not something to accumulate? What if our attitude shifts so that we don't define success by counting how much money we've captured? What if we give up the idea that money will do our bidding? What if we decide that we'll give money a pass, recognizing it for the windmill it is? (Remember Don Quixote ran his sword at the windmills he thought were opposing soldiers of great strength. They didn't fight back, and it was his own absurd tilting that unhorsed him.)

If we had free trade, a free and equitable exchange of resources around the world, one of the unintended consequences would likely be that we wouldn't have any more war. And if I had a free and loosely held attitude about money, I'd be more likely not to let either its lack or my work to accumulate it be the death of me.

When we're looking for money, we see little else.

185

"This is nobody's show but yours, always has been, always will be. Nobody has ever held you by the earlobes. Nobody has ever caused your life to be one way or the other. It's been your show from the outset, designed by how you were flowing energy, designed in every moment of every day by how you were feeling."

It's a funny-looking picture—somebody holding you back by the earlobes so you won't get ahead, find a good job, get married—whatever it is that you've set your heart to. It's such a funny picture, in fact, that envisioning it is a good tool. Try this—when you're tempted to think that your boss or your mother or whoever is holding you back from what you really want to do and be, picture them tackling you, throwing you to the ground, and holding you there by your earlobes.

If you're not laughing yet, I hope you're smiling. Now that you're smiling, feel the energy that you're attracting, feel what you might do with that energy. Remember that you're not really being held back by your earlobes or led around by your nose.

Let the feelings flow, let the bad ones go. Let the good ones in, and live your life according to the well-being that is your birthright.

When you feel like someone else is holding you back, picture yourself flying.

186

"You don't have to change it; you just have to stop focusing on it! Is it tough? Yes! Can it be done? You bet!!!"

Most of us have a laundry list of things we don't want in our lives: things we'd rather not have happen to us, things we wish we could stop doing or make other people stop doing. It might be a list you think or talk about every day, or maybe you never say it out loud because the moment you do, you are filled with paralyzing dread.

That dread is real; you know you cannot possibly change all the "bad" things on the list to "good" things, and there are a million reasons why not. But here's the best news you'll get this year: you never have to change another thing, *ever.* In fact, all you have to do is stop focusing on the bad things (notice I'm not saying *deny* the bad things exist, because denial is just another kind of focus, and a very powerful kind at that).

I just read that fewer Americans are on a diet now than at any time since the 1950s, and though I think we have a big health problem on our hands tied in many ways to what we weigh and how we eat, I almost jumped out of my seat, saying Hallelujah! Diets are about change by force and by self-denial. Change by crunching numbers, change by withholding food and forcing yourself to conform to someone else's plan. Your body longs to be healthy—it works best that way, is in less pain, and has more energy. So why cut off your nose to spite your face as you try to learn more habits that distance you from your natural rhythms, just trying to replace the old bad habits with some newer ones that might shrink your waistline by a couple of inches temporarily, but it always comes back? So I hope Americans are ditching their diets in order to think about something else (anything else!) that makes them feel good. Strangely enough, I'm thinking the pounds will come off in the process.

I don't have to change it, I will not deny it. I will change my focus and find my happiness.

"See your world and all who live upon her as abundant and well, and you will help her to get there."

Why is it so difficult to see the world as a place that will give us all we need to live in harmony with ourselves and others? Maybe because we're not individually or collectively very tuned in to thinking that way. So what would it take to start? It would take one person with a bit of clear vision. That person could be you, me, the guy next door. That clear vision could be an idea to start a neighborhood recycling program. I heard recently about a person who did that. It started with a block-party toy exchange. It grew to a twice-annual garage swap—people brought clothing, furniture, books, children's items they didn't need or want anymore. And people took what they needed. And everyone felt like the world was a good and friendly place for a day.

Or seeing clearly could be participating in a community garden. Or it could be picking up trash along the highway one day a month. Or it could be working in an election. Any positive gesture we make toward peace and abundance comes back to us in ways we can't even measure.

Seeing the world as an abundant mother is believing in the world as an abundant mother.

188

"As you think about them, see them the way you want them to be. If there's anything within them wanting to move forward, your bursts of positive, loving energy will have a strong influence on their thinking, feeling, and being."

I once heard the saying "Any two of us are smarter than any one of us." It seems particularly apt when we're talking about wanting to move forward, to create more positive energy because, as we've learned, positive energy creates more positive energy. The positive energy we send adds to theirs and the growth is geometrical. Two plus two becomes four, double that, it's eight, sixteen, and so on. Of course, energy can't be poured into a calibrated cup and measured. And that's one of the wonderful things about it. Positive energy moves in our lives and that of the people we send it to in ways we can neither control nor predict. Yet if we go with the flow, we do have a positive influence on others and ourselves.

There's a lot of talk these days about unintended consequences, most often a negative result of some do-good action set in motion. Well, in sending positive energy out to others, the positive unintended consequence is that it increases our own openness and positive energy, always. Inevitably. And both of us take a few more steps toward becoming who we want to be.

I picture _______________ coming into her own full self and [add a few words of description here].

189

"Talk tenderly to yourself every day. Out loud."

One of the best-known and frequently quoted passages of the Christian scriptures is "Love your neighbor as yourself." Most often (in my experience), that Bible verse is used to caution people to be nice to each other—to consider who their neighbors are (generally some individual or group we're being cautioned to be nice to even though they're "not like us") and to treat them in some way that we have not considered treating them before (maybe bringing them soup or perhaps not shooting at them). And when we hear a sermon like that, we can go away feeling like we'll take on the chore of loving some abstract someone out there.

So what if we were to turn the verse around. "Love yourself as your neighbor." And what if we were to think of people we really do love—our friends, our family, the people on our block, at work, in school, in our town. And when we meet those people, we say a nice hello. We smile. We ask how they are. We offer Vitamin C and concern if they have a cold. We offer words of encouragement if they're feeling down.

What if today you tried a little experiment of noticing how you greet and talk to everyone you meet? That's part one. Part two is to pay attention to the running dialogue you greet yourself with—say, waking up in the morning. Is it, "Good morning, self, it's a beautiful day." Or, is it, "Gotta hurry up, too much to do, c'mon move, move, move." Noticing—that's parts one and two of this experiment. That's the easy part. The fun part is part three—which is saying something nice and loving out loud to yourself—once in the morning and once at night. Minimum. Now repeat for thirty days.

Being a loving neighbor to yourself renews you. Spread the word.

190

"Practice flowing energy. Practice flowing it to your Wants, or practice just flowing it. Learn to turn it on at will . . . in any situation . . . wherever you are . . . whomever you're with . . . whatever's happening. You control your life by controlling your reactions to life."

You can flow energy in any situation, any time, any place. No matter what. No matter what. No matter what. It bears repeating, because there are so many moments in our lives that seem so awful (or plain blah) that we just can't muster the feel-good spirit.

You're walking down a street littered with garbage. Turn on: "Look, somebody ate a banana and got all that potassium."

You're headed to the dentist's chair with a mouth full of painful cavities. Turn on: "I can feel it now, the freedom of biting down on whatever I want, pain-free and healthy."

You're looking at an IRS audit. Turn on: "The money I want needs a clean and clear path to flow to me, and getting things straightened out will brush away whatever's blocking the flow of energy in the form of money."

In short, you can be relentless about flowing your energy wherever and whenever you want. If you can't muster something to flow to about your present situation or circumstances, then flip the switch to something simple that you can be thankful for and flow appreciation to, even if it's as basic as a glass of clean, fresh water.

You may not get to choose all the circumstances that come your way, but you have the gift of choosing your response, no matter what.

191

"If you truly desire a less bumpy walk in your daily life, you gotta give that energy of yours more outlets, more things to flow to in order to keep it moving."

Some days feel less inspired than others. The routine is fine, but it's still a routine. The energy is flowing, but not in particularly new and exciting ways. There's nothing wrong, but maybe things could get a little more right.

One of my favorite exercises* to shake things up again and get the juices flowing involves writing down options—lots of options. First, go through the basics: identify what you Don't Want and, from that, figure out your Want. Then sit down and get to work making outlets for energy. Normally, we can think of about ten, maybe fifteen options about a particular Want, but this is going to really push you. Think of and write down eighty-eight! At fifteen you're going to feel done. As you make it to thirty, you may hit a wall entirely, but keep at it, even if it takes days or weeks. Write down options that seem to make no sense (sometimes those turn out to be the most inspired!). Somewhere along the line, you will notice that the energy you've been flowing is branching out in all kinds of crazy and wonderful directions, and probably coming back at you in the form of some interesting synchronicity.

You can do a smaller version of this exercise about little things all day long. You can send out as many options as you can think of ahead of a

*Adapted from *The "Excuse Me, Your Life Is Waiting" Playbook* (Charlottesville, VA: Hampton Roads Publishing, 2001), 217.

business meeting, or a soccer game, or even a trip to the supermarket. Provide as many conscious, positive outcomes as you can muster, and, while you might not get in return the exact details you're projecting, you will have paved the way for your energy to go where it needs to go, and you'll probably be pleasantly surprised by the results.

Push yourself to create more options, and your energy will accept the challenge.

192

"Find new ways to feel a little better every day. Be creative. Be inventive. Be outrageous."

There is a secret to feeling better. It's not a very well-kept secret. Most of us have known it for years, maybe since we were children. (I'm talking about feeling better "feelings," not recovering from surgery, say—except come to think of it, the secret works for that, as well.) And here it is revealed—to feel better, all we have to do is to make the choice to feel better and then to keep making it.

Why I think we've known this since we were children is that when we were children, we got over our playground crises or the tragedy of not being able to stay up late. We knew in our cells that there was no real payoff to holding on to that hurt. But then, somehow, when we get older and maybe the hurts get more serious, we find a payoff to feeling badly—maybe someone else's sympathy or just our own perverse pleasure. So we hold on to feeling bad.

To keep making the choice to feel better is (1) to remember to do it, (2) to choose enough ways to keep our critical minds distracted, and (3) to choose ways that please us—not our mothers or spouses or whomever. I can't tell you what to choose; I can only encourage you to choose to see the flowers, to breathe deeply, to read a book, to connect with a friend, to take a walk, to make funny faces at yourself in the mirror, to say thank you for being alive. Choose as if you're a child—sobbing one minute and blissfully hugging your teddy bear the next. And if, in any one day, say today, you think of more ways to feel better than you need, well, write them down for a rainy day.

Today I choose to feel better by filling in my own blanks.

193

"Most of us don't let ourselves believe something can happen unless we can see ahead of time how all the pieces are going to fit together. So start watching for clues. Watch for the masterful coming together as all the missing parts take form and start dropping into place like magic."

When I read this bit of wisdom, I think about all the time, money, and energy we waste planning, worrying, "what ifing" every little thing that could go wrong—even with a small plan. We make contingency plans for what happens if the first contingency plan doesn't work—and people who are good at making contingency plans to the third degree are called executive planners. And in the cynical part of my brain, I think they make a lot of money for making lists of disasters waiting to happen.

Recently I was talking on the phone with my cousin, who's the mother of eighteen-month-old twins. We were trying to make a plan to get together, and I sort of fell into the "what if" this and that. She said, "Well, I don't make plans any more, and things just sort of work out." Of course they do, and of course they did (and we had a wonderful Saturday in the park).

When mothers pay attention to the clues of babies, the days come together in a different way from what you imagine. I've known "type A" women who couldn't adjust and, if I do say so, a lot of them don't look very happy. So, I've been thinking lately about working organically—wanting to take on a new project, not knowing exactly what it is or whether it will be a book or teaching a class. I've got myself a little notebook, and I'm just jotting down related ideas and quotes and bits of information that seem to relate.

Magic happens when we pay attention to the feedback from our daily lives.

194

"We've become such a defensive species, our entire lives revolve around fearful credos of Be Careful, Be Cautious, Be Safe, and Secure. Heaven forbid we should ever let that guard down!"

In the dark reaches of time, when we roamed the plains, hunting big, dangerous animals with rocks or spears or other primitive weapons, we seem to have developed an automatic response. Danger! See it out of the corner of your eye—about to be attacked. Adrenaline rush. Fear. Fight. Or flight. It's a response that served us well as a species then.

Babies, toddlers, small children hear it all day long—"Don't touch. Hot." "Street. Stop." We have to teach our children to be careful in traffic. We teach them not to eat soap. We teach them to put on a coat before they go outside in winter. These are lessons we need to learn. We develop an internal voice that tells us whether we're safe and when we should take care.

But sometimes our adrenaline and our internal voice lie to us—we're in no immediate danger. We could take a chance—whether it's a physical chance, say to learn to rock climb or skydive or swim, or an emotional chance to risk loving someone after a heartbreak. Letting our guard down and taking some chances can lead to unexpected places—starting our own company, writing a book, learning to swim. And if enough of us let our guard down enough times, perhaps we can stem the tide of fear.

Where's your guard right now? Can you move it down a notch?

195

"Money equates to not enough . . . which equates to lack . . . which equates to Feel Bad Vibrations . . . which faithfully supplies us more of precisely what we don't want any more of: lack!"

The Beach Boys sang the song "Good Vibrations." It's a peppy song, full of the beautiful close harmony they're known for, with very simple lyrics. Good, good, good vibrations are a beautiful thing to feel—between ourselves and others. Among large groups. And in our own hearts. No matter what kind of material resources—and money—we have or don't have, when we feel the love we don't feel the lack.

People get weird about money, and a lot of the time, very few—no matter how many digits in their bank accounts—think they have enough. You might say it's the metaphysical law of money. But, there's a way to begin to feel differently about money and about lack.

It's simple and it's called gratitude, because as much as money creates a feeling of lack, gratitude creates a feeling of abundance. Do I feel the lack because I can't buy my friend a birthday present? Or do I feel the gratitude by writing her a poem about how grateful I am to have her in my life? And that's the magic of gratitude, because I did that once, and a decade later my friend says it's the best gift she ever got.

Cultivate some gratitude in your life and feel the good vibrations.

"The good news is we don't have to get in there and dig up all our moldy old beliefs about money to allow the abundance to flow; we only have to override them."

It doesn't make any difference if your mother grew up in the Great Depression when oranges were a treat only at Christmas. And her Aunt Nettie bought a house for each of her children after WWII because she had kept her money out of the bank and in the mattress. It doesn't matter if your father grew up in a house where if you had money you spent it, and when the rent came due, well then, the rent would be due and maybe there would be some way to find the money to pay it.

So, whether you believe that there's never enough, or always enough, or only other people get it, or that you have to spend it to have it, or that you can only have enough if you save more than you spend, it really doesn't make any difference. We all have beliefs about money. Who knows when we formed those beliefs? Or exactly where they came from? Likely they started before we were really old enough to remember. And were reinforced by sibling rivalry and stories from our parents and grandparents. Getting to the root of where we got them would take a lot of time and energy. And then we still wouldn't have any new beliefs.

Abundance is like beauty—it's in the eye of the beholder—and different for everyone. One sure thing is that money is not the same thing as abundance. So when we override our fears, worries, guilty feelings about money, we begin to see the blessings and joy available to us. As we do that we spend even less time in fear and worry, and, lo and behold, we feel more joy and blessings.

May I bless what I have as I seek what I want and I need.

197

"No matter where you are, you can always turn on with some kind of warm feeling if you really want to."

Walking to work on the third day of a winter storm that's left filthy, slushy ice everywhere (and it's seeping into your boots). Sitting in a dentist's waiting room with a mouth full of "needs work" and an empty bank account. Or just having a day in the dumps, where everything's a little rough around the edges, and even those bright flowers on the table are looking washed out and drained of life and feeling.

You have so many choices: you can wallow in your misery, you can block it, you can pretend it isn't there, or you can convince yourself it's the end of the world. And those are just a few. How about none of the above? How about letting yourself feel all of those feelings and then still finding a way to turn them around? You don't have to do it all at once. And please don't kick yourself for being miserable in the first place; that won't do a thing.

How about opening up your awareness to one single thing? It can be anything—a pebble, a fallen leaf, the tip of a pencil. Examine it and think about its unique qualities, its story, the space it takes up in the world. Flood appreciation to it for just being. Most of the time this is all you'll need, a foothold opening up your mind and energy to the good flowing all around you all the time.

When everything is sending you to a down-and-out place, try opening up to the vibrations of one single, simple thing.

"We are not here to be forever addicted to observing negative conditions; we are here to create our own experiences the way we desire them to be."

Or, as my mother might say, "If you're not going to help cook dinner, get out of the kitchen." Another pertinent cliché (and remember clichés got to be clichés because they're true) is, "You can be part of the problem or you can be part of the solution."

Who among us can't get into making a laundry list of what's wrong with the world, our jobs, our lives, our friends, our families, and, yeah, even ourselves? It is addictive. Maybe at first it seems as if it might provide some comfort—I can console myself with the fact that other people, the country, the world are worse off than I am. But that can be kind of like an alcoholic taking one drink. Pretty soon the bottle is empty and the binge well underway. And I've wasted an hour bemoaning the way things are.

Part of recovery from addictive behaviors is finding substitute behaviors. And there are lots of substitutes for observing what's wrong in our lives. (Trust me on this: observing what's wrong is *not* necessarily the first step to fixing it.) Taking a walk, calling a friend, listing what you've accomplished and what that's going to lead to, offering up a wishful, hopeful thought or prayer for a newly elected government—all those things are positive. Helping cook dinner.

Today I'm going to be part of my own solution.

199

"The more we give our attention to the things we want to EXclude, the more we INclude them in our vibrations."

Don't even think of an elephant. I bet you can't spend the next five minutes not thinking of an elephant. This old saw is so well-known that it's become shorthand for things we don't want to pay attention to—the elephant in the living room. The drunk uncle, the family dysfunction, the gambling debt—whatever it is that's an unspoken family secret. It gets bigger and bigger, not only because it's not spoken about. It gets bigger and bigger because not speaking about it, pretending things are different, takes a lot of energy.

So, too, it is with putting our attention on things we want to exclude—bad habits, weight gain, negative attitude. Naming them once and letting them go is one thing. Reciting them over and over as a litany only draws our attention and our vibrations to their existence.

I've had many friends who describe this process as they try to not smoke tobacco. Thinking about wanting to smoke leads to obsessing about smoking, leads to smoking.

It's time for me to turn my excludes out to pasture and invite my includes in to stay.

200

"Until deep desires are touched and released, a life can do nothing but stagnate."

A desire released is not always a desire achieved—at least not in the controlled or limited way we might have imagined it. Neither of my grandmothers went to college. The one, although she regretted not having the opportunity, was a lifelong reader and learner, avidly curious, and, for a religious lady of a certain age, open to new ideas. The other graduated from high school at the top of her class at age sixteen. She was offered a full scholarship to a school forty miles from her home—there were only two problems with this: the school was run by a religious denomination not her family's own and, as the youngest daughter in a large family, she was the one traditionally designated to stay at home and help her mother and father as they aged.

I never even knew this story until I was an adult. What I did know is that this grandmother never seemed at ease in the world. She was pretty much closed down to new ideas—for herself and others. I don't know that her life would have been different if she'd admitted that she would have liked to have gone to college. I do know that she resisted her adult children's attempts to get her signed up for any classes or elder hostel programs. And I'm pretty sure she didn't have as happy a life.

When I acknowledge my unfulfilled desires, they have a way of becoming fulfilled.

201

"Every moment we feel good in the now, we affect the outcome of the next moment."

This is and is not like having a magic wand. If what's going to happen the next moment is that you're going to be declared redundant at work or find out that your favorite aunt has cancer or any other kind of news that's less than welcome, your attitude isn't going to change that news. What it is going to change, though, is your reaction to it. And that makes all the difference.

Feeling good when I get that kind of news allows me to see it for what it is and react accordingly. If I feel good and centered in the present moment as I walk into my boss's office, I'm likely to affect the way she delivers the news, making the whole exchange less awkward for everyone, making her more likely to go to bat for me to get the best possible severance package, making it possible for me to go out on my own, which I've been intending to do for some months anyway.

Of course, there are a million other scenarios, but the real point is how I feel in each moment affects the way things go. Now each of us has, say, sixteen to eighteen waking hours in a day times sixty minutes (if we call a minute a moment), so that's around a thousand chances to not only choose to feel good in one day, but a thousand chances to affect the next moment bringing something good into our lives. And that doesn't even count our sweet dreaming time.

Moment by moment I choose to feel good.

202

"In fact, the electromagnetic energy of blame is so potently charged as it flows from us to others, it can cause those who are usually fairly dependable to mess up all over the place."

Simply put, the best way to get someone to do a bad job, to fail to meet expectations, or even not to show up is to blame them for what they've done in the past, are doing now, and might do in the future. C'mon, that's so obvious—no one would do that. Yet, it's so ingrained in most of us to look for who did what, point the finger, demand the retribution, or, at the least, the contrition, that we don't even see how much we blame others and ourselves.

We blame the woman ahead of us in the deli line for making us feel irritated because she takes ninety seconds to make the clerk go through all her options three times, instead of seeing that maybe she needs attention or is having a hard time making up her mind. This actually happened to me just the other day. Then I blamed myself for getting irritated, and then I dropped my sandwich. I probably won't ever see that woman again, but she knows that people blame her. She's done this before. She's likely even blamed herself for it and then, of course, done it again.

Energetically, when we blame people, we engender more of the same behavior we blamed them for in the first place. Everybody feels less comfortable in their own skin and does stupid things.

When you feel yourself releasing blame energy, whistle.

203

"It you want to change something,
change the way you feel about it,
then well-being will abound."

Say you want to clean up your clutter. The clutter is driving you nuts, you can't find anything, and important papers are getting lost forever in the mess. You want to change the situation of having cluttered space, and you want to change the behavior that clutters your space. Those are two big changes, and, if you sit and puzzle over what steps to take to get to that change, you're probably going to lower your vibrational frequencies, which is only going to make things harder. Especially if you then dive in and start throwing things away in some harried way.

Instead, approach the problem from the back door: don't worry for the moment about changing behavior, or moving stacks around. Instead, write a new script in which you are a character living in your space. The space makes you happy, and information and energy flow freely in and out of the door. There's no need to hold on to excess paper, because the stuff that you need floats to the top and the rest is carried away. Really feel the release of letting things go, and relax in the knowledge that you find what you need right when you need it.

Next time you look at your clutter, bless it. Change the way you feel about it—it's a work in progress toward the new script you've written.

"Stop talking about your illness and causing your body to degenerate even more. Start talking about how your body is rejuvenating, and open your valve to allow it."

It's always something—bodies age and they do degenerate. There are the sniffles and the small aches and pains. And there are the bigger ones. There's one theory that pain is our body's way of making us pay attention—don't put your fingers in the fire, it's hot. Don't run after you've fallen and twisted your ankle. That makes sense and that's something to pay attention to.

But paying attention isn't incessant complaining. It isn't running a woe-is-me, I'm-so-sick tape in your head. And it isn't talking the hind leg off a dog, as my grandmother might have said, dominating any conversation you can with a recital of your symptoms and your pain level and how you can't do this, that, or the other thing.

A change in attitude is like a healing bath. Tell others about that change—about how you're taking care of yourself. About how you had a good day yesterday. About how good it feels to exercise your sprained toe, to keep the fluid moving. And, literally and figuratively, your body does what it can—which is a lot—to heal itself.

I celebrate my body with positive talk—to myself and others.

205

"The greater part of our being is operating in a frequency, or rate of vibration, a tad unknown to us at this time; that we would call *reeeeeeeeeally* happy."

There's an old song about getting to know all about a person that comes to my mind. While this song is about a person getting to know another—and feeling really good about it—it occurs to me that the same sentiment could just as well be applied to ourselves.

As we open up and invite good energy into our lives—and more energy comes—and we begin to vibrate at a higher energy, we begin to get a glimpse of what's possible.

We may not even get to *reeeeeeally* happy in this lifetime. Or we may, because the more we get to know ourselves in this state of openness, the more we're going to like ourselves. And the happier we're going to feel.

This is a happiness not based on external circumstances of money, status, power, possessions. This is a happiness that depends only on our, bit by bit, realizing on a conscious level what our subconscious—or spirit—or mind—or Higher Self—already knows. The universe vibrates happiness.

I open myself to feeling the vibration.

"The truth is that *the universe doesn't give out Certificates of Authentic Inspiration;* it only gives out feeling. . . . Learn to trust the way you feel."

Wouldn't that be nice? You have a stupendous, wonderful, great idea. And you submit it to the universe's Committee for Certificates of Authentic Inspiration. And then you wait. You get a message. They are backlogged, they have so many great submissions at this time of the year. They will get back to you in six weeks.

Three months later, they send you a form letter. They are very sorry, but your inspired idea does not meet their current needs, and, therefore, they will not be granting you a certificate. You are crushed. You had what you thought was a great idea. It made you happy just thinking about how you would proceed once you got the certificate. You had a plan, you couldn't stop yourself from sharing your inspiration. Man, you felt good, and here you are crushed. Or, three months later, they send you the certificate and invite you to the awards ceremony set for six months from now. By then, they're sure your inspiration will be put into action and they can't wait to hear about it. Trouble is, you've already forgotten it. You're simply not interested in that idea any more.

Silly as this little scenario sounds, isn't it what we sometimes try to do? Instead of trusting ourselves, we turn to others for ratification. Rarely does that come without cost—everybody has an opinion. And our inspiration doesn't remain our own for long. So when you're longing for a certificate, sit quietly. Review how your inspiration makes you feel—happy, energized, eager to start action, yet also calm and sure of yourself?

Training myself to trust my feelings is just about the best inspirational training I can get.

207

"If you wake up feeling great, pump it. If you wake up feeling lousy, change it."

Sometimes it feels like you woke up on the wrong side of your life—ever get that way? You can hardly peel yourself off the sheets, even if you've had plenty of sleep, and every day is a struggle to stay awake and aware. Think back to a time in your life, I'm sure there was one, even a single day, when you jumped out of bed well-rested and excited to face your day. Maybe it was the day of a school field trip when you were a kid, maybe it was your wedding day, maybe it was the day of your Broadway debut (in your mind or for real, either one!).

Those mornings are great—there's no struggle to wake up because we are flowing our energy of excitement and love forward into a day we plan to live to the fullest. If you start a morning like that and keep your energy flowing, you can move mountains (or cement lifetime bonds of love, or wow an audience of thousands).

On the days that are less exciting, you can still wake up with enormous spirit and energy. If you're regularly waking up feeling lousy, it's time to write a new script about your job, or your sleeping patterns, or even something as simple as the light in your bedroom in the morning.

Choose to make changes in your feelings that will bring more and more days where you practically bounce out of bed to greet the world.

208

"Passion comes from the excitement of having something in the making. Contentment, on the other hand, comes from looking at something already achieved, more like a satisfaction. Contentment is positive energy, true, but it's not a fuel; it won't take you anyplace. It is not an energy of creation."

So what's the point of resting on our laurels? What's the point of stopping to smell the flowers? If contentment isn't an energy of creation, how is it a positive energy? These are questions that could make my head hurt if I thought about them for too long. I did ponder this quote for a good long time, though. And I came to the conclusion that we need both contentment and passion to create.

Contentment is not the engine or the fuel, true. It is not the energy that drives our creation. It *is* the energy that opens the way for passion. It allows us to see the world and our place in it as positive. It allows us to open the channel for passion. Horse and buggy. Chicken and egg. Passion and contentment. They go hand in hand.

I remain content in the knowledge that I will find fuel for the project.

209

"Look instead for valve-*opening* statements such as 'I don't know how it's going to turn out for you, but I know it's going to be fine.' 'I never worry about you, I never worry about us, because I know whatever is in store will be good.'"

Worrying is worse than a waste of energy. Worrying creates negative energy. Worrying is, in the words of one of my grandmas, "borrowing trouble." She told me that when my dad was a teenager and he was out with the car, she made a conscious choice to go to bed and go to sleep. She said that at first she had to tell herself that she was doing it "in case anything bad happened." If it did and she had to go to the hospital or something, at least she would have had some sleep.

Eventually she got to the "it's going to be fine" part. And it is going to be fine, in a no-matter-what-happens sort of way. When we stay in the present moment and open to the energy around us and between us—whether that's parents and children or friends or spouses, we can begin to create the good that's in store by seeing the good right in front of us.

Some people have to make a list of disaster scenarios, as my grandma did, on the way to accepting that outcomes are both out of our hands *and* guided by the energy we put out into the world in the present. The important part is opening beyond the disaster scenario to envisioning the scenario we want, and, even more important, the surety that whatever comes will be fine.

In the words of Julian of Norwich, "All will be well. All matter of things shall be well."

210

"What we're talking about now is honest-to-God unconditional love, something I'm sure not one in fifty million of us has ever understood."

Would we know it? Could we know it? What would it feel like? I once heard a sermon on the Biblical commandment that we should love our neighbors as ourselves. I'm telling you this was a huge revelation to me—huge. The gist of the sermon was that we might look at how we treat other people—we are kind to them. We ask them if they're hungry or thirsty. We feed them. We tell them to sit and rest a bit. We give them our time, energy, and attention. How often do we love ourselves as we love others? Show that same caring concern? I think that's one thing that unconditional love is about.

Another, it seems to me, is allowing ourselves and others to simply be. Unconditional love doesn't engineer. It might encourage—us or others to get in touch with our true selves. But it doesn't make a project of it, nor does it withhold positive energy and affection if those changes aren't forthcoming in the way our minds imagined them.

One wonderful thing about unconditional love is that it's a work in progress. As we unleash our positive energy, as we write the script of our life as we want it to unfold, we learn more and more about love.

I keep the energy moving, and that is love.

211

"If there's need to forgive, there had to be judgment or blames preceding that need, otherwise there'd be no reason to forgive. And judgment and/or blame means we're focusing on a Don't Want."

Lew Smedes wrote several books on forgiveness. I recommend them. Recently I came across this quote, "To forgive is to set a prisoner free and discover that the prisoner was you." It seems to jive well with the idea of judgment or blame. What a surprise that the person imprisoned when we don't forgive, when we hold on to our hurts, when we proclaim who's at fault to anyone who will listen is ourselves.

Yet, as soon as we say it, why, yes, that's obvious. Of course it is. Obvious, easy to understand, maybe even easy enough to remember if I put my mind to it. But not, alas, so easy to remember to put into practice.

So let's think about "Don't Wants." And focus on them. What does that get me? "I don't want to feel bad about what you did to me anymore," I say. How could I take the focus off the Don't Want and find a better Want? "I want to do something fun with you, something that makes us both laugh out loud." There's progress. What else do I want? And how do I get it?

By forgiving you, I set myself free.

212

"If it's people you're concerned about, open your valve to the greatest love you can muster, and flow it out to those beings of your concern. See them in their states of perfection, rather than lack."

A simple meditation practice is to picture warm, glowing light surrounding and protecting folks you're concerned about. Picture them not stoned, or drunk, or troubled in any way. Picture them not angry and wrangling with you and others. Picture them at ease, looking rested and happy.

If you have never tried this, it takes a bit of a leap of faith. And the easiest way to see if it works for you is to try it. It can ease relations between you and someone you've been at odds with. It can give you a sense of peace and well-being. And, as we know, peace and well-being tend to generate more peace and well-being. Ultimately, it makes me act with more goodwill toward myself and others.

The world can be made a better place by the simple act of letting our love flow.

213

"But the most thrilling thing to me was that up or down, fear of any kind was clearly taking more and more of a back seat. The down days had no specific focus of Don't Wants or stress, just basic doldrums."

Mama said there'd be days like this—gray-sky days. Days when nothing seems to get done and the minutes crawl by. By opening ourselves up to our fullest lives, we feel like we're risking everything. What if things don't work out the way we want them to? What if we fail? What if . . . ?

What we find out soon enough is that when we're present to ourselves, open to sending out and receiving energy, without specific expectations or fears, everything goes more smoothly.

There's nothing really to do to be open to ourselves except to be open to ourselves. If you're having trouble, you might do something like put a rubber band around your wrist and snap it when you find yourself drifting off to disaster land. Or maybe there's a word or phrase—"I can come back to now"—that you repeat to yourself.

Doldrums don't need to send me into a tizzy.

214

"Ignore how someone else is flowing their energy, and pay attention to your own, only your own."

"Mom! He's bugging me! She's calling me names! He just stuck his tongue out at me! She just hit me!"

"Aaaaghhh! Will you kids just ignore each other and leave it alone?!"

When we think of ignoring someone else, we think of building a wall to block out something obnoxious that someone else is doing. If we can build that wall—put on headphones, go in another room, or just shut down completely, we think we've successfully ignored that other person, even though if we dwell on the thought for even just a second, it's easy to get all worked up again pretty quickly. By ignoring someone, we're usually turning up the dial on our resistance and/or our denial, all of which we know by now is going to get in the way of vibrating positively.

So how do we accomplish this while ignoring "how someone else is flowing their energy"? This is like Lynn's excellent teaching about forgiveness. If you forgive without forgetting, it's going to turn around and bite you. If you "ignore" someone's energy but underneath it's still bugging ya, you've just invited that nasty energy into your home and handed it a big old super snack to grow on.

I'm pretty sure Lynn's not advocating ignoring other people—just their energy flows. You can notice it, you can know it for what it is, but you must not take it on as yours. Negativity is like a parasite, always looking for a fresh host. So, if anything, in order to truly ignore someone's flow, you'll probably have to turn on your powers of perception even more as you see that people's energies and circumstances are not the sum total of their identities—encounter them on their most basic energetic levels—move beyond whatever surface crud they are believing and cultivating, and meet them at their core energies.

Respond to a negative churner only from your deepest self or not at all, and be shocked by the results for you both.

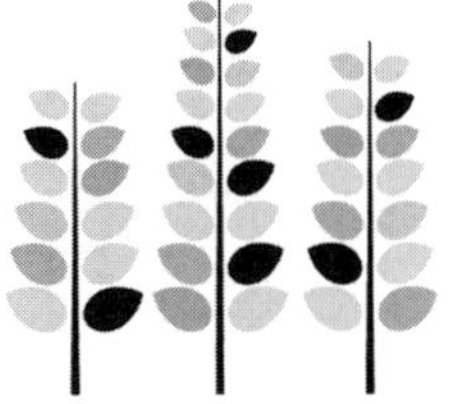

215

"As long as we live in these bodies, down days are going to happen."

It's a material world. Madonna, famously, told us so. And I'd be willing to bet pretty much everything I own that even the Material Girl, with all her material accoutrements, has a down day. As long as we live in a material world, even though we may begin to understand the laws of metaphysics, the laws of physics are at work.

For every up, there's a down. And, thankfully, for every down, there's an up. For every lunge ahead, there's a push back. Trying to avoid having down days is a fool's errand. Sisyphus-like in nature. We will never get the rock up over the hill. It will always roll back down.

A better expenditure of our energy is probably deciding how to react to down—whether it's the down and out of grieving a death or the loss of love, the loneliness that won't end. Or the down and out of being ill. Or just a day when, seemingly inexplicably, I feel blue. What do I do? Take a nap, buy a flower (even if it doesn't make me feel immediately good), say a prayer.

Oh, yes, and acknowledge to myself: down days are going to happen. And tomorrow is another day.

216

"Give more time to your subject, and get off the fact that it hasn't happened yet. It's forming, it's happening, it's on its way. Believe it!"

Have you ever lived near a child who's planted a seed? Children approach waiting for the seed to sprout and then grow from a single slip into a plant that branches out in a number of different ways. Children don't have much sense of future. For them, tomorrow might be ten minutes from now or it might be next year. Some of them get anxious—asking ten million times when the seed will sprout. Others get discouraged—the seed will never sprout. Still, others seem to take it on faith and in their stride—they might check on the plant once a day, carefully observe, be the first to notice—and rejoice at the little green slip.

It's those careful observers that it's good to emulate when we're waiting for something to grow in our hearts. It seems like a simple thing, doesn't it? It's so obvious as to hardly be worth taking up the ink and the space on this page—but, yes, we can be like children. We don't need to worry ourselves that it will never happen. We don't need to ask everyone within sight—our friends, mentors, spiritual teachers—if it will ever happen.

All we need to do is consider the miracle of the seed—it sprouts, it grows leaves, it bears beans or tomatoes or flowers—whatever it's meant to bear. And that process all leads to producing more seeds that produce more fruit or flowers, related to the first. That's the way of the world. Our projects and our thoughts reach out to connect us to the universe to produce good things for ourselves and for others.

Seeds and miracles all sprout in their own good time.

217

"Be aware of the very real obstacles you're creating with your resistance to Source energy."

It behooves us to pay attention to our "I can'ts . . . ," "I won'ts . . . ," "They won't let mes . . . ," and "It's impossibles . . ." We have a lot to learn from them. And perhaps the hardest lesson of all is that we do create most of them quite simply with our own resistance.

Sometimes, yes, there are what seem to be external obstacles between us and our goals—someone else gets the job I had my heart set on. Someone else rents the dream apartment first. How do those very real setbacks or changes in course become obstacles, though?

Exactly—by our responses to them. I can lament the unfairness of a colleague's promotion or I can take it for the message it is: to do what I need to do to find the best job for me.

Being open to Source energy connects me to the energy from within myself and from the world around me. When I spend time and energy bemoaning circumstances, I can create bigger obstacles for myself.

The good news is we can clear obstacles simply by shifting our energy.

218

"Prayers for the sick rarely work. When we see the one for whom the prayer is being offered as being deficient in some way, we're coming from a place of lack. We are viewing that person as deficient in some way when in fact they are every bit as adequate as any power in the universe. They've just forgotten; and for a time, so did those of us doing the praying."

A prayer or an energy thought sent to someone who has any kind of illness, mental or physical, can be reframed so that it doesn't concentrate on lack. When I picture my mother in pain and ask that she be relieved of that pain, I draw attention to the pain, not to the healing of her body or her mind. If, instead, I ask that she absorb healing energy into herself, essentially create a healing (not necessarily a cure, I might add), then I'm adding to her own power.

This is very good wording for ourselves, too. When we see ourselves as being deficient or we're blaming ourselves for tragedy or hardship or illness, we are viewing ourselves and our circumstances from a place of lack, which serves to bring more in.

It takes some practice to find words and ways to pray from a positive point of view—for others or ourselves. Yet the very practice of finding those words—with an open heart and a nonjudgmental attitude—can bring us to a place where we can see how to ask for and look for the positive energy that will bring us—or others—through a crisis or an illness. It's especially important to remember that this is not about will and control, for those, too, are about lack, implying that we need something more to power on through.

May [I or another person's name] feel the flow of [my/his/her/our/their] healing light.

"You can not bulldoze something into place and get the results you truly want, no matter how hard you push and shove. Does this mean we stop doing? Of course not. We just substitute inspired doing for wasted doing by stopping our constant knee-jerk responses to everything. . . . Action becomes a joy instead of a 'have to.'"

I recently watched a three-year-old boy and a five-year-old girl—siblings—compete for attention from their mom and their grandma. The little girl was sitting on her mom's lap. The little boy tried to push and shove his way onto her lap, too. Mom suggested that he go and sit on Grandma's lap instead. Off he went—with his big sister, not to be outdone, right behind him, trying to push her way onto Grandma's lap. Neither one of them got what they ostensibly wanted—alone time on the chosen lap. What they both did get was to annoy each other. And maybe that was the point, after all.

When our actions are pushing and shoving, how often are we trying to do somebody else out of something rather than get what we want? Just those words—Push. Shove. They're hard words—getting somebody or something out of MY way. Bulldozers have their uses—building roads, clearing away debris after a catastrophe. And every once in a while in life we may need some bulldozer action. We may need to create a flat, clear space, with no garbage and no baggage.

Once we've got that space, it's time to separate our actions from our reactions. Inspired actions are simply those we take a breath before taking—and in that breath, we ask ourselves: Is this an action that serves my higher self? Or is this an action that tears me (or another person) down?

As I practice inspired action today, I check my progress toward what I want.

220

"Quit trying to find yourself. Begin, instead, to allow yourself. A grand life is your right. You *are* your life; therefore, you *are* your right."

My mom used to have this cartoon in her office by a woman named Claire Bretecher, at least that's the name she remembers. She also remembers that one of her best friends cut it out and just handed it to her at a time when she was complaining a lot about her life and wanting to make a lot of changes. The cartoon shows a young woman who's going to get a good haircut, do something about her thighs, find the job and the man of her dreams—and then, the punch line goes, she'll really begin to live. I'm sure I'm not doing justice to the humor of it. But the sentiment has sure come back to me at various times.

A man I know tells a pretty typical childhood story. The youngest of about six kids, he was on a family trip to the zoo. He got interested in the sign that monkeys were that way and just quietly wandered off. He couldn't understand what all the fuss was about. He knew where he was and where he was going—the way to the monkey house was clearly marked.

So, where are you right now—lost in a maze or right where you're supposed to be? Are you lost—or following signs that lead to a place you've never been before? Are you looking to live a wonderful life just as soon as? Or are you living one right now?

I allow myself to see the life I am having right now.

"Our goal now is to change the way we *react* to our unwanted conditions so they cease being the focal point of our lives."

It's a cliché—the definition of insane is doing the same thing over and over again, and expecting a different result. It's a cliché because it's true. Okay, so maybe insane is a bit over the top. But whatever my unwanted condition is—being single in a world of couples, being married unhappily, being in the wrong job—it's a long litany. It could be something small—the husband who leaves the toilet seat up, the wife who pushes back the car seat when she gets out. And we all know our own unwanted conditions because we pay so much attention to them.

We're discussing a condition we can't change—probably not overnight and probably really never—since mostly what we're talking about when we say "unwanted conditions" is other people's behavior and/or circumstances that are out of our control. So, okay, focus on the condition, but in a slightly different way. What can I control?

Aha, my reaction to the condition. And how could I do that? One way might be to make an option list. Try something different. Take a breath. Take a walk. Take stock of what you do like in your life.

For every circumstance there may be a reaction, but it's a reaction I can choose.

222

"During those first ten days, I didn't think I was going to make it. The more I had to flip-switch, the more depressed I became that this vibrant person (me) whom people had always viewed as being so positive, up, and happy, was nothing but a common, run-of-the-mill worry-wart, the kind of person I used to tell people to stop being!"

I knew a dog once that was trained as a watchdog. Well, poorly trained. The dog was anxious, neurotic, with almost no social contact. It would slam itself to the end of its chain over and over again, barking and growling at everything and everyone, and was such a nervous wreck that it could hardly digest the food it wolfed down every day. This dog was conditioned to think that everything around it—sounds, smells, vibrations—was a sign or source of danger. In some ways, the dog did the trick—nobody messed with the lot the dog was assigned to protect, but eventually the neighbors' complaints against the owner for the noise and the neglect of the dog led to its removal and an uncertain fate, and no protection for the property.

In fact, you don't have to train most dogs to be watchful—it's their natural state—the training is in encouraging specific responses to various possible threats. A truly effective and healthy watchdog can move around quietly all day long, interacting in a relaxed way, checking things out, listening, sniffing. This dog is simply free to rely on its own genetic instincts, programmed through millennia, to stay attentive to real danger from a relaxed state and then spring into full action only when necessary.

All of which blows to pieces the theory that in order to keep ourselves safe in mind and body in a violent, unpredictable world, we'd better stay on our toes in a constant state of worry and anxiety. We must be ever vigilant, the thinking goes, for danger lurks around every corner. Drop the worry, we think, and we lose our suit of armor. Turns out that suit is too cumbersome for our own good, and we'd be better off trusting our guidance, which will keep us out of danger every time, either by avoidance or by the right action at the right moment.

Take off your suit of worry and fear, and replace it by tuning in to the inner voice that knows how to keep you safe.

223

"You want more passion?
Then follow your joy!"

"If you're happy and you know it, stomp your feet." What pure, unadulterated joy to watch a two-year-old shout out this children's classic, stamping his little legs as hard as he can. A later line in that song goes, "If you're happy and you know it, then your face will surely show it." Okay, that's so obvious it seems barely worth stating. But when was the last time you stopped to pay attention to pure joy, to look—figuratively or literally—into a mirror to see the joy showing?

When we stop to look at our joy, we discover things about it. Is it fleeting? Maybe. Does it occur accidentally? It might feel like that in the moment. Can we figure out how to bring more of it into our lives? Some people would say, yes, and to that I say a resounding *Yes.* No qualifications.

It's pure and simple as a child's song. Clapping our hands when we're happy generates more happiness. Doing work that makes us happy generates more work, and pretty soon we're passionate about what we're doing much of our waking time. (And for doing those things we're not passionate about—say, cleaning the toilet or washing the dishes—if we're passionate and happy in our daily lives, we're more likely to feel the burden of those far less.)

When I'm happy and I know it, I'm going to tell myself so.

224

"If you do decide to embark full tilt on this thirty-day turnaround, you could be facing a major battle with your fears. Old habits die hard, and your fears are not going to like it that you're thinking about cutting them loose."

Okay, so it's time to dust off some of your moldy old beliefs and get started with some fresh scripts. Sounds easier than it is, sure, but it's not impossible.

First take a good hard look at the belief itself. Produce a little inner TV documentary about the belief that explores how it got started and evolved into its current state. Talk to yourself in your mind or out loud about the thought patterns that emanate from this belief, and how you really feel when you're thinking those thoughts. Then think about the circumstances in your life—both wanted and unwanted—that might be linked to this belief.

Once you have a pretty decent picture of what your belief is, how it got started, and what kind of havoc it's wreaking on your life, you have a foundation for changing it. If you try to change it before you've sorted this all out you may have some success, but my guess is that the belief will come raging back after some limited gains. Beliefs usually change in one of two ways: the first is an *aha!* moment that feels like a complete, immediate turnaround from which you never go back (think George Bailey in *It's a Wonderful Life*). And the second is longer and more arduous, a process of changing your belief habit in fits and starts through tiny, everyday actions that eventually pile up into a total life change.

I have found that this second process includes some setbacks that can really throw you for a loop. The change in your eating and exercise plan that crumbles as you sit in front of the TV all day, nursing a pan of brownies. In those dark moments, I always try to remember that those setbacks are really just the moldy old beliefs pushing back because they are being seriously threatened. So believe it or not, those setbacks are a good sign. It means you're giving those nasty old beliefs some hell, and they're being challenged enough to really do some thrashing and kicking as they go down. Just get your valve back open (even if you have to switch to another, easier topic), and, as your energy flows, watch those incremental changes blossom into a glorious new set of beliefs.

Don't panic when an old belief rears its ugly head—you've done your homework and you know all about that crummy old thing, and it knows it's on the outs for good.

225

"Didn't it ever strike you as bizarre that our lives should be so tough when we're all so brilliant?"

We have cures for most diseases and yet plagues still ravage entire continents. We produce heartier, healthier crops than ever, and children still starve. We've sent humans to the moon and beyond, we've conquered so much of what makes day to day life difficult for human beings, but a paradox remains: the more brilliant our circumstances, often the worse off we feel.

I read an interview recently with Madonna, who was struck by this paradox when she visited Malawi in Africa on a mission to bring aid. As she met resilient orphaned children and witnessed the everyday joy of people in the thick of grief and tragedy, she wondered to herself, *Who are we meant to be helping?* She went there to make a difference in people's lives, but came home feeling we need to make a huge difference in our own lives. We are educated, wealthy, satiated, and largely untouched by tragedy—so why the widespread misery?

Why? Because we've managed to collect all of our brilliance into a cycle of fear and worry that perpetuates itself. Instead of the necessity that people in tough circumstances face—to live through it and make the best of it—we feel the lack of that directive and so we invent neurotic, winding paths to keep ourselves unaware of the true emptiness of many of our lives. It's time to take a step back and realize that our brilliance at fixing problems, or denying them, ought to be tempered by a new brilliance, one that helps us find joy in our situation no matter what it is right now, and more importantly helps us map our true paths to ever greater happiness and success.

Remember a time when you found a way to be happy in the bleakest circumstances.

226

"We made sure whatever dreams we did secretly harbor were tidy and small—for two reasons: (1) so as not to offend that big roaring judge in the sky, and (2) so that if the dream didn't come to pass, we could handle the pain. 'Dream small, hurt small' became our way of life."

"Dream small, hurt small." Over a lifetime of denying who we are and what we want, of thinking if we just live as if we can't be seen, if we keep our secret (maybe not "normal") talents hidden under a bushel, then we won't have any major disappointments. Well, that all depends on what we mean by major disappointments, because, really, what living like this amounts to is that our life is one big disappointment.

How did we get so committed as human beings to a god up in the sky who spends all his time and energy thinking up things for us not to do, ways for us not to use the bodies, brains, and spirits he supposedly created for us? This doesn't make any sense.

Dreaming big doesn't necessarily mean we'll win the most marbles in the corporate game, go home with the handsomest (or prettiest) partner, invent the cure for cancer, or write a bestseller. But one thing is absolutely 100 percent for sure—we won't do any of those things or a number of others if we don't dream big.

From now on I'm going to dream big and loud.

227

"Ask to be filled with those things the soul longs for."

There's a kind of wanting that invites mediocrity, or, to put it another way, a kind of wanting that shuts down your ability to see the infinite possibility all around you. If you single-mindedly flow your attention toward wanting one material possession, you might get it. But you also might not get it precisely because you're so focused on the detail of that narrow want that you might miss out on reams of opportunities that float by you in the form of intuition and synchronicity.

By all means, want away for small things, but also want—and ask for—some biggies. You don't have to know what they are consciously, because your soul has all that information stored up from eons and eons ago. Then, all you have to do is dial in and allow yourself to see the possibilities, whether they're pointing to your smaller conscious wants or to something bigger and more sustaining. Who knows? You might get both!

Small scale wanting is fine, but why not broaden the scope of your Wants to include desires that are so deep, you may not even be able to articulate them.

228

"Don't think it, feel it."

The brain scientist Jill Bolte Taylor had a stroke and, while it was happening, she had the unique ability to understand the event from the point of view of her scientific background. At some point after the stroke, as she describes it, a feeling of infinity came over her, and she was consciously worried that she may never fit back into her own small body. Her stroke had shut down the language and self-consciousness center of the brain, and she describes full immersion in the deep inner peace circuitry of her right brain, and it was nirvana.

Our brains can cause us a lot of pain when they get into patterns of obsession, neurosis, or fear. They can make us feel separate and separated, alone.

But they also contain the most basic knowledge we have—that nirvana that Dr. Bolte Taylor talks about—and there are ways to consciously emphasize that part of our brains and our thinking.

Through drawing and visual art, we can explore the capabilities of that part of our brain. Through meditation, we can be space and time travelers in our own minds. Most of all, the brain functions by "use it or lose it," so to stay nimble and connected, you just have to do a little bit every day.

I will find a new way to explore the feeling side of my brain today.

"We are not at the mercy of events that transpired in our childhood unless we believe we are."

That was then and this is now. But if we believe we'll never be loved or happy or fulfilled or creative because we were told that as children, then we never will be. There's no self-fulfilling prophecy that carries quite so much weight as those we took on in childhood. And the questions aren't how many do I have? What are they? Why do I have them? Those just reinforce our beliefs.

The real question is how do I look at those events in the light of the present, let others and me off the big old judgment hook, and go on, freed up from believing that I'm shy or stupid or scattered. Or whatever it is that I believe I am.

Some childhoods are worse than others, and I'm not trying to make light of the effects of post-traumatic stress from physical or mental abuse. Yet I have known people who have gone through pretty horrendous childhoods and know that they have made a choice, are making a choice, not to be confined or limited by those circumstances.

I make the choice not to let my own beliefs limit me.

230

"As long as we see ourselves as victims of circumstance, we will never gain the emotional experience of the event, and shall repeat it in some way or other over and over and over."

There's a process for looking at our own victimhood that asks us to look at the person we think made us a victim and asks us to figure out how *we* got *them* to do that. It took me the longest time to figure this out and accept it. I never asked to feel miserable for a full year when I got dumped by a boyfriend. It was his fault. Losing a bid for a job you wanted? Not getting chosen to serve on a board? Being picked on when you were a child? Getting passed over for a promotion? Even getting a chronic disease?

It must be the fault of someone or something else, right? But, remember: we always, always, always have a choice. In any situation in which we're tempted to feel the victim, to blame someone or something else, to play the woe-is-poor-me role to the hilt, we can choose not to. We can be sad or angry. Then we can pull ourselves together and figure out what's next. We can steer ourselves to calmer, safer waters. If I feel powerless at this bump in the road, I will feel powerless at the next.

Read this loud and clear—there's no time like the present to stop being a victim.

231

"I'm talking about the freedom to exist as we desire, the freedom to acquire, to be outrageous, to prosper, and even to excel if that is a desire."

If you are the one attracting everything in your life, and only you, does that make you the totalitarian dictator of your own existence? Is this an exercise in benevolent control and suppression?

Well, if you've read this far, you probably know my answer. *NO!*

The power of attraction is about freedom, which is the opposite of control. The freedom to choose your path, the freedom to connect with the power of your own feelings. Personal freedom requires sacrifice and release; it demands connection to others, to our collective experience. It thrives on honesty and openness.

A dictator may feel free in the subjugation of others—he might feel like his destiny is being fully realized, and that because he can do whatever he wants that he is living through the power of his own desires and wants. Of course, we can all see that the emperor has no clothes—the dictator may have power over others, but he is controlled and consumed in turn by his own fear, or by the fears of the culture he's helped to create.

Guess what—you don't get to be the supreme dictator of your existence, barking out orders in a system of control and intimidation to line up each and every circumstance you've been hoping for. You don't get to divorce yourself from the needs and wants of others. You have to tread a careful line between indulging your old habit of trying to please everyone and embracing a new program of taking responsibility for your own existence—releasing those around you and your circumstances from any blame for your condition.

Release the impulse to control, and replace it with the power of freedom.

232

"Practice flowing appreciation to street signs, brick buildings, red lights, or other outdoor objects as you're driving."

Now, you will think I've gone off the deep end for sure. Standing in my bathroom, brushing my teeth, I just managed to flow appreciation to two unused water valves that stick out at a funny angle from the wall. I have no idea what they turn on or off, and the only thing they've ever been good for is the occasional shin-busting bruise. While I brushed, I imagined them in an art gallery, just as they are, totally useless and wonderfully absurd, and it made me smile. Ping! Ten more seconds of flowing positive energy.

It doesn't matter what fool thing your energy flows to—just do it! Do it while you're driving, do it toward things that have zip to do with you, your life, or your Wants. Think of it as weight lifting to become a better swimmer or basketball player; just flex the muscles, see how far they can go, and maximize their range and power. Then when you're ready to flow to something you really care about and are invested in, let 'er rip!

And in the meantime, all that positive flow to bowling balls and public transportation and room fresheners and keyboards will boost your energy level, your immune system, and maybe even help you hit more green lights as you drive. You never know.

Flow, flow, flow your thoughts, everywhere and anywhere!

233

"Stop with the 'issues' game. Having issues is nothing but an excuse to stay in negative vibrations."

Well, issues might be a good comedy routine too. But enough with the tired mother-in-law, wife, husband, father, boss issues. No, seriously, folks, issues are for magazines—some of them publish a monthly issue, some biweekly. If you can't stop the issues game cold turkey, at the very least laugh at yourself.

Why do I need my issues? What are they serving? They're excuses, reasons to remain a victim—I can't do or have something I want because something or someone else—with whom I have an issue—is preventing me from it. Or, even more likely, did prevent me when I was a child—you hear people say they have an issue with risk-taking because their mothers (who may have been dead for decades) some many years ago screamed at them for jumping off a log into a stream.

Now seriously, doesn't something like that take a lot more energy to hold on to than to let go of. And, once let go, well, you can jump in the water and play. That will bring on some good vibrations.

I get good vibrations by creating them.

234

"Intention, strongly placed, leaves no room for anything but joy."

In our culture, "wanting" often has all sorts of guilt and negativity attached to it. Maybe we don't need that thing. Maybe it's not "spiritual" to want nice things. Maybe we should remember the starving children and not be so selfish. Or maybe we should remember the starving children, intend ourselves a nice fat bonus, and give a bunch of money to buy food for those children. Wanting is a good thing, not a negative thing. But it can engender strong feelings of inadequacy and guilt.

If you're having trouble with "want," think about what Grabhorn calls "strong true intending." To intend and mean it liberates the negative feelings around the wanting into a positive force.

Let's say you want a new job because you want enough money to live on. Take it to the next level. Intend that you find a job that uses your skills for the common good, that provides you enough resources so that you can use some of them for doing good works near to your heart, and a job that makes you happy. This is intention, and the intending and the realizing of it create joy—in you and in others.

My intentions are buoyant.

"Since happiness and well-being are synonymous, that means there's a part of us—the biggest part—that knows nothing but unconditional, timeless well-being."

We are bigger than we think we are—and not alone. The bigger part of us is our energy body that surrounds and moves out from our physical bodies. The biggest part is that our energy body melds and interacts with the energy that is creation. We are bigger than we think we are—and not alone.

Granted, we don't always feel that. We're in our little cave bodies—trying to get warmer, thinner, richer, healthier. It's as if we're in a prison. We have limited freedom in this body.

And when we begin to realize that we have access to a much, much bigger, freer being, our whole perspective from our physical body changes. We may still have aches and pains and disappointments. But the space and energy they take up is not nearly so large. Well-being becomes more than a word. It becomes a way of life.

I welcome my connection to all creation and the well-being that it brings.

236

"'The worse it gets, the worse it gets,' remember? A constant flow of annoyance over anything will, sooner or later, turn ugly. It must. Like attracts like."

So, the question is, do I want it to turn ugly? Because if we want ugly, we know exactly how to make it so. We just keep reciting how bad it is. We chant that litany: the guy who cut me off on the corner ticked me off, the lady who dithered in front of me in the grocery line—couldn't she see I was in a hurry, the insensitive rich you-know-whats who don't care that kids are going hungry, the stupid politicians who keep on lying to us. (Maybe because they think we want to hear lies?) At any rate, the more we let annoyances build up in our minds and bodies, the more annoyances will come our way—to be counted and coddled. And the bigger the UGLY will be when we finally blow up—usually at some poor, unsuspecting person.

Or do we take it out on ourselves? After singing the "nobody likes me" and "nuttin' is going my way" songs, what do I do? Spend too much money? Take a drink? Eat a mound of candy? And by doing that, what do I attract to my life—this is not a trick question. What I attract is a cycle of whining, complaining, overdoing, feeling badly, feeling worse, and start it all over again.

One of my grandpas, who wasn't the most positive guy on the face of the planet, was full of homespun wisdom/advice. One cliché he particularly favored was how sorry he felt for himself because he had no shoes, until he met the man who had no feet. On days when it's really, really hard for me to feel positive about much of anything, I, at the very least, try to go a little way—the negative positive if you will. Well, at least I have my feet.

What can I do to divert the flow today?

237

"With our constant negative focus on the illness, we're cutting off the most important ingredient available to reverse the condition: the curative powers of our higher frequencies."

Whistle a happy tune and think a healthy thought. If you're not a believer, it might not cure you, but it's for sure not going to kill you. Yes, allopathic and alternative medicine are resources we can and should avail ourselves of when we have an illness. However, there's something else we can do, no matter what our circumstances.

Tune in to the higher frequencies, open our minds and hearts to the possibility of healing and well-being no matter what our physical circumstances. Depending on the condition and your physical and emotional health, do what you can to open your valve to positive energy. Take a minute when you think of it. Do a longer meditation. Be thankful for your breath. Invite friends and family into the process. Find positive words and feelings that work for you. You'll recognize them because, as you begin to use them, you'll feel better.

Find an action or a sound that jump starts positive energy for you.

It's hard to feel negative when I whistle.

238

"One of the best ways to [help a Want magnetize in] is to talk about the 'whys' of wanting something. The What defines, but it's the Whys that charge your battery and start the juices running."

Let's look at the steps of deliberate creation again:

1. Identify what you Don't Want
2. From that, identify what you Do Want
3. Get into a feeling place
4. Allow it to happen

Lately, when I have been going through those steps, I get hung up on number three. The Don't Want is staring me in the face, the Want is plain as day, but the feeling place just trips away every time I think I'm on the verge of pinning it down.

So I start asking myself, Why. And the Whys invariably lead me to one place: freedom. I'm not talking about patriotic freedom, or freedom that's unaccountable to other people. I'm talking about a feeling I get, when I get far enough into the Whys, a feeling that tells me there is no further to go, that really a Want is a kind of openness of mind, body, and spirit that provides even as it protects, that energizes even as it calms my fears.

The only reason we ever really want anything, whether it's a material possession or a relationship or a new mindset, is because it will help us build that freedom that is our natural state of positive vibrations, the feeling that feels like we are home and yet we can travel anywhere we need to go with ease and without fear.

The What is your map, the Why is your full tank of gas. Enjoy the trip!

"Remember, need is from fear, desire is from excitement. They are at opposite ends of the vibrational pole."

Why is it that some people, who are given every opportunity and seem to have unlimited potential, seem to falter and fail in adulthood when they were meant to succeed? And how is it that many people who have made great achievements in their lives were written off as kids for being untalented, dumb, or unlikely to go anywhere?

Of course, it's not always the case, but why is it that people's destiny is so often a far distance from what was considered their potential? Imagine those child prodigies who excel at something beyond all expectation—music, math, spelling, etc. Often the original spark or passion that led these kids to initial success is all but snuffed out as they grow up. Their energy changes focus at some point, turning from the original excitement of exploring and developing their talents, and pointing in a new direction toward the relentless need to prove themselves over and over again, often to adoring and/or demanding parents or other adults. Much of their energy eventually gets funneled into "I must be good enough, I have to please them, I have to show everyone I'm the best." And the more thoughts and feelings go in that direction, the more fears they engender: "What if I'm not the best? What will happen to me? Who will I be?" The fears, of course, bring the feared consequence, and the original passion (which is creation) is sapped, leaving them in a holding pattern—or worse, a total standstill.

This happens to many of us to a greater or lesser degree, with a dream, a new project, or a relationship. Our focus on the desired outcome leads us away from the infinite source of our potential in the first place—our passion! Whether you start at the top of the heap or at the bottom, this passion will lead you to ever greater heights, so stay connected to it in every way you can.

Where do you draw the line between the possible and the impossible? Why?

"Emotionally spend the money you want, again and again and again to give the energy outlets into which to flow. You can't say 'give me X amount of dollars and *then* I'll decide what to do with it.'"

Hey, if it worked for Kevin Costner in *Field of Dreams,* why won't it work now? But it's not just one hit movie from two decades ago that teaches us to be specific and persistent in catching our dreams. The character in the movie knew exactly and specifically what he wanted—to build a baseball field to which all the old-time greats would come (most from the other side) to play ball. It was the perfect field, and it was the perfect dream because he was specific in what he wanted and persuasive, even dogged, in his actions to make that dream come true.

What is it you need or want money for? Let go of the guilt of wanting and the guilt of asking. In your mind's eye, picture yourself writing the check for a down payment, for back rent, for a new and beautiful pair of shoes, for the perfect haircut. Make a shopping list. Picture yourself ordering the items on it. Make a to do list. Picture yourself doing what you will do with the money when it comes. Picture yourself sitting down with your loved ones to decide what you're doing with it. Have the discussion. Decide.

As you make your list of wants and needs, be as clean as you can in your intentions. Let go of feelings on not deserving or guilt at having what others do not. Let go of all that. Know that your plan is made in a spirit of contributing to the greater good.

In my mind I spend the money that is coming my way.

241

"Just open your valve no matter what, no matter what, NO MATTER WHAT! The rest will take care of itself. Another guarantee."

"Lifetime guarantee!" You hear that a lot on late-night television, especially associated with kitchen gadgets that peel, pare, grind, grate, and sing and dance if you program them correctly. Send money now and you get the thing, plus a lifetime guarantee. Whose lifetime? They never say that. I always imagine the thing works until it doesn't, and that's the end of its life—so the end of the guarantee.

The kind of guarantee you get when you open your valve, no matter what happens—the peeler, parer thing could cut off the tip of your finger and you could have to wait three hours in the emergency room while your guests finish cooking and eating the holiday dinner—if your valve is open, the very, very, very least you'll get out of the experience is a holiday story to tell for years to come. Who knows what else? People have made job contacts, met their spouses, had inspirations for creative projects while sitting and waiting in less-than-pleasant-circumstances, such as emergency rooms at holiday times.

Take it to your bank: My valve is open and everything will take care of itself.

242

"Watch for clues that things are happening, for concurrent events, for synchronicity."

A woman I know has been known to say, "Don't put too much belief in astrology and numerology—everybody has to be born sometime and named something." However, part of her work as a spiritual teacher and psychologist is to train people to pay attention, to unseal the set of sealed instructions that Danish philosopher Soren Kierkegaard says we come to earth with. Noticing patterns in our lives is one way to open those instructions and figure out what we really need to do.

There are at least three steps to being on the lookout for synchronicity. The first is knowing that these things are happening, whether you see them or not (twenty-five signs saying Memphis, when you're thinking of moving to Minneapolis, cross your field of vision in three days). The signs are there. The second is noticing. It has to register in your conscious brain that you're seeing all those signs. The third is interpretation. Seeing those signs might mean you're meant to look into moving to Memphis, where you don't know anyone. Oh, wait, it might also mean you're supposed to call the person whom you exchanged cards with in the airport, someone who lives in Memphis. An executive in your field who knows of a job in Minneapolis. Interpretation is everything!

What kind of frame of mind does it take to watch for clues? Well, here are some that won't help much: self-absorption, being consumed in our own anger and pain, walking down the street and looking only at our feet—literally or figuratively. When we're putting one foot in front of the other, trying to get somewhere, sometimes the best thing to do is to look up and around us for signs.

Look, see, interpret, repeat—until it becomes second nature.

"But don't get caught up in the words or you'll end up like an inside-out pretzel. Just stay tuned to how you *feeeeel* when you say or think something."

I have often thought that if I could change my vocabulary, I could change my life. If I could let go of a few choice ugly words (like *should, hate,* or *fear*) that I could eradicate everything that those words connote or stand for, and I'd be in the middle of a whole new ballgame. I've even tried disciplining myself to force the issue, and, after some initial positive results, I sputter out. The words may be gone, but what they represent is not.

It's like a new diet—we think that if we follow the prescribed eating and exercise plans that all will be well. And it often works—the weight comes off and we're thrilled, and then we slowly put it back on, failing to realize once again that no one diet has ever changed what needs changing: the relationship we have to food, our bodies, and our self-images.

The diet, like the vocabulary, is just action—not intention. And intention is more important than action in all arenas (except maybe calling your mom on Mother's Day). You can say almost anything and as long as the right kind of feeling is behind it, your words can be understood and powerful beyond what you could imagine.

Don't swallow your voice for fear of uttering the wrong thing—there are no wrong words if they come from the right place.

244

"Let's say there's a bunch of things in a partnership we don't like, some big, some just trivial little things we might even think we're ignoring. But 'little' does not exist, and 'little' is usually our biggest problem."

One way of looking at this is that little problems, focused on, grow up to be big ones. You can ignore the open cupboard doors just so long; then you hit your head on one, and open warfare breaks out. The "You nevers . . ." and "You always . . ." fly through the air until it's thick with acrid energy.

Lynn Grabhorn also wrote, "If something is big enough for us to label, even if that label is 'little,' there's no way we can say we're ignoring it or accepting it. We're focusing on the bloody thing, so obviously we're flowing energy to it and making it bigger." So if you say your partner is a little messy, sloppy, late, inconsiderate, or whatever, what are you to do?

Well, one is to stop. Simply stop with the labels. Two is to look at your own response to the offending habit or behavior. Why is it nagging at you? What triggers it to blow up? "How can I let go of my need to control another person?" is perhaps one of the most important questions in human language.

So before those little things become big, it's probably time to talk about them and then let them go.

245

"Is it easy? No, it is not the least bit easy to switch focus away from a roaring illness, or pain, or unwanted weight. But you can talk yourself down a little bit at a time. You can open that valve a little bit at a time and reverse your body's direction."

Does it happen overnight? No. Will things ever be the same? Probably not. Can you let yourself breathe into your pain for ten seconds? Maybe. Can you forget your pain for twenty seconds? Let yourself try. Let yourself off the hook.

If laughter lets you forget for a minute, put yourself in the way of laughter. Get some funny movies. Ask friends to send you jokes. If you can't sleep in the middle of the night, see if there aren't some home videos or pet tricks on TV.

Find a mantra. A simple one. "Let light surround me. Let my spirit be open. Let my body heal." That's a sample. Find what works for you. And then write it down, and post it prominently so that when you're in the throes of your pain, you see it and say it, preferably out loud.

I remember that when I'm open to well-being, more well-being can get in.

246

"Sometimes the process is fast and electrifying; other times so slow it seems like lifetimes pass before I get myself talked out of a downer."

There may be a rhyme or reason to the timing of change—but it's not of our own making. That is to say, we can't schedule next Tuesday at two o'clock to be when we start to feel better. Or when the results of our latest scripts for our lives start to kick in. Nor can we control the form in which good things and good feelings come to us.

It helps me to remember that time is basically a manmade invention. Yes, every second is the same length as every other second, and there are sixty of them in a minute and sixty of those in an hour—small bits of time, all nice and even and of the same duration if you're watching them tick away on a clock. But if we're in physical pain or enduring grief, then those same sixty minutes can feel quite different. We all know this, and, yet, when it comes to time seeming to pass so slowly when we're waiting for the good stuff or waiting for the bad stuff to be over, we act as if it's a big surprise.

So what to do while waiting: take a nap, take a walk, make a pot of tea. Meditate. Chant a mantra that helps you open your heart to the changes that will come.

To everything there is a season, and it's time for me to remember that.

247

"Stop joining bandwagons of grievances loaded with closed-valve, disconnected being. Flow your energy to what you do want, and affect the whole."

An old friend of our family's jokes about getting together with friends she hasn't seen for a long time, and they all spend time doing what she calls their "organ recitals." My heart this, my stomach that, my gallbladder, liver, back, knee, hip—get it? Complaining about their organs and other body parts. Finally, someone figures it out and the talk shifts away from complaining about what's going on with them physically into the happier realms of things old friends have to talk about.

A little bit of organ recital or any other kind of grievance litany goes a long way. We can probably always finds someone to listen to our complaints—well, not really listen, but sit quietly waiting their own turn to complain. We're not having any kind of meaningful exchange, and we're not really affecting any whole or part of our lives.

So the alternative to a bandwagon of grievances is what? A bandwagon of cheerleading? A bandwagon of brainstorming new ideas? A bandwagon of meaningful conversation? A bandwagon of celebrating the day? Any and all of the above.

Strike up the band and let your energy flow.

248

"Get off your case. If you goof up, so what? Just decide to change it."

So, here's an idea: stop asking yourself what's the worst thing that can happen. Ask what's the best thing that can happen? So you inadvertently copied your boss on the email to your friend about what an idiot your boss is. That's a pretty big goof-up by anyone's measure. What's the best thing that can happen?

So, you yelled at your kids. So, you ate more than you intended yesterday. So, you fell off the wagon after being sober for a long time. From small things to large. You have a choice. You can choose to beat yourself up. You can also continue to continue your self-destructive behavior, all the while telling yourself how self-destructive it is. Or, you can let yourself off the hook.

What, exactly, is letting ourselves off the hook? It's not pretending we never did it. And it's not pretending the world is going to end because we did. Apologize to your boss, and maybe you'll get fired or maybe you'll be able to have an honest and open talk about what changes you'd like to see in both your behaviors. (And maybe you'll find the job you've always wanted, one way or the other.) Talk with your kids. Let them know you goofed up. Funny thing about how we try to appear perfect to our children—we're not doing them any favors, and they certainly can see through the act. Changing behavior is a decision for the moment.

What decision for change will I make today?

> "So as hard as it may be to swallow, it becomes a matter of looking at *our own* valve, *our own* reactions, *our own* energy flow, because as long as we're glaring somewhere else . . . not only are we inviting more of the same, we're blocking all the good things we'd like to see in its place."

Is it possible that I don't understand my life because I am always trying to understand it? That is, I'm always trying to put it in context and understand it by comparing it to other people's lives. Is it possible that my choice about how I am trying to make sense of my life is somehow robbing it of sense?

I'm not advocating an unexamined life, or going into denial about your circumstances. But something happens when you spend a lot of time comparing yourself to others or imagining yourself in their lives or their circumstances. You can't compare without passing judgment in some way—on yourself or someone else—and judgment in this case is akin to blame and guilt.

It keeps me busy, thinking about my life and whether I'm doing things right and looking around to see if someone else is doing it better or worse. It's sort of like watching too much television—it passes the time and takes some mental energy and it feels productive. Actually, it couldn't be further from productive action. All that busy-ness and analyzing and weighing has one net effect: it blocks energy flow in my life and keeps my own dreams and plans and Wants from taking root and growing.

Resist the temptation to compare your situation to anyone else's and funnel all that energy back into your Wants.

250

"Start small to flip-switch from a negative to positive vibration. Soon that small thought will gain the momentum necessary to launch you into a major Feel Good."

Okay, let's be honest. I don't have it in me to be a Goody Two-shoes. I just don't. Say I go to a gathering of people I don't know very well and I put up the façade—well, it's pretty laughable to begin with, and then when I get home and cop to all the awkwardness and nerves I was stuffing underneath my sweet exterior, I crumble in a heap on the floor. Another casualty of Pollyanna thinking.

Get into flowing positive energy. Does this mean be nicey-nice to everyone you meet? No. Does this mean think only happy thoughts? Heck, no. If that's your natural state and you feel comfortable there, by all means, go right ahead and the rest of us grumps can consider ourselves very lucky that we have you in the world to balance things out. But there is no formula, no vocabulary that flows energy better than any other, so don't try to live up to some expectation of what a positive person looks or sounds like. I know some real curmudgeons who are rough on the outside, but strangely easy to spend time with. They somehow don't draw you into any negativity because for all their outward saltiness, at their core, they are true optimists, funneling their energies into their love for the world and the people in it, in the best way they know how. These same curmudgeons tend to have a wicked, lively sense of humor—maybe the best measure of good stuff flowing.

Regardless of your disposition, what you can do, even if you have to do it through gritted teeth and an occasional snarky comment, is to live in this world and stay open to experiencing that *whoosh* of sensation and energy pouring around us all the time, the balance of which is tipped towards the well-being of everything on the planet, *including us*. This is true positivity, and it trumps the negative every time.

Being yourself is a positive act all by itself—and trying to be anyone else wastes time and energy.

251

"Allow yourself time in each day to dream, desire, imagine, intend, want, and time to flow energy to them all, flow energy to them all, flow energy to them all."

I had a teacher who reminded his class that no human being can sleep without dreaming. Whether or not you remember your dreams, or think they mean anything in relation to your waking life, you simply cannot be alive and stop dreaming.

And yet we walk around during the day as though the world might as well have been created inside our conscious brains. We trust our waking thoughts, our sensible deductions, far more than our intuition, our gut, our Guidance. We think we can plan, push, and willingly act our way into or out of any situation, and then we're taken off guard when it seems like invisible forces are shaping our lives. So we buckle down and work harder, or we throw up our hands at the loss of control.

These invisible forces—we label them either benevolent when we win the lottery or nasty and sour when they get us fired from the job we need to pay the bills. But what if it's none of the above? What if our dreams, both asleep and awake, are a tapestry of passions, desires, and fears that create the road map of our life stories every day of our lives? What if we invest some time in reading that tapestry a little more closely and finding the spots that don't agree with us in the core of our being, and reweave them?

The energy of one moment of your life, its sources, its power, its projection into the future could be analyzed and dissected, and the resulting conclusions would fill volumes. Each moment is so full that you would go mad trying to wrestle perfection from any one—so it's time to take a moment and open up to that vast unknown power. Open up to your dreams, your unconscious energy, and give it some credit for the path you are taking.

Acknowledge the power and complexity of your dreams, and stand in awe of the tapestry of your life. This will help you release the iron grip of "control."

252

"Whether male or female, there is within you a softness, a gentleness, a sweetness so beautiful you might weep from the feeling, were you to touch it. . . . This sweetness has nothing to do with personality. . . . It has to do with you, for it is what you are."

Sweetness. The seed of who you are. The perfect gift from the universe. Your angelic self, your highest consciousness, your finest vibrations, the light within you.

No matter what your current circumstance—poverty, shame, loneliness, anger, boredom—there lies within you a source of life and living that is your boldest champion and your closest ally. No one can take it away from you, you can't even take it away from yourself. No situation or action can dull its brilliance. You may hide it well, bury it deep, and think it's gone, but it will always be there. And it may be the simplest thing in the world to access. Just sitting quietly, knowing it's there, will bring it immediately to the surface. What's more, a single moment of feeling the pulse of that energy can override thousands of hours of negative being.

The challenge, of course, is to call upon the strength to *live* from this place. The practice is to find the open door to this power source, and keep it open. You will find it, lose it, and find it again, probably many times. That's the struggle and, ultimately, the joy.

Reacquaint yourself with the indelible spirit at your core—that being of unlimited humanity, empathy, understanding, and peace. That is what you are.

253

"Realize that your present difficulty is only a small part of you, and the rest of you is doing quite well, thank you."

We are spiritual beings having a physical experience, as the saying goes, and part of what that means is that we are greater than the sum of our parts. The part that's an aching joint. The part that's feeling sad. The part that's having trouble with a family member. The painful and difficult parts have a way of drawing attention to themselves—which is okay—we need to take care of our headaches, whether they're physical or emotional.

But those parts don't get to steal the show. And when they threaten to, we can have an arsenal at the ready. One thing that works well is the simple list, maybe added to once a week, maybe daily, maybe only intermittently. It's the "Just fine, thank you very much" list. And, on it, I write the things that are going well.

So when this little hitch at work, this little downturn in self-esteem, tries to take over as if she's diva for a day, I can haul out my list. I acknowledge her, but I don't let her take over. I don't let her get me down.

I know that I am bigger than the sum of my parts—especially my hurting parts.

254

"So as hard as it may be to swallow, it becomes a matter of looking at *our own* valve, *our own* reactions, *our own* energy flow, because as long as we're glaring somewhere else—past or present—at all the stuff we don't like, not only are we inviting more of the same, we're blocking all the good things we'd like to see in its place."

Truth. It's simple, not always easy. It's a kind of "I get it already" that I don't do myself any favors when I blame my parents for not teaching me the value of a dollar. Blaming my spouse for not loving me enough isn't going to get me more love. And blaming the government or corporations or the system for making it impossible for people like me to succeed, make a living, or have a nice place to live isn't going to get me any of those things, either. Putting all my focus on blame or shame or naming someone or something else as the source of my woe—it's easy to understand intellectually that doesn't work. It's a little bit harder to put into practice.

Simply put, we need to look at our own stuff—how we act with our spouse, how we play victim to the system—and then we need to let it go. When we take our focus off the problem or the hurt . . . when we don't lash out with sarcasm or in anger . . . when we admit our mistakes and move on, we unlock the deadbolt and the good things move into our hearts, minds, and lives.

Today I'm letting go of old gripes to make way for new goodies.

255

"Should we stop protecting ourselves? No . . . Later, maybe, but not for a while, until the hang of this new vibration becomes so ingrained in us, we simply *KNOW* we are okay and will always BE okay. Meanwhile, if a guard dog will help us relax into well-being, terrific. If new locks will help us relax into well-being, terrific. Whatever it takes."

It won't work to abandon your old beliefs before you are ready. There are some really great reasons for taking care of ourselves in the traditional ways—with locks, seat belts, doctor visits. Maybe some enlightened monk on a mountaintop is ready to do away with all that, but, if you're not yet, don't sweat it. Use the tools you have right here and right now to get all warm and fuzzy and to feel safe. That's okay.

Our safety, or lack of it, comes from our beliefs. Our beliefs form the core of our vibrational force, which brings in everything we're sending out. If you feel like you "should" let go of some safety mechanism (physical or emotional) and you force it before you're ready, you could be vibrationally advertising a vulnerability to the universe. Then, when you get smacked around by some unwanted circumstances, you may run back further into your defensive safety zone, worse off than you were before.

Keep yourself safe in the ways that feel best to you, even as you learn that your safety is ultimately tied to your well-being.

256

"We come up with the only possible choice, and it still feels lousy . . . What do you do then? You go for the one that feels best, even if it doesn't feel terrific. There's a difference between a 'No' that shouts to you, and a 'Yes, this is right,' even if that 'Yes' doesn't sing."

Choice is a wonderful thing and there are often many more choices than we think we have in any given situation, but sometimes none of them feel like the big winner. In fact, often this is the case. If you feel you have really explored all the options and the only viable few are still unappealing, the work of your choosing shifts in some way to how you are going to choose to handle your decision once it is made.

So, yes, you go with the one that feels better, even slightly, than the other ones. Then you have to forgive yourself and your conditions and remember no one put you in this box but you, and there is always, *always* a way to keep your valve open. That is, it won't be in your best interests to make the choice halfway just because it's not ideal. If you do that, you're pretty quickly going to get bogged down in regret and inaction. Try to acknowledge the crumminess of the choice so that you can fully dive in, so then your focus can shift to how to make the resulting situation into something that you can be happy with, or at least at peace with.

When we decided to put our ailing cat to sleep, it was that sort of decision—not one anyone wants to make, but once we made it, we could go about preparing the warmest, safest passing we could for the little guy who had given us so much joy. Fretting over that choice was holding us back from the real task at hand of helping him go.

A lousy range of choices can still bring us to a peaceful outcome if we flow good energy to the important stuff.

"Play with it all, but remember, this is all very, very new, so please, please, please don't get discouraged."

When we're trying so hard and so earnestly to allow this new way of thinking to take root in our lives, it can be easy to get disillusioned, especially if we don't see concrete results right away. The whole process is so simple on the surface that we feel dumb or inadequate when we fail to keep it up, or fail to find our inspiration to keep going with it. Or maybe we feel like we got it at the beginning, but we just can't sustain and maintain it, and then a cycle of guilt and blame sets in that brings more negative energy, and then we're well into a tailspin.

If this happens, just let it go. Stop trying to "do" anything. Stop playing around with new ideas or new ways of looking at problems. Stop trying to flow energy. Because you can't manufacture perfect positive feeling. You're going to suck at this sometimes, and sometimes the best thing you can do is let yourself grind to a halt.

So if this happens, please just go play. Do something that feels fun to you, no matter what it is.

Play hooky from the serious, dour business of changing your life. It will do wonders.

258

"An old belief—or any belief—is nothing but a vibrational habit that we respond to like trained seals."

One of the biggest stumbling blocks we encounter on our way to changing our lives is the idea that our beliefs constitute who we are. It's easy to understand why we think this—our beliefs are indeed the soil from which any thought or action in our life must spring. And most of the time our actions and our thoughts feel like the sum total of who we are.

But there is another, deeper part of us—the part that philosophers and theologians and artists have tried to disclose since the beginning of time. No matter what we call it or how we describe it, this deepest core of our being is what connects us to everyone, and everything, on the planet. Whether it's energy or soul or consciousness, this core is essential and therefore in some way unchangeable. It is who we are in our most basic state, before and outside of our bodies, above and beyond our thoughts and deeds.

Our beliefs may emanate from this deepest core of us, and indeed the most powerful beliefs usually do. But beliefs can also come from any number of other sources including our families, society, religious traditions, education, and superstition. But we often don't distinguish between who we are and what we believe, and this keeps us in thrall to beliefs that may or may not be serving us, because they feel so essential to who we are. So we need to be meticulous in our examinations of our various beliefs, sorting out what came from where and what each belief is bringing into our life. Is the belief that we have to "keep our guard up" really warding off danger, or is it inviting calamity to dinner? Is our fear of suffering and pain opening a back door for those very things to sneak in?

Be comforted by the thought that belief is most often habit—and habits can change!

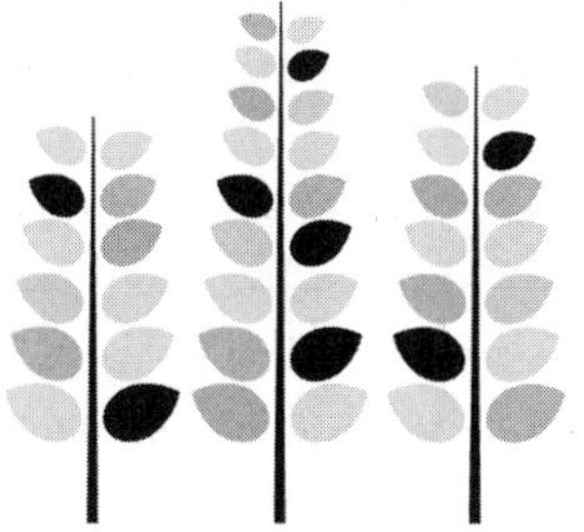

259

"Remember that nothing—*nothing*—is more important than feeling good, even if it's just feeling better."

Each of us has a few things that we long for to bring us comfort when we're in pain: foods that Mom made us when we were sick, things we do to feel better when we're blue. Sometimes they can feel silly or unnecessary—do I really have to have a popsicle when I have a sore throat? If it makes me feel better, of course!

Mahatma Gandhi said, "As long as you derive inner help and comfort from anything, keep it." There is no right or wrong in the comfort game, just what makes you feel good. Feeling just a tiny bit better counts for a lot, too. You have a right to that comfort, and a responsibility to take care of yourself and to let others take care of you.

Enjoy the small comforts: tea, poetry, crossword puzzles, swimming, a good book. If you suddenly feel guilty, like you're not doing enough or you should be doing something big and meaningful instead, just remember that comfort is a shortcut to feeling good, and that is the single most important thing you can do.

Take care of yourself, and feel better.

260

"You MUST go into action! There is never a time when you just sit back and say to yourself, 'Well, I've placed my order with the universe. It's out of my hands.' *No way!* Once you begin to get an inkling of how to proceed, or get your first idea, or see someone who suggests something . . . once things begin to happen, no matter how unrelated they may seem to be, you MUST engage that idea with action."

If you placed an order in a restaurant and it didn't come, how long would you wait for it without doing something—like flagging down your waiter and asking him? If you landed a contract to write a report, how long would you wait to start doing the research and putting your ideas down on paper? Probably not very long in either case. Yet, in matters that some people call "spiritual," when they've asked for help or for something to change in their lives—to find a new partner, say, or a new home—they think the next thing to do is just what Grabhorn cautions against—to sit around and wait for something to happen.

And then, they're disappointed. It was spiritual. I had the inspiration during meditation. It was meant to be and it didn't happen. I must have done something wrong. Or, this connecting to the universe stuff is all so much hooey. Disappointment—once again.

None of us—nobody on this planet—needs more disappointment. We need to be encouraged to dream our dreams. And we need to be encouraged to take the next step, to engage our dreams, to work with them, talk to them, nourish them, make them come true.

Making my dreams come true is never "out of my hands."

261

> "Creating a new script is nothing more than making up a grand little daydream and stepping into it emotionally. That's the important part: you've gotta get into your daydream *emotionally* or you're just blowing hot air."

There are many teachers and theories of acting—and they usually fall into two basic camps. Often great actors work in one way or the other: from the outside in (that is, building behaviors and using the external look and modes of being of the character to get at the core truth) or beginning from a core kernel of truth in themselves that they then develop into a fully realized outer performance of actions, gestures, etc.

Great acting is storytelling in its most vivid form, and the story becomes more real than reality in some ways—we can learn things from plays, music, and art that would pass us by in our everyday lives. Often a performance or piece of art will almost knock us off our feet with an *aha* moment. The power of the truth in storytelling is ancient; it's literally part of our humanity.

But no matter how you get there, from the inside out or the outside in, acting is really living truthfully in imaginary circumstances. And in order to get to the truth that will magnetize in the desired circumstances that aren't in your life yet, you're going to have to get into living your script in every way you can like the greatest actor who ever lived (luckily, it should be easier for you since these are *your* wants and not a fictional character's). You make the script, and then learning your lines is the very least of it. You have to explore how you feel in that script, what your sensory experiences are in that script—what it smells like, sounds like, tastes like to live the life you've always wanted. You have to let it bring you to tears or make you laugh out loud, and don't bother censoring yourself, because you are your only audience.

Get into it—with your mind, your body, and the whole range of your emotions. The more detailed you are, the better it will turn out.

262

"You must do something each day to physically engage your idea."

Rome, as they say, wasn't built in a day. A little bit at a time. Break it down to build it up. You're getting the picture, right? Any one of us can do great things. We can bring our big ideas into the material world. And none of us can do it like a wizard in a children's magic book. You know, presto, change-o, appear-o!

As Grabhorn writes, to manifest an idea, "You must go into action . . . you must engage! No matter how small the engagement (action), no matter how little the amount of time, even if it's just a phone call or two each day, or a listing of your ideas on paper, or an actual outline of your project, or a trip to the car dealer, or real estate agent, or dog pound, or buying some small thing that's related to your idea. . . ."

To most of us, I think, this idea of doing something small toward achieving our goal and manifesting our idea is a relief. For one thing, it is a natural and gentle way beyond the block that many of us experience when we first start to get whammed with great ideas and then get overwhelmed by fear that little old me will never be able to do this big thing.

When I think I can't build a castle I know I can place one brick.

263

"Your Guidance system is doing all it knows how to get you where you want to go to follow your Original Intent. So give it a chance. Tune in and listen up; that Expanded Self knows what it's doing."

I'm sometimes a bit behind the technology curve, so maybe it's not news to most people that you can throw a GPS system off track by not listening and not giving it a chance. I was in an unfamiliar town with a colleague, and we needed to make our way back and forth across town to several different appointments. So we rented a GPS system with our car and dubbed the sultry voice box Gypsy. We turned her on, and off we went.

We made our way to the freeway exit near our hotel without incident. But that's when things got tricky. Road construction, exit closed, we drive past. Gypsy recalculates. Or did she say recalibrate? At any rate, take this exit, turn left here, right there. Oh, oh, recalibrating again. There were so many twists and turns, frontage roads going one way, that pretty soon we were hopelessly lost practically in sight of the hotel, and Gypsy seemed to have gone into a tailspin.

Of course, she wasn't the one who'd gone into that spin. And she wasn't the one who lost sight of this simple original intent—to get to the hotel in the fastest possible time. Nor was she the one who stopped listening. Now, I know a computer is not my highest self. But I did think about my listening skills that day. Not being able to slow down and listen to the computer whose only point of existence was to serve my needs—hmm. Could that be a lesson for other parts of my life?

When I don't know what to do, I know I can slow down and listen to my higher self.

264

"Don't try to label how you feel when you're down. Stop calling it guilt or frustration or whatever. Just know you are out of sync and find a way to get back in."

It's tempting. Oh, it's so tempting. It's the stuff that melodramas, soap operas, and navel-gazing novels are made out of—I'm sad, lonely, depressed, guilty, frustrated, and not good enough for anyone to love me. And, furthermore, I'm like this because my father wasn't home enough, my mother doesn't understand me, my kindergarten teacher didn't realize I have a learning disability—or whatever. In the end, pity parties are useless. They don't make us feel better. They don't win us friends. And they sure don't get us in touch with our true heart's desire.

So what is this temptation to linger in the shadows? Sometimes we even brag about how badly things are going and how out of sync and sorts we are—got up on the wrong side of the bed, broke the coffee carafe, cut my foot, was an hour late for work, missed a meeting, broke a fingernail, spilled lunch down the front of my new shirt. Have we gotten enough attention yet? Because on days like this, it seems like I'm (1) trying to get someone—anyone—else to pay attention to how hard my life is and how brave I am to sadly march around in it or (2) trying to get my own attention to what fun it would be—but it's NOT—to wallow in my mishaps.

The alternative to living out a day like that is living out a day like that with a different attitude. Okay, so the coffee pot broke. If I'd slowed down right then and there, I might not have even cut my foot. But at some point during that day, even if it's when I carry my bedraggled self off to bed that night, I can review the day, paying attention to its lessons, without judging myself or others.

There will always be "days like this," and it's what I do with them that counts.

265

"You are far greater than your body, so never doubt you can do this thing. Laugh more at everything and lighten up."

There's that old saw. "Laugh and the world laughs with you. Cry and you cry alone." Now, as it turns out, current research says that some crying is good for us. Cleans out our physical and emotional bodies, removes toxins. So, maybe we should learn to cry together and get rid of some of the toxins. And, after we cry, let's laugh.

Laughing, to my mind, is right up there with babies being born and the sun rising every day, to count as a miracle on this material plane. I wish I could say that when I encounter an obstacle or have what seems to be an overwhelming task, one my body's not up to, that my first inclination is to laugh. It's not. And it could be. But usually after I've had my meltdown, felt the burden of my own limitations, cried my eyes out, I begin to see how ludicrous my small objections are. And then I remember to go out looking for something to laugh at. Generally, I don't have to look very far.

The other day I came across this quote from Jean Houston: "At the height of laughter, the universe is flung into a kaleidoscope of new possibilities." In my mind, I pictured myself laughing, and I saw the sound coming out of my mouth as bright and shifting shapes and colors. I felt a release somewhere down in my belly, and I knew I could go on with my day.

Let yourself remember the best laugh you ever had.

266

"Passion. We've talked a lot about it. It's one of those words that sounds great, but what does it mean? How do we get it? And do we really need it? Here's your clue: passion is creation!"

Many artists, writers, performers know that you can talk a thing to death—pretty easily. Talk too much about a story you're trying to write—especially to a naysayer, even a well-meaning one—and the thing can fall apart in your hands. Ditto a character you're trying to create for a performance, a piece of music, a painting. So, the point is that talking about passion for creating your life is not passion for creating your life.

Passion sounds great—and, indeed, what does that mean? One way to define and find our own particular passion is to try a creation litmus test. Suppose you think you've discovered your passion to grow orchids. You look up books on cultivating orchids, you buy a few. Maybe you even buy a small plant to start with. Then you get busy. You forget one week to water them. You never did buy that food stuff you're supposed to give them, or clear away a space in front of the window where they'll get the best sun. So you have lovely purple flowers that last for a few months. Sometime before the plant stops blooming, you've probably figured out that you don't really have a passion for raising orchids after all.

Another way to discover our passions, our creative genius, is to look at our past. When is a time I felt fully alive? When did I feel like I was in the moment and flowing with the moment? What was going on at those times—not only what was I doing, but what was I feeling, how was I looking at my world and the people in it? What kind of energy (or passion) do I want to bring back into my life?

Passion is creation and creation feeds passion—it's a cycle that feeds itself and me.

"It means 'I don't need conditions to be just right to be happy. I'm not going to pay any more attention to your silly habits, because I don't need everything to be perfect for my love to flow to you.'"

Feelings are the vibrational core of our body and soul. When we understand this, we can begin to really pay attention to *how we are feeling.* This goes beyond moments of jealousy, or fits of silliness, or a frustrated tantrum. Those are details, and while they can be important and are definitely worth going through and noticing, they can never define the broad undercurrent of your existence.

But for many of us, this is exactly how we live. We amount to a strung-together formation of grievances, lost hopes, and petty misunderstandings, as well as heaps of fearful responding to conditions we believe are beyond our control. Occasionally, we stumble on a moment of elation, or find something or someone who temporarily makes us feel like we're on top of the world. If those moments aren't grounded in a larger experience that connects us to the power of our deepest feelings, we may be really lost. Even the best feelings are confusing and ultimately disappointing if there's nothing to make them feel real.

That reality can only come from complete trust of your own self. And that trust can only come from truly loving yourself. No small task, let me tell you. The good news is that you don't have to know yourself (you don't even have to really like yourself) to love yourself. Because this kind of love is your most basic vibration, and it doesn't have anything to do with thoughts. It's all about feeling, and it's way beyond that.

I remember that it's not what I do or know or have that makes me lovable—it's who I am.

268

"For a relationship to change to your liking, it's gotta be: Focus *off* the condition; Focus *onto* opening the valve . . . yours."

This is actually a pretty simple concept. If we focus all our attention on a problem, we don't have any attention left to focus on a solution. Yet, when we're dealing with relationships, especially close ones, our tendency is to focus on the thing we think is the problem—whether it's that the other person is being stubborn, or doesn't see the world the way we do, or likes the room to be warmer or colder. (Seriously, people have gotten divorced over that.) If all we think about is that we can't live together, then we probably can't.

How much sweeter would the world be if we stopped to open up to the love and the kindness and the good things that abound—in our everyday encounters with ourselves, our loved ones, and anyone we meet? If we focus on how we like being with that person, maybe we put a sweater on and stop bickering about where the thermostat is set.

Opening a valve allows us to see possibilities. It allows us to see ways to compromise. And it allows us to be kinder to one another. When we're kinder, the condition is going to change for the better. It's inevitable.

Today I'm paying attention to what will make change possible—my openness to it.

269

"Place your intent that you are going to lower your resistance to 'shoulds and shouldn'ts,' and that you're going to learn how to receive. Make it a Want: 'I want to learn to receive.'"

There's a lot—tons, megawatts, kilobytes, whatever big measurement you want to name—of energy that goes into what amounts to this: We should abolish *should* from our vocabulary. Or we shouldn't use *shouldn't.* It kind of reminds me of something my grandma used to say, "Ain't ain't a word and I ain't supposed to use it."

Seriously, folks, there is very good reason to let go of the "shoulds" and "shouldn'ts." And there are a lot of resources available to help accomplish that—both on abolishing the conditionals and focusing on the "I Wants."

This is serious work, and it sometimes helps to have a light touch when doing heavy work. So, here's a little eyelid-blinking meditation. You can do it anywhere, anytime—in a meeting, at dinner with friends, in line at the supermarket—whenever you hear an internal *should.* Blink your eyes, and say, "I want to learn to receive." Just that. In the blink of an eye, big shifts are made.

I want to learn to receive.

270

> "The body, after all, isn't separate from the universe, so when we think a thought, the vibrations run through the body as well as everywhere else. If those vibrations are in harmony with our body's intrinsic programming for well-being (open valve Feel Good), then the cells thrive."

What's good for our world is good for our body, what's good for our atmosphere is good for our spirit, what's good for the universe is good for us. It's as simple as that. (Remember, simple isn't necessarily easy.) Also remember energy flows both ways.

When we "pollute" our bodies with junk food with little nutritional or aesthetic value, we're polluting the planet. When we dump garbage into our brains—negative thoughts, for example—we're sending those same negative thoughts out to every living thing in the universe. When we recycle, pick up garbage off the beach, use low-energy light bulbs, walk instead of drive—we're doing something for the planet, our fellow human beings, and ourselves.

If you can't think of this as literally true—that any polluting to ourselves is polluting to the planet, that any polluting to the planet is polluting to ourselves—then at least think of it as a metaphor. And when you think good thoughts for yourself—open your valve—think good thoughts for the tree in the backyard. When you open your valve and feel your cells thrive, feel the cells of the water thriving as well.

Sending out good energy—and receiving it back—is what life is all about.

"Watch your excuses."

Here's an interesting idea. Don't try to stop making excuses. Don't blame yourself for making excuses. Don't make a big deal out of making excuses. Don't judge yourself for making excuses. Just watch. Sounds really simple. And I suppose it may be for some people, because it is, in fact, a simple idea.

By watching what behavior we engage in and then make excuses or apologies for, we find the bumps in our lives. Say I want to change my eating habits. I resolve that I will eat more vegetables, less refined sugar, not so many carbs. Maybe things go well for a day or two, or less or more—and then I have a really bad, awful day. Everybody wants something from me. So, I'm tired and hungry, and maybe crabby and lonely. I make all these excuses, and I eat six cookies. What happens next is really interesting.

It is, really. I can watch my excuse of eating what I didn't want to eat—turn my attention to it without judgment. Or I can judge it—get madder at myself, feel worse, eat more.

Watching excuses and not letting them control my behavior opens the way for me to change my behavior.

272

"Stop trying to fix anybody else; that's valve-closing stuff. You don't have to fix anything; you just have to stop thinking about it."

To try to fix someone else is one of the most frustrating temptations known to humankind. It simply cannot be done. And it is always, always a lose/lose proposition from here to Sunday. I mean, think about it. The stereotype is the woman who marries a man because he's a bon vivant and he makes her laugh—something in his spirit attracts her. But then she discovers that he drinks too much and can't hold down a job. Eventually, maybe this guy is going to need to quit (or at least cut down on) drinking and figure out how to attract some money into the family coffers. But who's going to have to do that?

That's right. He is. The woman who tries to stop her husband from drinking will have a much better life if she stops putting her attention on the problems and looks toward how she is going to attract what she needs in her own life. Just because you love someone doesn't mean you are meant to try to remake him—or yourself—into an image of what you or your parents or society thinks he should be.

Say it out loud: I don't need to fix anything. I just need to stop thinking about it.

"So when inspiration hits, or an idea for how to further your Want just happens to slip in one day, start thinking in Can Dos rather than Yeah Buts. Never mind the How Tos, they'll come once you relax into that higher frequency."

"Yeah, but" is probably one of the ugliest word combinations in the English language. It doesn't feel good to say it; it doesn't feel good to hear it from someone else. So, why does it pop up so readily whenever something new comes along? Is it the newness that scares us? The unknown? I think so.

Inspiration is almost always something new, or at least it feels that way. They say that even the most genius discoveries tend to be the result of someone able to see and rearrange some previously known elements in such a way that a totally new picture becomes clear, using the same old puzzle pieces. I find this thought so comforting because it means that in order to make any new discovery, either in our personal lives or in a broader arena, all we have to do is sit back and let the puzzle rearrange itself into inspiration. You don't have to pore over the individual pieces, you just have to get to that higher frequency and let in the Can Dos.

Then, of course, the hard thing is turning down the volume on any Yeah, Buts that come your way. And they will. We are wired to think of what might go wrong, to plan for the difficulties ahead. But use those instincts as tools, thank them for the insight, and let them go. You don't have to even bother shooting down those Yeah, Buts, just acknowledge their contribution to the contrast of the situation and move on. Re-center yourself in the Want that brought in that inspiration in the first place.

Even the wildest inspirations are completely valid, and you have permission to let them run their course without pausing for any Yeah, Buts.

274

"It's all energy. That's all this world and universe is. You can either be its master or its victim."

There are circumstances in this world that are difficult to understand—war, famine, brutality, child abuse, rape, murder. And it can take a lifetime of meditation to come to understand the relationship between being a victim and choosing our destiny. I do not pretend to know exactly what it all means, but I do know that there are many energies circling through my life, and my energy flows through my life and beyond it in ways I couldn't plan or articulate.

Lately, I've begun to see that the small choices we make—the prayers we send up, the energy we send out and let in—not only affect our own lives, but that they can be cumulative and can affect the energy of the world. If enough people make enough small choices not to be victims, not to let the circumstances of the world get them down, make them apathetic, then the flow of energy increases and the circumstances of people's lives change.

I think of the first line of a folk song/hymn that my dad used to sing: Let there be peace on Earth and let it begin with me. And as I repeat that line in my mind, I become more master than victim.

What simple way can you become master over the energy of your life?

275

"Think about your daily appreciation item when you're *not* in fear. Think about it every minute you remember to do it. That kind of concentrated, high-vibrational focus will do more to break up your habitual worry vibration—faster—than you can imagine."

My father died suddenly shortly after my sixteenth birthday, and my response to that loss has informed, consciously and unconsciously, everything about the rest of my life.

As the initial shock of his death started to recede in that first year, I made what must have been a semiconscious decision. As much as it was possible I would remain as I was when he died; I would try to not grow up. This would honor his memory, the logic went, because he was so important to me that I would not be able to go on without him, except to go through the motions of daily life, to do what was expected, and to let the passage of time happen around me.

Several years later, I justified my failure to go through any real grieving process and my reluctance to dive into and live my own life with a kind of false gratitude. Again, the strange logic flowed: I'm grateful that my father died, I pretended, because it has made me who I am. (Never mind I deeply hated myself and was in no place to feel any kind of gratitude.)

This is, of course, the last thing any parent would want for his child, and the worst possible way to honor the memory of my father. Now, I think of my dad almost every day, and, while I am still heartbroken that he is gone, I am starting to find a genuine gratitude—for his life and my own.

Gratitude in name only won't cut it—true gratitude lives and breathes through our decisions, our dreams, and our actions.

276

"Ask yourself constantly, 'How am I flowing my energy?' 'How am I flowing my energy?'"

Your Wants should be articulated, worked through, pored over, very detailed affairs. The details give your energy plenty of avenues to flow down, and the more energy, the better. But no one conscious mind can comprehend the power of all the energetic flow in the universe in any given moment.

So much as we would like it to be, the power of attraction is not quite like ordering a hamburger (or veggie burger). You might order extra cheese and mushrooms and a bun toasted to just this side of burnt, and really the more detailed, the better. And you'll get your burger, but it might be a bit different from what you expected (probably even better) and it might come out of the blue, from an angle you never expected.

You make your order, and then when it doesn't come right away, you think, "Where is it? When's it going to get here already?" The key is to release the impatient, controlling aspect of your expectations, and learn to appreciate that your Want is on its way. Don't get frustrated with the slow waitress, because that's just going to hold it up longer. Try to avoid thinking how it's going to make its way to your table, because you really won't be able to guess and that'll slow things down even more.

Order up the life you want to your exact specifications, and then remember it's on its way, in some form or another and from any possible direction.

277

"We cannot hold ourselves above responsibility for what is happening around the world today, for the planet mirrors the predominant vibration in which it is encompassed."

You may have built yourself into quite a worrywart by this point in your life. And reading and thinking about the power of attraction, you're sure to have encountered some more things to worry about. That you've created your own and your family's illness? That people who pass on in car crashes or become victims of violent crime have created, or cocreated with those around them, the circumstances of their own tragedies?

It's a pretty extreme slippery slope, and, in my belief, this kind of thinking is both a gross oversimplification and an exaggeration. Furthermore, it's probably the single biggest booby trap you'll come across as you learn to let your energy flow and magnetize your wants into being. If you're inclined to think that tragedy is on the way because of something you did wrong, then you most certainly are setting the stage for some ugly energy flow through your extreme guilt, blame, and fear.

At the core of this teaching is the idea that you create your own life. This is a powerful idea, a positive idea, and one that I know can lead you to a happiness that may be unfathomable to you now. You are a powerful magnet, and like attracts like, so as you crank up your vibrations, you will be thrilled by the wonderful things that start pouring into your life. And the powerful magnet that is you gets to live in this universe for a time in a physical body, a world in which everything is emanating vibrational energy—other people, animals, plants, even inanimate objects. You are not the only show in town.

Yes, you create what you send into the world—this frees you from dumping responsibility for your circumstances on other people or things. The freedom of taking the reins of your life energetically is a huge gift—why would you turn around and squander it on the superstition that everything "bad" you do is attracting a car accident, a broken leg, or worse?

Don't let the idea of cocreation of tragedy become its own vicious superstition—this has as much or more power to close your valve as the worst of your fears.

278

"So here's the flash: Continuing to live life as a victim of circumstance forever focusing on what's wrong with everything and everybody, will never, ever, bring the life desired. It will only bring one thing: more of whatever it is we're wanting so desperately to change."

Are you ready for it? You are a *nag.* Yes, you. You are a total pain—just like your mother, whose nagging you to finish your chores or your homework managed to make the tasks even less appealing than they were in the first place. You know how it feels to be on the listening (or blocking out) end of nagging. It inspires countless variations, schemes, and deceits to get out of the labor. It invites an endless waste of time and energy spent in any direction *other* than what the nagger wants.

Quit nagging. Right now. Quit looking at each negative aspect of your life and turning it over disapprovingly, making mental notes and suggestions about how it might be remedied. Quit fixing other people's problems in your head. Quit figuring out who's responsible for the shortcomings and disappointments in your life, and take a deep breath as you realize there's nothing to figure out. It's you; you're responsible. Now take another deep breath, and get on with the business of bringing in the life you truly desire. Not through lists of others' faults and your own, not through gentle nudging and guilt-inducing suggestions. Not through fear or intimidation or superstition. Any of this will simply heap more junk onto the pile.

Think of all the time and energy you'll claim back into your life when you quit spending it stacking garbage and start putting it into the things you really cherish and love. Think of the rush of excitement when the lists of ugly circumstances get shorter every day just because you stopped giving them all your attention and started putting that focus on what really matters.

Every time you feel the urge to nag, stick your tongue out at yourself, yell "No!" and/or have a good laugh.

279

"Instead of thinking about it, feel about it."

In some support groups, especially those related to addictions, people talk about "stinkin' thinkin'," the kind that sends us into a spiral of despair, anger, grief, depression, or bingeing on food or alcohol, or whatever our downward spiral of choice is. We all pretty much have an ongoing dialogue in our heads. This dialogue—or thinking—is, in and of itself, neither good nor bad. You wake up in the morning. You remind yourself that while you wait for your coffee, you want to do your stretching exercises. Then you get out of bed, start your day. Brew your coffee, sit down, read the paper, eat breakfast. And somewhere in between bites of toast your brain says something like, "You are so stupid. You can't even remember for ten minutes that you need to do your stretching exercises. You're going to be a stiff old lady if you don't do these."

And it goes on. That is stinkin' thinkin'. We also tend to use it when we're trying to make a decision, choose a new course, or a new path. Choose between two jobs. Choose whether or not to continue in a relationship.

One way to get out of the thinking-something-to-death routine is to do what Lynn Grabhorn suggests—feel it. This could still be a dialogue—imagine yourself in the new job. How does that feel? (I once turned down a job offer after four interviews because every single time I walked into the office, my stomach hurt. And I didn't like the starched smell and sound of my would-be boss's white shirts.) Do you find yourself smiling when you think of one path? Do you find yourself tired when you think of another?

Our bodies and our senses provide clues to feelings and to making decisions when we pay attention.

280

"We accept that we are not separate, not alone; we are one with All That Is."

There's an old saying: we're born alone, we die alone. I've never really liked that saying—or believed it. First, the born part—our mothers were there, weren't they? And the die part, well, it's hard to imagine that the energy of connection and love we've built through our lives doesn't extend beyond this material plane.

Ah, the energy of connection and love that we've built—that's the crux. Or maybe the way to connect the dots, close the circle—the circle that comes back around to itself. It rolls like this—I accept that I'm connection. I let myself feel that. Once I do, I reach out—I connect to others and to the deep inner core of myself on a genuine basis. And I feel even less alone. And I reach out more, more and deeper connection. Feel less alone, more connection.

When we make a conscious practice of building our feeling of connection, we're storing up for the times when we get down, feel a bit isolated. We're learning to flip a switch in our psyche that reminds us that no one is alone. Ever.

My circle remains unbroken.

"A belief is nothing but a habit of thought. You can always tell you're having one of your habits by how you *feeeeel.*"

Good. Bad. Exhilarated. Down in the dumps. Frumpy. Happy. Sad. Grumpy. Let me count the ways. As human beings, we have a more extraordinary range of feelings than we usually give ourselves credit for or pay attention to. And that is unfortunate, to say the least, because our feelings are like the best road marker, psychic global positioning that ever could be invented.

Okay, so I believe all people are good and kind at heart, so why am I feeling so pissed off when the clerk who waited on me talked on the phone to another customer the whole time? Hello, I'm metaphorically waving my arms around, pay attention to me. It doesn't cost you anything. Well, I'm feeling annoyed because I'm being ignored, duh. And one of my habits is probably to stew about that and not to say anything or do anything differently.

So I've paid attention to my feelings enough to recognize the habit that I get into when my belief in people's innate goodness and their actual behavior are dissonant. Next I can decide what to do with that feeling. I can continue to stew, thereby reinforcing another habit (and not all habits are bad, but this one isn't doing me any favors), or I can choose to do something else. Maybe ask the clerk to finish with me before she continues on the phone. And how I feel then is another marker. And so on and so forth, throughout the day.

To pay attention to my feelings is to pay attention to the present.

282

"Most of us think of blame as the melodramatic pointing of a long, crooked finger towards one who has done scandalous wrong. Yet we're actually into blame just about every waking moment of our days . . . we blame from sunup 'til sundown and never think a thing about it."

Blaming is in the air we breathe. Our culture is practically built on blame. Our government certainly does it—or individuals in our government, which amounts to the same thing. They do it to grab power or to explain why they haven't lived up to their promises. We learn to do it as children, but I don't think it's intrinsic. If we don't blame a child for spilled milk—an accident—and other small things over time, is it possible that that child will grow up with two things: (1) less of a sense of guilt and (2) less of an inclination to blame others when things don't go his way?

I recently discouraged myself by trying to count all the ways I was blaming other people—and the petty things I was blaming them for. One day, I managed to do it until about mid-morning. Then I had to give up the exercise. It was too much of a downer. I blamed the management company for not taking my call about a broken dishwasher (on the weekend); I blamed their employee for scolding me for calling and making me feel like a child with no rights; I blamed a house guest for not sympathizing with me and the other one for telling me what to do (hey, I didn't say this was rational); I blamed myself for not handling the whole situation better. I also blamed myself for not meeting a deadline last week at work and, just for good measure, in advance for having to take time off to deal with the broken microwave next week. Then, for good measure, we got into a little discussion at breakfast about airlines and airport security—in which we managed to blame just about everybody who ever worked in or near any airport in the country, not to mention the bureaucrats who made all these fear-based regulations to begin with.

The alternative is not to think about these things. It's good to understand that our government is into fear-based ruling and that's what airport security measures do—they don't really prevent terrorist attacks. We need to understand so that we don't behave the same way, don't give a lot of time and focus a lot of attention on getting back at those people.

Today I'm going to look at each time I blame as an opportunity to make a different choice.

283

"So whenever a feeling of being trapped comes over you, call an immediate halt to everything, go inside, ask for guidance, and begin to listen for the choices that are always, always available."

All it takes is a minute, or a fraction thereof. The more frequently we do it, the better we'll get at it. It can become second nature, and we can choose not to suffer the feeling of being trapped for more than a minute.

I've found that it helps to have a trigger word, something I can say out loud to myself almost anytime or anywhere. "Moment" is a good one. You can say it out loud at a meeting, and then excuse yourself if you need more than that moment. Go to the loo or get a drink of water. Any word that's neutral to you will do.

If I'm alone and have the time, I take three deep breaths, consciously clearing my thoughts with each. I'm not so much looking for choices instantaneously, but for the realization, the reassurance that choices are available to me. That they will come.

Knowing I have choices gives me the power to explore my options.

284

"The universe responds only to vibration, not words."

There used to be a commercial for some kind of margarine—or maybe it was butter—both of which come from natural sources. The punch line was, "You can't fool Mother Nature." Well, we can't fool the universe, either. Or we can try, but it doesn't really work.

If you say you want to make a change—respond only to the positive, open up your heart and your valve, attract whatever it is you want—but your words are complaining and doubting, you're creating a vibratory situation that is *not* conducive to that change happening.

But I've changed my vocabulary, you say. I don't use "should." I never say "can't." I've banished negatives, dammit. Well, so you say. Listen to your attitude. That's what the universe hears.

When my words and my attitude align, my intentions come home to roost.

285

"Your physical proximity to harm, and your vibrational proximity, are two different things."

If this weren't the case, there would be no such thing as accident prone, or daredevil, for that matter. We all needed to learn as children not to put our fingers in the fire. Much of the rest of the fear of physical—or emotional or psychic—harm that we learned doesn't really serve us very well.

Sure there are "dangerous" situations. Women, for instance, should maybe avoid unlit streets at night. But if I am a woman and I find I need to walk down a street after dark, I can adjust the vibration and energy I put out to minimize my proximity to harm.

When we find ourselves feeling in harm's way, we can take a step back. If we tend more to the "accident prone" end of the vibrational continuum, we might want to push ourselves a bit, examine the reality of the threat, see if we can breathe through standing on a ladder when we're afraid of falling off, for instance. If we're more to the "daredevil" end of the vibrational continuum, we might want to take another step back and ask ourselves whether we really want to jump out of this particular plane—literally or metaphorically.

When it comes to harm's way, staying in tune with our energy is all important.

286

"We always get whatever we need to support our beliefs, good or bad."

Self-fulfilling prophecy is a two-edged sword. When we believe we're not worth getting what we want and need, we aren't. And vice versa. Good or bad. Positive or negative. So our task is to work with our beliefs.

Times when I feel like I'm expecting (or dreading) bad things are times when I know I need to take a step back from the day and look at what I'm expecting and why. My mother believes that Christmas is a sad time of year. She readily admits that this is one of her biggies in the "bad" category—and that's usually what she gets. So this year, she's consciously watching her beliefs—closely—as they arrive, about what's going to happen over the holiday. And actively imagining that it's a good time—for family, for kids, for giving up expectations.

Once we see that our beliefs are causing what we get by way of support from others and the universe—in other words, once we've replaced an old negative belief with a new positive one—it becomes easier to do that again and again.

Take a small negative belief and list what it's brought you—now flip it and see what happens.

287

"Listening daily will evaporate our blocks."

Busy, busy, busy. Kids need time and attention. Work. Friends. Family. House. Run, run, run. See Dick and Jane run themselves ragged. And every Dick and every Jane both say that there's no time to do what they really want, be who they really are. Well, no, we don't. As long as we let ourselves run ragged without taking even five minutes a day to listen to our own wise Guidance, aka Intuition, we will continue to be blocked from implementing our heart's desire.

Five minutes, really, it doesn't need to take any longer than that. Sitting, listening for the small, still voice from within. And, as we listen, that voice grows stronger, more self-assured. And the guidance we offer ourselves moves those roadblocks as if they were cotton puffs.

When I met a roadblock I couldn't move, go over, or around, I just about gave up a dream. So I sat for five minutes a day, reminding myself of my goal and asking the question, "How am I keeping myself from doing it?"

Remember, help is at hand. Ask for guidance and listen for the answer.

288

"If you have a problem, talk it out to yourself for ten or fifteen minutes every day. Explore it out loud until you've found out what's troubling you and you've talked it down."

I don't know about you, but I normally have two ways to solve a problem: butt my head into it again and again, hoping the fool thing will crack open, or stick that same head as deeply in the sand as I can get, hoping that things will have sorted themselves out by the time I have the courage to look at them again. You can see the shortcomings of each plan of attack.

A third, more useful, solution is to set aside a bit of time every day for your problem. You can even set a timer, if that helps you. Take ten minutes out of your day and begin to talk out loud about your problem. The out loud part is important, because when the words to describe your problem are trapped inside your head, they can feel very big and powerful. Hearing them out loud dissipates some of that energy. Try talking to yourself the way you might talk to a child who's just woken up from a nightmare; soothe and reassure. When ten minutes are up, stop talking about your problem and get back to the other important stuff in your day.

By giving your problem some time and space to be heard, you quit denying and you also take away its power to become an obsession that lasts all day and all night. Taking away that power means a solution is on the way.

289

"The point is not to try to LIKE everything: that would be contrary to why we came here. The point IS, however, to change our attitude about those things we don't like so they'll become no-things in our experience, and we'll finally stop attracting any more of what we don't want."

If you told me you loved and embraced everyone and everything, and were one with this world and all its various madness, I would tell you that you're a big fat liar!

I have a friend who constantly expresses just this sort of attitude. She spends a lot of time in deep meditation, praying for the earth and bathing the negative energy around her in a white light. But I still get a major kick out of watching her get cut off in traffic. She immediately goes all high-pitched and angry, and then just as quickly, she tries to cover it up with a deep sigh and a smile. She knows I think she's a piece of work, and we can laugh about it together.

Go ahead. Get mad in traffic. Snarl at your spouse every once in a while. Get really worked up and angry about a political cause or a social injustice. But don't get so lost in those feelings that you can't reduce them to nothing in an instant. Every negative thing (just as every positive thing) in the world thrives on the attention and energy we give it. So you need to be aware that every moment of hating something, or being angry about it, is like giving it a potent fertilizer. You're better off when you can acknowledge those feelings, feel them fully, and then change your reaction to them.

Find a real way to let it go.

290

"The meanest and greediest people in the world are those who really want to feel good, but don't know how. They're in a living hell with no idea how to get out, or even the awareness that they have that option. One thing is for sure—our hate against them—no matter what they may have done or are doing—is only going to make matters worse. For everybody."

When I read this excerpt, I think about politicians who use their positions of power to make a lot of money for themselves and their friends. Or about corporate moguls who don't care if their products are harmful to people's lives and health—so long as they're profitable. Even these people give lip service to the fact that money doesn't buy happiness. Yet they really believe that living in the lap of luxury is their god-given right. Their god shows them favor by providing for them. A sort of "he who dies with the most marbles wins" mindset.

If these people did feel good, does it make any sense that they would continue to accumulate, especially at the expense of others? The misery they visit on us and others is real. And it's a good thing to vote them out of office, stop buying their products, protest, and, in any way we can, stop their behavior.

At the same time, we need to remember that expending energy on hating them, lashing out with a like kind of energy that's grabby, or violent, does only one thing. It brings us more into the orbit of their negative energy. And it does no good for ourselves or our world.

I fight negative energy and behavior with a positive attitude.

291

"The importance of putting this fear to rest is no small thing, because even if we get all of our other Don't Wants switched to Wants, but then leave that one scary thorn in our side called death, we still have a fear vibration affecting everything, along with a mighty uphill climb to enjoyable health."

Don't want to breathe. Don't want to die. What do those two statements have in common? Well, if we're living, we can't not breathe. We can't avoid breathing. We have to breathe, that's part of the condition in which we exist in our bodies. And another part of the condition in which we exist in our bodies is that our bodies die. So dying is as natural as breathing.

Sit with that. Dying is as natural as breathing. Breathing is as natural as dying. Our bodies breathe—we don't (most of the time) think about breathing. We do it. Our bodies do it. So perhaps a way to think about dying, to begin to alleviate the fear vibration, is to think of it as something entirely natural and inevitable, like breathing. Something not to be feared.

If, bit by bit, we can breathe through our fear of death, we can neutralize the negative vibration that prevents us from living fully and healthily while we are alive. Transform that vibration into neutral. An unknown will happen to us, to all of us.

Consciously breathing can be a good way to put the fear of death to rest.

292

"So isn't it interesting that the biggest fear we continue to vibrate, and then stuff away to vibrate even stronger, is the fear we have of death?"

Although it's not widely practiced, there was a time when some Christian monks slept in their coffins. And some Buddhists take on the pose of the corpse and try to sleep that way. While there are different explanations for how and why these practices are carried out, one thing they surely must do is make the practitioner more aware of the fact of death, that our bodies die.

Yes, our bodies die. And all the work we do to transform our fear, turn our thoughts and feelings to giving and receiving positive energy, will be for nothing if we don't transform our fear of the biggest unknown—death. And, really, that's all it is—an unknown—an experience we don't remember having before, may not have had before.

To work with my fear of death is to enhance my life.

293

"The universe is a better organizer than you could ever think of being, so give it a chance and stay out of the way. You've given the universe a task, you've sent out your magnetic energy, now settle back and allow the manifestation to unfold."

Just sit back—why is that so, so, so hard to do? And why is the fidgeting around that we all do from time to time so much easier to see in other people than in ourselves? I started working on a writing project with a colleague. She is a person who pretty frequently mouths the words, "We've put it out, now we just wait to see what happens." The next words out of her mouth—or on my email—go something like this—"Do you think we should rewrite the proposal? Should we change the order of the chapters? Don't you think we should make it shorter? Is it too short? Will people get it?" I finally had to tell her I wasn't going to talk to her about the project until we heard back from the folks we'd sent it to—any one of whom could help us bring it to fruition.

And then I started my own fidgeting. And I found myself picking up the phone, thinking I'd just call one of the people we'd sent the proposal to. Her response, "For heaven's sake, I've had it less than forty-eight hours." I remembered that the next day and stopped myself sending any emails or making any more phone calls.

A lot of time went by, about two months I think. And we still didn't have any movement on that proposal. We were both getting antsy, didn't want to talk about it when our spouses asked questions. What happened next? Well, we waited another week or so, and then the phone rang. Someone I worked with at a temp job long ago was now a book editor and she'd seen a collaboration my friend and I'd published in a magazine and wondered if we'd ever consider turning it into a book. Whole different subject from the original proposal that was never sent to the old temp friend, because who even knew she was an editor now? Apparently the universe did.

Sit back, put your feet up, and relax while you wait, and remember the universe doesn't follow our schedule outline—and it almost always turns out better.

294

"You can be nasty, you can say mean, hurtful things, but your choice does not affect my choice, which is to keep my valve open and feel good. I am no longer blaming my negative conditions and/or your negative habits for the way I feel!"

Period. Amen. Or, as my grandma used to say (and almost everybody's did and we should pay attention), "Sticks and stones may break my bones, but words will never hurt me." It's not that they don't have the power to hurt me, but they have that power only when I let them.

Understanding that somebody—anybody—else is not responsible for how I feel is the first step. It's the I-get-it-in-my-head step. Not voicing in word or action any blame for what that person did to me is another step into positive energy. It's something we can do at any time—and anytime we think of it—in the middle of an argument, in the middle of the night when bad feelings are keeping us awake.

Reading this quote from Lynn Grabhorn aloud can be energizing. Try it. Put some emphasis on "keep my valve open and feel good." Go ahead, feel it. Give it up. Let go of that blame.

Words may never hurt me, but they sure can help set my positive energy free.

295

"Now let's say that we've decided to forgive somebody. How nice. Here's the flash: Forgiveness is a releasing of *our* resistance to positive energy, not the transgressor's at whom we are so benevolently aiming our forgiving smile."

There are some truly horrific transgressions in this world. And sometimes to bring things into perspective in our own lives, it can be instructive to look at them. I don't know, for instance, how a mother can forgive a drunken driver who kills her child. I don't know how a woman can forgive a man who beats her. I don't know how a country or people can forgive a government that tries to annihilate them. Yet they do. There is a woman in Massachusetts who arranges for children of Nazis and children of Holocaust survivors to come together in small groups, to meet and know each other, to forgive themselves and each other. This can't be easy. It does happen.

To forgive someone is to give myself a present. It is, indeed, to release positive energy. In the case of the woman who started the survivors' group, the positive energy she released affected not only her life, and not only the lives of the children of the survivors and, maybe especially, the children of the transgressors. It's just about as sure as anything is in this life that the positive energy released by her efforts has affected thousands of lives in ways she'll never know. That's what releasing positive energy can do.

True forgiveness is about how I choose to feel, about creating positive energy for myself.

296

"It goes without saying that the exalted position of forgiveness can come about only after one has first convicted. Which means the way we usually look at forgiveness is not much different than blame. Which means we rarely genuinely forgive."

One of those human interactions seen in public most likely to make me cringe is watching a mother berate a child who has done something to annoy her or act out. It can be knocking over a grocery display or hitting another child on the playground or some offense that isn't apparent, at least to me. "Say you're sorry," the mother says. Or some version of it, in an increasingly harsh tone if the child isn't immediately forthcoming. Sometimes the first mumbled "sorry" doesn't extract the pound of flesh. "Say it like you mean it," Mother says, often adding, "That was really naughty." And, then, finally, you guessed it, something like, "Don't ever do that again." Grudgingly. "Apology accepted. You're forgiven."

This kind of small interaction happens a lot. We've probably all been on the giving and receiving end of it more times than we care to count, or even think about. And, truth to tell, it's way harder for me to come up with an example of forgiveness that's not transaction-and-judgment based. I know I've read stories about such forgiveness.

What would that kind of forgiveness look like? What would it do? To the other person? To me? When I forgive my friend for ruining one of my pans by burning cranberries in the bottom of it, I don't even say I forgive you. She says she wants to replace the pan. I say, "It's old. Let it go. It was an accident." I think she feels better. I know I do.

Today I take the first step to telling forgiveness and blame to take a hike.

"As any small, unimportant aggravation begins to snowball into something major from our continued focus and negative energy flow toward it, we'll start to get more of other unpleasant things on that same wavelength, as well as enlarge the petty thing we've been grousing about."

Remember those cartoon snowballs that start at the top of an improbably long hill, getting bigger and bigger as they gain speed on the way down, frequently swallowing up anyone and anything in their path? That's it, the snowball that ate New York City. That's the snowball of negativity we can attract. Pretty powerful, huh?

Complain about one friend not calling you to another friend and then another, and, pretty soon, no one is calling you. So, you call up one of them and complain that you're lonely and no one loves you anymore, and, pretty soon, they're not only not calling you, they're crossing the street to avoid you.

Letting go of unimportant aggravations doesn't automatically mean we attract positive energy, but something has to fill the space where that negative energy isn't. What do you think it will be?

What would happen if I started thinking about something else?

298

"These days just about everybody knows that the state of one's physical health is connected to the state of one's mental health."

Twenty years ago, Norman Cousins published his groundbreaking book *Anatomy of an Illness,* in which he told the story of his own healing from a debilitating and life-threatening illness through laughter. Jokes and funny movies became a part of his treatment protocol—and the idea spread like wildfire. In addition to laughter, anything that soothes us, makes us feel more loved and loving, connects to others, and lifts our spirits is likely to help us heal faster. So that's one direction of the flow of energy between our mental and physical well-being.

The other is something every grandmother who ever made a pot of chicken soup has always known. When we're sad, lonely, angry, frightened, and not getting what we need in life, we open the channel to physical illness. It's not fair (or accurate) to say (for example) that we bring on cancer. But many studies show that unhappy people are more prone to any number of illnesses from common colds to raging arthritis to who knows what all.

Knowing that attitude can both accelerate and impede the course of an illness in our bodies gives us a tool to work our way back to healthy or to stay healthy in the first place.

All we need to do is choose to use it.

"Every doctor on the face of this planet knows that illness soars once the diagnosis is given. Fancy that!"

Does this mean that we shouldn't tell grandma she has stomach cancer? Probably not, but how we tell her and what we tell her it means can make all the difference in whether she's with us for five more months or fifteen more years. I have a sister's mother-in-law story. When my sister was pregnant with her second child, her mother-in-law, who had just gotten divorced after a long, unhappy marriage, was diagnosed with Stage IV breast cancer and told she had weeks, maybe months to live, although they could try some new experimental treatment. My sister's son is now a senior in high school, and his grandma is happily remarried and enjoying her almost-adult grandchildren.

We've all heard about the diagnosis "terminal" that turns out to be wrong. And, even if it's not wrong, how a diagnosis is delivered can make all the difference in how fast the disease progresses and in how the sick person feels.

Of course, our bodies will die some day. So, in a way, we all have a terminal diagnosis. So what? What we do with the life we have now, the energy and love we create, the work we do, the well-being we attract to ourselves—that's what counts. So letting ourselves feel mired down because someday this will all be over, well, that's just like getting sicker once we know the name of what's making us feel poorly. It's a reaction to an illusion.

I refuse to be a victim of the circumstances of my diagnosis.

300

"You can't screw this up. You can't make a mistake or a wrong decision. It's impossible. In fact, you never have made a mistake; you only invited lessons to help you get out of vibrating negatively. Now you know!"

Well, that's a relief. How many times in life have you been incapacitated, unable to make a move because in a past situation that your brain is telling you is similar, you "made a mistake"? Among other things, this is a lesson about how words affect our being.

Think of the words we can use to teach a child not to touch the stove. We can say it's "wrong" to touch the stove because it's hot. Or we can say something to the effect that touching the stove isn't a good idea because of the very real danger of being burned. The first articulation, repeated over time and in other circumstances, tends to lead to a child thinking he's wrong or stupid or making mistakes. The second tends to lead to a child who understands that she can make the choices that are good for her.

If you were a child who was taught more by the "wrong" method than the choices method, there's no time like the present to remind yourself that you can't screw this up, that you can look at your lessons and learn from them. You can choose not to put your hand on the metaphorical hot stove.

I invited the lessons in, and I can show them the door when I'm done with them.

301

"Keep writing outrageous new scripts."

Everybody should be so lucky as to have an Auntie Mame—and if we don't have one, there's no time like the present to develop our own inner Auntie Mame. That's who can prevent us from getting stuck in a rut, especially a stuffy, what will others think if we . . . (fill in the blank) rut; that is, do anything that's not commonly accepted as normal in our communities. If we keep doing (a) what we think other people do, (b) what we think other people think we should do, (c) what we think our mothers think we should do, we'll never get to (d) OTHER. And "other" is the only place to get to when we're trying to live our own creative best lives.

So, how exactly do we go about writing those outrageous new scripts? For a long time, I thought something that psychology calls "reaction formation" was the best (maybe only) way. If my family expected (a), well, then I'd do (b). In some circles, this is known as "acting out." And, in some (not so many, but some) circles, it's trying out new ways of doing things, new ways of looking at problems, new ways of seeing the world. And that's writing an outrageous new script, whether it starts in reaction against something or as an impulse to find something for ourselves.

Outrageous may or may not be wearing bright purple feathers in one's hair. Or dying one's hair lime green. At a gathering of wanna-be hippies, to be outrageous might be to dress like a banker. The point is that an outrageous script is one that says, "I can be myself and do what I want. I don't have to accept my family or society's expectations."

I am free to figure out what I mean by outrageous and then do it or be it, if I want to.

302

"I am simply no longer willing to sacrifice all my Wants and dreams and well-being for self-indulgent negative feelings over some stupid negative event."

Is there anything harder than letting go and moving on? Eating a huge piece of chocolate cake when we're on an eating plan that doesn't involve chocolate cake and does involve our long-term health. Taking a drink when we know that often leads to another and another, and a day of feeling lousy—or worse. Picking a fight with a friend just because we didn't get enough sleep last night. Knowing that this is an unfair world and seeing our elected leaders do things that benefit only a small minority. Each and every one of these things and a lot more you could think up, probably on the spot, are difficult, if not impossible, to let go of. We feel angry, sad, bad, mad—and we revisit the event—and we feel even more angry, sad . . . well, you know the drill.

What exactly do those feelings get us? Do they make us healthier in the long run? Do they give us back the day we lost to a hangover? Do they make us less sleep-deprived and back in accord with a friend? Do they change the world, elect politicians more in line with our values? No, no, and no! They do not. They take up energy we could be using to be healthier and happier and more effective in the world. So, what would it take to let go of them?

Two things come to mind—a decision to let them go and a replacement for them. I ate cake, okay. I let it go. I take a walk and eat a carrot. I get back on the plan. I remember my Wants and dreams, whatever they are, and I do something positive toward them.

My well-being is worth more than any momentary rush I get from feeling badly.

303

"So be gentle with yourself, take it easy, play with the energies, become curious, laugh more, smile more, experiment."

I just read that there's some new thinking about "senior moments," those lapses of memory that become more and more frequent as we get a bit older—forgetting your keys or the name of the guy who sings that song. Scientists used to think that they were just another in the line of cruddy things that happen as we age, that we were losing brain function or intellectual capacity. Well, they're thinking now it might be the exact opposite. Rather than the brain emptying out as we get older, the synapses are actually so full of memory, information, experience, and connections that the brain takes a while to sift it all out, and, as we get frustrated, we reinforce the time it takes to recall the desired bit of information, and by doing that the brain learns to repeat that frustration each time we search for that info.

The connections in our brains are good things, of course, and there are some ways to stop the cycle of slowing down the recall process. Things that may sound silly, even: like use your left hand to brush your teeth if you're a righty. Do your nightly routine backwards (and, yes, go ahead and eat dessert first). Drive a new route to work. These all fire off new sequences of synapses in your brain, which helps it function better. And a delicious side product of all these fun new things is that they can jostle that same brain into a new thought or two, maybe even an inspiration. Or they can help you break an old thought pattern of worry or negativity.

Put your brain to work on a fun or even silly new task, and free it up to do its job.

304

"But of course it's fashionable to talk about what's wrong with everything instead of what's right, so we're more easily drawn into negative vibrations than positive, sliding unwittingly into the 'ain't it awful' conversations."

A friend told me once in a pretty blunt way that my negativity was the single biggest problem in my life, and that if I couldn't get over it (or at least try), she wasn't interested in hanging around to be my friend. And what do you think I flowed right back at her? More of the same, you bet! We had a big, nasty blowout and didn't speak for quite a while.

I walked around in a funk for quite a while, stewing in my own broth. I knew she was right, and yet that knowledge just made me even more dark and moody—not only was I hopelessly negative to the point of destroying my own friendships, but I didn't even have the self-knowledge to figure it out on my own! Imagine where that vicious cycle landed me—squarely in the dumps.

Then something strange happened. A last-minute change in a project I was working on meant that I had to throw myself wholeheartedly into work to take advantage of a particular opportunity. It was so hectic and last minute that I didn't have time to build up a resistance to it or to second-guess myself. And I didn't have any time to think about my own moodiness or the fight with my friend. Without knowing it, I was pouring positive energy into my work as I went, and it was overflowing into other parts of my life as well. I picked up the ringing phone one day and it was my friend—she almost hung up because she apparently had dialed the wrong number and thought she was calling someone else. But we now know there are no accidents. I kept her on the line and had a chance to apologize and start the process of patching things up with her.

In the middle of a deep funk about a particular problem, do whatever you can to flip to something—anything—positive. Even energy spent away from your problem will help bring it to a solution.

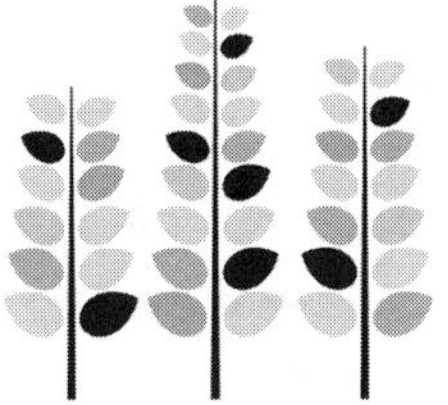

305

"The truth is, in our everyday natural state, we have the sacred ability to maneuver this thing called 'our life' to be any way we want it to be. *Any way!* Bar nothing! From a happy family to a filled-in ozone layer."

This is not the way it has to be. Remember that just because it's what *has been* and what *is*, there is no reason it's what's *going to be.* History tells us that we can expect the same result in the same circumstances over and over again, until suddenly things change. Progress happens, revolutionary thought or action (or, yes, feeling!) changes the world and everyone in it. In fact, when you take the long view, change is the only constant.

When we feel enclosed by our circumstances, when everyone around us has the same set of beliefs, when we are bombarded by horrifying news and depressing realities, we adjust our frequency to what surrounds us, and everything in our lives sinks to the low levels we perceive. But we are not our circumstances, or at least we don't have to be. We are driving the ship, it's our hands at the wheel in all things, and we can maneuver the vessel anywhere we want to go.

Think of your most outlandish dream for change in your life or in the world. It is possible. It is doable. It is easier than you think. In fact, the hardest step in getting there will be getting yourself to the place where you *know* it's possible, you know it so deeply that just by knowing it, you have already begun to turn the wheel toward that goal.

When it comes to what's possible, there is no limit beyond what I can imagine to be true.

306

"Remember that 'needing' something to change will always flow negative energy and hold it to you. Finding a way to become excited about what it will be changing into will flow positive energy and get the desired revisions started."

The hard way or the easy way—it's a choice. When Florence Scovel Shinn wrote *The Game of Life and How to Play It,* she laid out a unique way to choose positive flow. (It's a wonderful little book, and I highly recommend it.) The main idea of the book is that when you want or need something to change in your life—whether that's enough money to pay next month's rent or to meet your life's partner—you make a demonstration. You choose the way to bring that thing into your life.

The example that I most remember from the book is the woman who wanted to buy Christmas presents for her friends and family. She didn't have enough money to buy the presents, but she did have enough to buy the wrapping paper and ribbon. So she did just that—and in the doing the positive energy flowed and she soon came into enough money to buy the presents.

Change is the one constant in life—and if we can find ways to look at that as the good news rather than the bad news, it becomes the good news. If you know you have to find a new place to live, it's all too easy to tighten up around the fear of never being able to find what you want. What would happen if you made a demonstration—maybe buy a new set of towels or a plant for the garden you look forward to having. What could it hurt?

Excitement is energy stirred up—and something will happen.

307

"Negative emotions are not 100 percent gone (they never will be for any of us)."

Have you ever watched sorrow on the face of a toddler—maybe he's bereft because his mother left him at home. Or a two-year-old having a temper tantrum. She's so mad that what words she has are likely to fail her, and she throws herself on the ground and kicks. These are negative emotions at their most elemental. Barefaced, unchecked. As we grow up, the idea is to check them—to learn to control our disappointment, curb our anger, quell our sorrow.

To a certain extent that's what makes our relationships and our lives work. But still we all have disappointments and sorrow. Things don't go our way and we get angry. These are real feelings. We'll have them. So the question is, what are we going to do with them? Wallow? Kick something or somebody? Yell at our kids or our co-workers?

It's not an inevitable outcome that Cain killed Abel. He could have been jealous and angry, and still made a different choice. It might have been hard to swallow. Nobody ever said making a different choice is easy. We have these negative emotions. We will continue to have them. And we will have to continue to choose what to do. We can wallow in them, or we can acknowledge them and try to discern what they're trying to tell us.

The next time you feel a negative emotion, try talking to it and then sending it on its way.

308

"That's when it's time to let it be okay—*let it be okay*—that your Want hasn't shown up yet. You know that it will, but it's perfectly normal that it hasn't . . . yet."

So many spiritual and psychological practices and theories tell us to stay in the present. Stay with what is in your life, even when it isn't what you want. Some theories or belief systems propound it's good for us—and good for a child—to not get what he wants. Maybe, unless what he wants are food and a clean diaper. Many years ago, psychologist Abraham Maslow articulated a hierarchy of human needs—with basic food, water, and air on the bottom, and more abstract meaning, fulfillment, transcendence being attainable only when those more basic needs were met.

I think the real problem is when that judgment comes into the picture—that little voice that says it's bad to want something. And there's an even nastier little voice that says we're a bad person for wanting. When that happens it becomes almost impossible to stay calmly in the present, to let it be okay. To remember that wanting is normal, that fulfilling our true desires is the purest expression of our time on this earth.

The trick is to develop practices or reminders that help us let it be okay. These can be very simple things. Take three breaths. Count to ten. Picture what you want. Say hello to it. Picture yourself wanting it. Tell yourself to remain calm in the face of obstacles and delay. Take a walk, reconnect to the feeling place in yourself—your "gut" or "heart"—that will draw your want in.

Today, this hour, this minute, I tell myself, it is okay.

309

"The moment you make that decision to change your energy . . . the entire universe coalesces *in that instant* to cascade well-being into every crevice of your physical existence. It dumps all over you, and around you, and through you."

Still think that beliefs can't *really* change? Sure, you say, I can *pretend* I'm not afraid of going bankrupt or losing my spouse or getting sick, but that's all just make-believe.

Well, let me remind you that your beliefs have changed many times over, though maybe not lately. Think back to a time, maybe recently, but more likely sometime in your childhood, when you suddenly or gradually came to an entirely new belief. Psychologists have mapped the developmental stage in which babies learn that they have selves that are separate from their environment—a pretty big belief change, going from a world in which there is no boundary between our bodies and the world around us to one in which we use our entire, separate bodies to explore the outside world in every way we can.

Or, an even simpler one—is there any doubt in your mind that there is not an actual, slimy, drooling monster under your bed? For many of us, that was a profound and terrifying reality for many years that either slowly wore away or simply vanished one day, never to return.

Monsters are not real, but they *felt* really, really real. What are the fears that feel real to you now? And what kind of feelings are you pouring into those fears? And what kind of crud are you thereby attracting? Allow me to suggest that those fears might be no more real than googly-eyed monsters. Really. Stop pretending to change—really do it.

Write a new script in which you remember how it felt when you used to believe one way, and how free and alive you feel in your new belief. And tell the monsters to stuff it.

310

"Wonder, preciousness, appreciation, gratitude, excitement, reverence, awe. Can you pull up those different feelings any time you want?"

Yes, you can! We all get stuck in whatever is in front of our face. We get mired in the pull of our here-and-now drama. We get trapped there because we like it there. It's an easier place to hang out because we don't feel responsible, either for how we got there or for how we're going to get out. In the center of that whirling emotional storm we forget that we have unlimited, immediate access to anything we want.

Some idiot cuts you off on the highway and you feel gratitude? Awe? Wonder? Well, if you can't find the wonder in that moment, in remembering that it's good to be alive, with the physical function that allows you to be driving in the first place, maybe you can find it in something totally outside the situation. Maybe the power of reverence and appreciation lives in a memory you have, a touchstone from your past, an achievement, a discovery, the birth of something new.

How do you get rid of all the anger and frustration of your present crummy circumstance? How do you stop wanting to speed up and run the guy off the road? You don't have to worry about that, it'll take care of itself when you get plugged into the higher vibrations of wonder and gratitude. It's like putting a telemarketer on hold. Press a button, mentally, and pick up a new line. Dive right into a new meaningful conversation, and the first line will go dead pretty quickly, completely forgotten.

Gratitude, excitement, and awe are on hold for you—are you ready to take the call?

"Every moment we spend feeling negative emotion, we deprive ourselves of the life force that is natural to us, heals us, and magnetizes our desires."

Okay, I get that. I think of a cup full of water. If you pour mud into that water, the mud, which is heavier, is going to sink to the bottom and the water is going to spill out. Allowing myself to dwell in anger or sadness, to harbor feelings of revenge, to feel like other people are getting more goodies or a better break than I am—all of that is pouring mud into my cup. Not only is it going to displace and pollute the nourishing, life-giving water, it's also going to settle and get stuck and be hard to clean up. Yuck!

Yuck, indeed. Now if I can just remember this when I feel myself spinning out, going off on a tirade. I don't all the time. I suppose I would be some kind of saint if I did. Lately I've been realizing that judging myself for feeling a negative emotion is almost as toxic as dwelling on the emotion. In fact, I think it's another way of doing just that.

So this morning, and each morning, I take a minute to remind myself not to dwell on the negative. And I picture my nice clean, clear glass of water without dirty mud in the bottom of it. I do this when I'm not feeling the negative emotion in order to lay the groundwork for remembering it, so it's accessible to me when I do.

Find an image that can flip you out of negative emotion.

312

"It's not going to take a genius to figure out that if we're feeling *anything* other than at peace with ourselves, as well as totally allowing and appreciative of our partner (good luck), our vibrations are going to be slicing away at that relationship, no matter how much we're convinced that since there's nothing wrong with us, it must be the other guy's fault."

Is there anything in the world more complicated than negotiating a relationship? Probably not. So why do we almost automatically, certainly without much thought, insist that someone must be at fault when we encounter a difficulty? And we only make matters worse, of course, when it's the other person who's at fault.

What if no one is to blame? Then what? We still have the problem that she's always late and he never picks up the towels off the bathroom floor. But if she's not accused of being a hopeless airhead, and he's not accused of being a thoughtless boor, then maybe there's a way to solve the problem. Or maybe the bad feelings the problem engenders are seen for what they are—not much on the scale of things. Okay, so we get this, so how do we give up blaming others or ourselves?

Ah, the key is in the quote: feeling at peace with ourselves. Simple, not necessarily easy, as they say in twelve-step programs. That's the practice and the key to any good relationship—feel at peace with myself, my choices—including how I choose to react and feel when someone else does something not to my liking. After all, whose life am I in charge of? Who's the person I have to live with 24/7 for my whole life? You got it.

Me. So an attitude and a practice that allow me to have a peaceful relationship with myself is the key to having a successful relationship with anyone else.

Make a list of the ways you've been warring with yourself. Write it down. Burn it.

313

"We can meditate, chant, play with crystals and incense, do yoga exercises, and proclaim our divinity forevermore, but for as long as we hold judgments against ourselves, empowerment and awakening will be nothing but words."

And meditating, changing, focusing with crystals or incense, doing yoga are tools we can use to reinforce our efforts to give up judgment. And I personally think each of us owes it to ourselves to use as many tools as are available to us to give up the habit of judging ourselves that most of us have been carrying around since childhood.

A lot of people will say it's human nature, even that we need to be able to judge ourselves (and others). How else will we ever stay on the straight and narrow, treat each other well, prevent mayhem in the streets, because nobody will be paying attention to their consciences? Or some such poppycock. Of course, we can know the difference between right and wrong—between telling the truth to ourselves and others without coming down on ourselves like a ton of bricks. When we make a mistake, something we might have judged ourselves for in the past, we can simply acknowledge that and go on.

And, chances are, we'll see that opportunity more readily if we've been meditating, chanting, etc.

I choose to use all the tools in my repertoire to stay awake to my life.

"We always have choices. If we can't find answers, it means we have overlooked the obvious."

And if we've overlooked the obvious, maybe we're not asking the right questions. We've all had times we felt painted into a corner—no money, rent due, bills overdue, too much work—we feel trapped and without options. Yet, while we're alive, we do have choices.

If the question I've been asking is, "How can I do this all by myself?" maybe I've overlooked that I don't have to. The question could be, "Would you help me?" or "Who would help me?"

When overlooking the obvious becomes a habit, we tend to drop into the depths of feeling overwhelmed or get lost in "woe is me" land. We let ourselves become the victim of our circumstances. That's a choice. See, we always have one.

Or we could make the choice to remind ourselves that we have choices.

315

"Feeling good is natural, but not normal to us right now. Anything less than that is unnatural, and sadly, quite normal to us right now."

Why does it feel so good to feel bad? Why is it satisfying to mope, complain, gossip, and dread? Partly because it's normal. And partly because we think we need it.

I had a friend say to me once, in the middle of a long tirade of frustration, anger, and uncertainty about my financial position, "What are you getting out of this?"

I snapped back. "What do you mean what am I getting out of this? Nothing! That's the problem. If I were getting answers, or getting more money, I wouldn't be talking to you about it."

"Oh no," she said, "human beings don't hold on to their troubles for no reason. You're getting something out of hanging on to all of this trash. Most likely an easy excuse to not try something new, something you're afraid you might fail at."

Oof. That one got me in the gut. It's stayed with me ever since. Now when I become conscious that I'm hanging on to something negative, I can evaluate what I might be getting out of that negativity, whether it's a rush of adrenaline, a momentary feeling of superiority, or an easy way out of a lot of soul searching. That's not to say I don't still have plenty of hangers-on, those feelings and situations that I claim I don't want but that I allow to set up camp and stay a while. I'm playing around with a new feeling of normal, one where I can feel good—even great—most of the time, and never look back.

What negative things are you carrying around, and what are you getting out of them? Consider the relief you'll feel when you jettison some of that extra baggage.

316

"Contentment (no action) feels okay, but passion (inspired action) feels better."

I have heard there are people who could go on vacation and do nothing else for the rest of their lives and be completely happy. I don't buy it. I used to go nuts toward the end of summer vacation. When people retire from their careers, there is often a long period of adjustment, sometimes accompanied by depression. The shift from doing something to doing nothing is foreign to us, and a successful life transition seems to be more about finding and embracing the next phase of what to do (not how to stop doing altogether).

We all need moments of rest. And there is a certain kind of psychic energy to moments of contentment—they refuel us and give us some perspective on whatever journey we've been trekking through.

I just heard this advice today: When you're not fishing, mend your nets. When you don't have inspired action ready to go, there is plenty to be done to regroup from the last adventure and prepare for the new one.

Go ahead and be content for a while, savor the peace and quiet while you gently mend your nets in preparation for the next outing, which will surely be more fun.

317

"Listen for your Guidance, and then act; never, never, never act before."

Don't go off half-cocked. That expression is pretty widely thought to originate with old muskets, in which the firing hammer had two positions—full cock, which was ready to fire, and half cock, which was a sort of safety measure. The gun was close to ready to fire—all a person needed to do was click the hammer into full cock, but it theoretically couldn't fire from that position. Except it could sometimes accidentally slip and fire.

I'm not much of a gun fan, despite coming from a Midwestern family, who, in past generations, relied on hunting to put food on the table. And from some of their stories, I know that hunting requires a sort of waiting until the moment is right. My grandfather probably would not have called it Guidance that he knew exactly when to blow his duck call and raise his gun. But it certainly seems to me that's what it was. On a successful day, he knew the moment.

To contemplate a course of action, even a small one, only after stopping to listen and consider, is really a pretty easy habit to acquire. We teach children to stop at the corner, not to cross the street without looking both ways, not to step into moving traffic, to wait for the signal to change. If we stop to think about it, we can teach ourselves the right moment and the correct and safe course of action.

Today I'll take a breath before I take action.

"Stepping out of victimhood is like coming home after a long absence, and being introduced to yourself for the first time."

Making the choice not to be victimized by any given situation can make a person feel twenty pounds lighter. Ten years younger. Able to leap tall buildings in a single bound. It feels that good. It can feel like Christmas and the fourth of July all wrapped up in one—great gifts and freedom, sweet freedom.

If you think I'm exaggerating, I can only say, try it, please. Choose to give yourself some time in a safe place where you can sit with yourself and be honest. What bad thing is happening to you? Say it out loud. Who do you think is responsible? (Yourself or others.) How are you responding or reacting to this situation that's making you feel like a victim? What other response could you have? Choose that instead.

Step out of your victim's closet into the bright light of day. The wonderful thing about this process is that we can repeat it at will, as often as we need to or want to.

I choose not to be a victim—I choose to be myself.

319

"If the action doesn't feel good, stop it."

Or, as the political commentator Molly Ivins said, "The first rule of holes: when you're in one, stop digging." It's deceptively simple, right? Any idiot would know they have to stop digging deeper if they ever hope to get out of a hole. But somehow when you're in the middle of it, tossing dirt over your shoulder in a frenzy, you forget all about that. The worst hole we get into is when something feels *bad,* but we have a belief that it's *good* or good for us (or worse, that we deserve to feel bad).

Keeping to an exercise plan with a shaky motivation is a good example—you have to lose five pounds fast, so you dive in. The new plan feels great at first, and then, a few days in, you get incredibly sore and tired. You push through that, 'cause you gotta lose that weight. Meanwhile, you're eating a bit more because you're burning calories, right? Then, if you manage to keep to it, within a couple of weeks or even a month, you hit a wall. You're bored, unmotivated to exercise, feeling guilty, and angry with yourself about the whole thing: the lack of joy, the extra pounds, etc., so you throw up your hands in disgust and settle back into your previous routine. Or, you keep going, digging your hole with obsessive determination.

This pit started early on—with a big Don't Want (I don't want those five pounds)—and only got worse from there. And, yet, by most people's standards and probably your own, you are doing the right thing—trying to lose weight by getting in shape; what's wrong with that? Nothing in the world is wrong with that, but think back to a time when you had a blast doing something physical that left you sore the next day: dancing, playing tag with your kids, hiking in the woods. That soreness doesn't feel as bad as all that guilt and shame, and, besides, the motivations were in place and you were having a ball. That is the kind of physical engagement you need to stay out of holes (and also the kind that will melt off the pounds)!

When you're having a blast, keep on going—even when it brings a bit of discomfort, it'll still be worth it.

320

"If something's bugging you, get over it."

You know the playground chant "I'm rubber and you're glue! Everything you say bounces off me and sticks to you." Same is true for energy. If you're sending out critical, nasty thoughts with the conviction that they are hitting your desired target, you're way off base. Anything that's bugging you, anything you find annoying or offensive, any situation you're griping and moaning about—you're simply not going to have any effect on it from that mindset. In fact, those negative feelings are just going to bounce right back to you and stick fast. Even if you're right, even if the feelings are justified, they're still going to be glued to you, not to anyone or anything else.

Time to get over it. It's not fair. It's not your turn, but do it anyway. Let it go. Because, if it's bugging you, you're feeding into it and creating more of the same, if not worse. If something's pissing you off, you're sending out party invitations for other obnoxious stuff to come on over. If it's making you mad, then you're running an advertisement that you'll take in garbage feelings and store them free of charge anytime.

You started it! So who's going to finish it? You're it! No tag backs!

321

"Calm down, relax, soften up, get natural, be closer to You."

As a kid, I rode horses a lot, taking lessons at a local stable and caring for the animals when I wasn't learning to ride. On a hot day after a long ride, it was great to take a saddle off and smell the sweat of a happy horse, brushing out the dirt and massaging those muscles. You could just feel the horse's whole body soften up, releasing the tension of exertion and going back to a more natural state.

We all need that time to cool off and calm down. If we can't let go of our stress, we're pretty useless. Even more importantly, if we don't take time to recenter after a burst of work or energy, it's like we lose a part of ourselves, leaving some of our energy in the task itself and not reclaiming it to renew our own stores.

Take a bath, get a massage, have a nap. Let yourself be more like you and less like your conditions, your to-do list, the task at hand.

322

"By all means go to your doctor, but watch your reactions, your fears, your denial—which means watch your valve."

Fear is an insidious motivator. A pain in the chest or the stomach, a headache can send us into a paroxysm of what we might have. Then between TV commercials telling us to look out for this disease and our doctors telling us we should have tests for things we've never heard of and looking up symptoms on the Internet—well, things can get out of hand pretty quickly. So when we have symptoms that cause us pain or concern, what is the best course of action?

A visit to the doctor can, in some cases, allay our fears. We're told it's nothing to worry about, or we know what we're dealing with and we can get treated. And it is good to get things checked out. What's not good is letting ourselves go into a tizzy before the results are back. Given half a chance, the "what ifs" will move in and make your life miserable.

So, yes, avail yourself of modern medicine or therapy *and* rely on your whole tool bag of valve opening. Don't pretend you know what's going to happen next. Don't let the drama of illness get you down.

My healing depends on keeping a level head and an open heart.

323

"Just state your Wants every day, write (and then speak) new scripts about your body, your health, your looks, your life. And pretend. Get into the feeling place of what you're pretending, and become one who is so aggressively flowing your own energy and vibrating in the frequency of joy that you override all that you—or anyone else—might have been flowing before."

If ever you played pretend in your childhood, now would be a good time to access those memories—not so much for the exact game you were playing, but for the feeling of being totally absorbed in being someone else—a famous jungle explorer or whatever you were. Once you've accessed that feeling, put your today's story into it. Go around your house *being* thinner or being the person who has your dream job or is painting a picture or writing a book. Try it on, like a costume. See how it *feels* to be that person.

Then put words on it. Say it out loud. "I look good at this (desired) weight." What health do you desire? What way of moving your body? Is it graceful? Lighter?

Say it. Write it. Spend some time "play pretending" it. Every day. Get that energy flowing.

I let joy flow into me and through me and out to others and back to me. Every day.

324

"The easier way is to stop fearing this atrocious manmade myth [death] and concentrate with everything we have on raising our frequencies to that Greater Part of ourselves which is the very essence of All That Is. Then we'd have all the heaven we could handle right here in our own little world, the way it was meant to be."

Stop fearing death, not stop thinking about it, but stop fearing the myth we have that we are only our bodies, that we don't have an energy and a spirit that are connected to all of consciousness. The "myth" of death is that we are separate. And that when our bodies cease to exist, we cease to exist.

Sometimes, the fear is that we won't have made our mark, affected the world around us. That our children or spouses will forget us (not likely) or go on without us (which one would think would be a hope, not a fear). Other times, the fear is something else. As we say or write those fears, though, they seem disproportionately small to the big fear we have of death and the way that fear can get in the way of living.

If it helps, do the worst-case scenario with death. What's the worst thing you fear? That it will hurt. Well, if it hurts enough, leaving our bodies and moving on might be a blessed relief, a healing.

May I feel connected to all that is.

"That's all there is to it. You replace the old negative script-vibration of 'I can't, I don't know how, I'm deranged,' with a positive new one that jams you smack into the enjoyment of having it now."

I used to know a woman who purposely misused words. One of her—and my—favorites was when she said she was sick of how her living room looked and she was going to derange it. And she did, enlisting all our help to move furniture around, take away some objects, introduce new color with a scarf, put a simple basket here, and, presto, change-o, the room looked and felt totally different. Deranging gave it a whole new lease on life. All this is to say if you're feeling deranged, turn it around.

Rearrange your vocabulary. I can't becomes I am. I don't know how, *but* I know how to find out. I am not deranged, I'm simply stumped, and I'm going to rearrange my thoughts and my circumstances until a solution presents itself.

Rearranging the furniture in my mind is hours and hours worth of fun. I can create a beautiful place to rest in. I can create inspiration to succeed at my current goals. I can create a breath of fresh air. And I can create a feeling of well-being. It all depends on what words I use.

Today I'm going to rearrange my feelings of derangement.

326

"And therein lies the cause of every downward spiral of any relationship that ever went sour; the relentless—though surely innocent—attention to disagreeable conditions, no matter how meaningless they may appear to be."

Gunk stuck on supposed washed dishes. Small hurts remembered from childhood—when your brother and father always got first choice of chicken parts. Your husband's socks next to the hamper, not in it. How much attention do we direct to these things? And how long do we remember them?

Since I grew up an observer, inclined to see and remember everything, I find it more difficult to let go of supposed hurts and little offenses than I want it to be. And I need to be vigilant about how *not* to pay attention. The exact opposite of what I try to do in the rest of my life. Or do I? Pay attention to the moment and then let the moment go, that is.

Holding on tight to anything—good or bad—is holding on tight. So, putting our attention on something to the extent we know that it's happening and how we're contributing to it or how we're choosing to feel about it is good. But holding on to it—bringing up a past good time as an excuse to feel sad now, or bringing up a past bad time—with the message this always happens, or even, perish the thought, bringing up a past good time and trying to recreate it exactly in this time—all of those draw energy into the vortex of the downward spiral.

Where am I putting my attention?

327

"I'm saying forgive at the drop of a hat."

Sometimes it's the little things. My mom and I both had landlord troubles this Thanksgiving. I got no response and she got scolded. She told me later that she ended up awake in the middle of the night, spinning out about how she felt because the guy she talked to from her management company scolded her as if she were a child. Was she in the right? Not in the right? She had twelve people for Thanksgiving dinner and her microwave quit. She called on the Friday, and no one returned her call. So on the Saturday she called the emergency number. An angry employee told her to wait until Monday.

I was trying to do two simple things—bake some sweet potatoes to take to a potluck and take a shower. For reasons that still aren't apparent to me, I couldn't get my oven to start and there was no hot water. I called my landlords and got no response—neither yelled at nor any hot water. So I cooked the sweet potatoes in the microwave and showered in cold water.

Despite our problems, both of us had great Thanksgivings, we agreed when we talked late in the day on the phone. Yet both of us had gone through blaming, being shamed, feeling guilty, and then coming around to "stuff happens."

Forgiving ourselves, forgiving landlords, sometimes it's the little things that add up to being able to just drop everything, improvise, and forgive.

Try it, it gets easier with practice.

328

"Stop thinking it can't happen. That vibration will guarantee it won't."

Possibility. A great word, a great concept, and one to be nurtured. To be fed, warmed up to, breathed on. One to bring to life. If we believe in possibility, then anything is possible. If we don't, then just about everything we try to do will fall apart at some point. This is a metaphysical law that is every bit as real as the law of gravity. (And no one really knows how and why that works, either.)

So, when we're tempted to think something can't happen, what to do instead? No nail biting. No blaming. No nay-saying. No rethinking. No turning the back and saying, Hmph—I didn't want it anyway. That won't help. Unless, after watching ourselves subvert our own efforts time after time, we finally get the power we have. And turn all that worry and negativity on its head.

You know how you sometimes lie awake at night, the worry that something won't happen, all the reasons it can't, cycling and cycling through your head? What about, one sleepless night, just letting positive messages cycle and cycle through your head—picture it happening. Your dream comes to fruition. How does it look, smell, feel? Where are you? What are you wearing?

Put as much energy into anti-worrying as you do into worrying and see what those vibrations create.

"Don't yearn. It's just a negative awareness that you don't have something."

In the event of a longing for something you don't have, don't just sit there—do something. Take a walk, drink a glass of water, count your breaths to a hundred, and then do it all over again. I know a woman who used to have anxiety attacks. They were frequently brought on by two different things that were really a kind of yearning. One was a negativity about time. She thought she'd never have the time to do what she wanted. Her yearning for more time made her anxious. The other was yearning for a different way of life—a more satisfying job and relationship and to start the family she'd always wanted.

She got some good advice about what to do when she felt one of these attacks coming on—sing. She says if she could just get herself to start singing, she was able to turn her heart and head around. She drew her attention away from her worries—that there would never be enough. She drew her attention to sending beautiful sound waves of song out into the world.

In her brilliant book *Drawing on the Right Side of the Brain,* Betty Edwards talks about negative space. The interesting thing about negative space when you're learning to draw a chair, which is the example I remember from the book, is that it defines the object. In the case of drawing, awareness of the negative space allows a person to draw a better chair. In the case of life, an awareness of negative space can help us determine where we are in relationship to where we want to be and what we want to draw into our lives. And we don't have to linger there.

Today is the day to find new ways to turn yearning into learning.

330

"Instead, if we can find something—*anything*—to appreciate about them, and plant the seeds of potential new growth about them with our positive vibrations, we open up a chance for change."

If someone is driving you nuts, or dragging you into their despair by constantly wanting to commiserate about their miserable life, what do you do? We are not heartless beings—we want to help. We want to make it better for the people we love. We even want to make it better for many of the people we've never met. We're genetically hardwired for altruism and fairness, and these traits start to really come out in us around the age of seven or eight.

Nothing that is so essential to who we are as a species can be wrong, but I think things get a bit confused in the application of that altruistic trait. When someone's in trouble, as much as we would like to or think it's possible to change them or make them better, most of us understand on some level that we can't change other people—they've got to do it themselves. Yet even as we hope for someone to make a change, or make suggestions about things they might try to get out of their mess, or even just lend a comforting ear to a litany of complaints, we may be making the situation worse, for ourselves and for the other person.

Here's why: if you think another person is in trouble, or has problems, or needs fixing, then you are feeling that something is *wrong* with them and thinking about them in terms of what they lack. And as we know by now, that lack will flow around them and you, drawing you both down. Instead, see if you can find something that is already in them (not something they want or are trying for) to appreciate and flow love to, and you will be giving them a huge helping hand. And any action you take to help them from this stance has the chance to help them in a truly profound way.

You can't change someone, but you can offer them a chance to change by simply appreciating something about them.

331

"It's okay! It really is. We've done it perfectly. Without our Don't Wants, we would never have our Wants. Now we just learn to turn 'em around on purpose, instead of by chance."

I, for one, spend far too much time scolding myself like a child for doing or thinking the "wrong" thing. In fact, when I was a child, I wanted so desperately to do things right on the first try that I would burst into tears, often before even getting started! Imagine how much fun I missed out on, paralyzed by the possibility I might make a mistake.

What a comfort, then, to hear that there is no such thing as a mistake. I don't have to beat myself up for spending the better part of the last forty-eight hours embroiled in every Don't Want under the sun. Believe me, I even knew what I was doing—and kept telling myself to knock it off, cut it out, and ease up on the gas. But telling myself was in the form of self-blame (aka, another Don't Want) so changing things around got more and more difficult.

Regret and guilt are wasted emotions in the law of attraction—because there is nothing to blame, and certainly nothing to feel guilty about. Whatever you do—don't stop the Don't Wants! There's a reason they are the first step of the four—because you need them to lay the groundwork for your Wants, and without them you'd be lost. (As a reminder, those four steps are [1] identify what you Don't Want, [2] identify what you Do Want, [3] get to your feeling place, and [4] allow it to happen.)

There are no real mistakes. Follow the roadmap to your Wants by reading between the lines of your Don't Wants.

332

"Gut-feeling, motivation, hit, intuition, sense, inspiration, impulse, urge, premonition, desire, imagination. It's all Guidance, the real You sending messages from the infinite intelligence You are, doing everything in Its power to pass on some ideas or direction before you shut down again."

Will the real me please stand up? How many of us get so mired in the many roles we play that we don't even take the time to admit we're feeling out of sorts because we haven't taken the time to get in touch with our internal guidance? We ignore the urge to sign up for an art class—and the jealous feeling we have when our friend turns up with a sheaf of beautiful drawings. We walk right by the flats of peonies and two months later wonder why we don't have any flowers in the yard. Or worse we completely forget that we ever thought having some color in our lives would be soothing and nurturing.

There's an old joke about Guidance and what form it takes. It's about the man in the flood—he doesn't evacuate. Then when the emergency workers come in a rowboat to pluck him from his second-story window, he refuses to go. Nor will he get on the helicopter when he's perched on his roof in the rising water. He drowns, goes to heaven, and asks why God didn't rescue him. And God says, "Well I sent an evacuation notice, a boat, and a helicopter—what were you waiting for?"

What are we waiting for? Is there a better time than right now to sit down and open my mind and heart? Maybe I won't hear something profound. And maybe it won't sound like my preconceived notion—I guess a helicopter wasn't that guy's preconceived notion of what God's salvation might look like.

I'm thankful for my gut feelings—wherever they take me.

333

"If you've goofed up, you've put Grinding Actions ahead of Source energy."

When a project falters, or a long-held dream falls just short of being a reality, you've goofed up. Look into the moment things switched. Go back through the events and trace when a delivery got misplaced, or a voicemail didn't go through. And then think about how you were *feeling* immediately before things started to go wrong. If you're honest with yourself, you can usually find it—a moment of indecision, fear, or guilt that got under your skin. At the time you weren't even conscious of it, or maybe it's even something you thought you had taken the time to explore and own, but for some reason it stuck to you.

Being fearful or feeling guilty feels so normal to us, and we are going to have to remember that they won't just go away—they will be hanging around for quite a while, but we have a new set of tools to process those feelings and tell them to get lost. Most likely when things get all fouled up, it's because we've reverted our priorities back to what they once were: work before play, perseverance no matter what, self-denial before self-gratification. When this happens, the first thing to do is stop everything (because uninspired action will just dig us a hole handy enough to fall into). Then you can realign with your Source energy by getting into the feeling place (and really feeling it! No pretending!) that got you into this action in the first place. Only then should you start up again, and you might get an interesting new lead or hint on the way.

I will turn my old priorities upside down.

"Take your treasured dreams out of that crowded old closet, dust them off with loving care, and give each one a long, hard look."

Every once in a while, there will be a newspaper story about buried treasure a family found in the attic when Grandma died—the dusty old painting that turns out to be worth thousands. Maybe you've finally gotten around to cleaning out the closet in the spare room—and found money in the pocket of a coat you haven't worn for ten years. Treasured dreams can be hidden just as well as the painting or the hundred dollars in a coat pocket. And even harder to find. But the rewards can be nothing less than a new lease on life.

While cleaning out an attic or a closet, not only might we find things of surprising worth, we might also find things we've simply lost track of, or maybe have never even seen before. Maybe not treasured antiques—maybe something of sentimental value. Not only that, we're more than likely to find things we want to sell, recycle, or donate. Oh boy, room for new stuff.

Taking treasured dreams out of the closet offers the same benefits. Maybe we remember that something we'd totally forgotten about. Maybe we find several dreams to let go of, making room for new ones. Maybe we find several we'd like to pursue.

Where have you put your most treasured dream?

335

"Expect it, listen, and allow the universe to bring it in."

Surely every one of us has a memory of a grade-school teacher whose mantra seemed to be, "Pay attention." Eyes forward, pay attention to the arithmetic on the board. Memorize this list of spelling words. Color inside the lines. There will be a test. You can expect that for sure.

They always say that school is meant to prepare us for real life. But the way that many of us were taught to pay attention, almost against our will, as if it were an unnatural thing, isn't actually all that useful. It leads to resistance. It leads to our minds being hyper-aware of what other people want us to pay attention to. It leads to frustration because we end up trying to force a result, often not even of our own wanting. It feels like we're paying out precious energetic resources we're not going to get back.

How do we take our early learning like this instruction to "pay attention" and mine it for what is useful to us? What if instead of "pay attention," we give ourselves the instruction to "notice"? What if my mind is the blackboard? And I look carefully to see what's on it? What if the spelling list is in my heart? And I spend at least as much time deciphering those words that I know to be my truth as I did memorizing someone else's words? What if I expect a test that will help me understand myself better and bring the work or art or peace or love that I want into my life?

What if I expect a rest from striving and just let things happen?

336

"If we say, 'I want perfect health,' and think emotionally about perfect health all the time, we'll either have it now or it will be on its way. But if we say, 'I don't want sickness,' and think emotionally about that often enough, we're opting for ill health because our focus is on the sickness."

The universe is like a two-year-old. Tell it not to do something ("Don't stick any peanuts up your nose, now") and prepare for the consequences (three hours in the emergency room with a screaming kid). The good news about two-year-olds' negativity, however, is that it responds astonishingly well to a little well-placed reverse psychology. You know the kind. "Don't you dare eat those peas, those peas are my peas and you can't have any!" Next thing you know the peas are happily slurped up and the child is laughing hysterically.

So the universe, like any healthy two-year-old, is obsessed with negativity, but pretty easily goaded into enthusiastic positivity. The trick is not in the words or the thinking, but in the *feelings.* In the peas example above, the end emotional effect is laughing hysterically. No thoughts about how good peas are for growing bodies, no lectures about children starving in faraway places. Just eating good peas, pulling one over on Mom or Dad, and having a great time.

Challenge yourself to stay on your toes in this tricky universe. Notice when your own negative thoughts are trying to take control, and redirect the yucky flow of anyone else's nastiness as it comes at you. In the end, it's pretty easy (and can be a lot of fun) to end up laughing through a face full of peas.

How can you hoodwink your universe into a feel-good result?

337

"It is impossible to solve a problem in the same frequency in which it was created, so you make a decision that for as long as it's with you, *that problem will no longer be the focal point of your life.*"

Not making a problem the focus of your life is not the same as denial. Everybody's heard about the elephant in the living room—the point of that story is that nobody's saying there's an elephant in the living room. In denial, everyone is making the problem the focal point of their life because they're not admitting that Dad has a little drinking problem, or Sis is using drugs, or there isn't enough money to pay the bills, or whatever the problem is.

So, no, we shouldn't ignore the elephant in the living room, but we don't have to groom it and feed it and obsess about it so it gets bigger and glossier and more entrenched, either.

So, what to do instead?

Try this: acknowledge that there's a problem. Say it out loud. Is it something I have the courage to change? What would it take for me to change it? Is it something I simply need to accept—accept and let it be because I have no control over its immediate resolution? In fact, I have no control over anything except the way I react to the problem.

For every problem there is a reaction that may eventually lead to an action that escorts the problem out of my life.

"Don't take anything that happens in your life for granted, good or bad, large or small. It came into your life because you magnetized it there, so pay attention to what you're creating."

There's a well-known Chinese proverb that goes "Be careful what you wish for, you might get it." Then there's a Rolling Stones song about not always getting what we want. Opposite ends of a spectrum? Two sides of a coin? Maybe. Or maybe two different ways of saying the same thing. Maybe what we get isn't exactly what we want. Maybe it's just slightly different and that makes all the difference.

I think of the fairy tale of the poor old fisherman who cast his net three times one day, and on the third casting caught a golden fish who begged for its life and promised to grant the man his wish. This man has no wish, but when he tells his wife the story, she has first a small wish, then she wishes for—and is granted—more and more, until she asks to be ruler of the sea. The moral of this story is most often stated as the fisherman's wife becomes greedy, asks for too much, and the fish teaches her a lesson by putting her back in her original state. And that's a perfectly good story as far as it goes. But what if we dig a bit? Why did the woman keep asking for more? And why did her husband ask for nothing? And what, finally, did they both attract to themselves that brought them back to their original state?

Those are questions I think about when I think about my life and what I'm wishing for—even if I never meet a magic fish. It's tempting to say that I didn't want the grief of a broken heart; the loss of a favorite necklace; I didn't want to feel sorry because a friend's stay was coming to an end, even while he was still visiting; and I was acting sad that she was leaving rather than happy that she was still there. We may not know exactly how we attract what we attract, but I think it's enough to know that we do, and that we need to pay attention to it.

What am I attracting to my life today—and why?

339

"The universe is a better organizer than you could ever think of being, so give it a chance and stay out of the way. You've given the universe a task, you've sent out your magnetic energy, now settle back and allow the manifestation to unfold."

Human beings have a pretty limited capacity to fully embrace suffering and remain open and buzzing. You need to be honest with yourself about the suffering in your life, you need to open the energies that you can, and then you need to LET IT GO. And I mean really let it go.

If you dwell on the creation of tragedy through energy, you will very quickly slide down a slippery slope into some very ugly territory of blame and guilt, both of yourself and others, which is the exact opposite of what is at the core of this attracting stuff. Knock it off. Worrying about bad things happening will not keep you safe. Obsessing about what you don't want is just dumping a heaping load of fertilizer on whatever nasty weeds you'd like to keep from growing.

You already have the key to your own safety and well-being (it's your natural state, after all!) and worry, guilt, fear, and blame only serve to deadbolt the door.

340

"We can become miracle-makers. The trick is learning to vibrate in harmony *with* our desire, not against it."

Let's say that I want to cook an omelet. I know exactly what I want to put into it—delicate cheese and fresh herbs. I whip up the eggs, I melt the butter, I put the eggs in the pan—and I turn the heat off. Nothing happens, no light, frothy, delicate egg mixture cooked just right. Without the heat, it becomes a mess, sitting there, congealing in the pan.

Same thing happens when I vibrate against my desire. Say I want to lose weight. I meditate about that, tell myself it's my desire, and then on my next trip to the grocery store, I buy candy and cookies and ice cream and potato chips. Those actions create a vibration in direct contradiction to what my stated desire is. Even if, in the end, I choose not to eat that stuff, I've created a vibratory situation in which I'm doing something like climbing Mount Everest rather than strolling up a hill.

I honor my heart's desire by letting my actions and my words be in tune with it.

"If it is not action taken in joy, it cannot possibly lead to a happy ending."

There is a particularly nasty strain of religious dogma that has been used for eons (and in many faiths) to keep us in a holding pattern of reverence to our own misery. This belief is a distortion of Jesus saying "the meek shall inherit the earth." We are told, consciously and unconsciously, that the more we suffer in this world, the more we will be rewarded in the next. So there's no reason for the powers that be to alleviate any misery or correct any injustice, because it will all turn out well in the next incarnation. And if we really internalize this message, we may even go around attracting more negativity to build up some positive payback down the line.

Going on our journey with joy is the best way to get to a joyful place. We don't get bonus points for suffering now in the hopes of later happiness. The inspired actions we take from a passionate, connected, lighthearted place will always trump actions coming from guilt, shame, or self-doubt.

Follow the path of joyful action to get to happily ever after.

342

"Intuition is our Guidance in action."

Sometimes we are so cut off from ourselves that we stop having gut instincts. Or, we have them, but because we don't trust them, they have become almost impossible to pay attention to in the cacophony of mixed messages in our heads. When this happens to me, I get feeling down on myself about not being in tune with my intuition. But, of course, that's not much help. One of the most useful things I've found to get back in touch with that feeling is to spend some time around someone you know who's a big believer in their own gut, someone who follows it, not blindly but with conviction.

The ability to be intuitive is as automatic to us as breathing; all babies are highly intuitive—they have to be because they have few other resources to process the world. So just being around someone who's in that zone will quickly remind us how strong our own connections to that Guidance can be.

Some people use pendulums, crystals, or other tools to help them get in touch with that intuitive force. I'm all for using whatever works for you—for me, I've found the only tool I need running down the whole length of my back. When I am crunched down and hunched over, I know that is a sign that I am flowing negatively, cutting off the mainline. Then, when the space between the bones opens up and my spine flexes tall through its curves, I know I'm home free—an antenna ready to receive the signals I need.

I will reconnect to my own all-knowing intuition, and trust it!

"1) Remove your focus from *any major thing* that is currently causing serious fear (worry, concern, anxiety, stress, etc.), *AND KEEP IT OFF!*"

This is the first of two steps of Grabhorn's introductory program.

Pretty much the best way to get a toddler not to play with something potentially dangerous is to distract his attention, to replace the scissors you're taking away with a ball or some other desired object. It occurred to me that that worked so well with children, I should try it for myself. For me, the danger isn't scissors, a light cord, the TV remote—it's worry about money, stress about work, thinking I'll never do enough or be enough or have enough. Phew.

So I distract myself. I've got the focus. It's on the worry. I have to put it on something else. This can be anything else. Some things that work really well are gratitude or counting my blessings. Other things that work are smiling at strangers, gazing at flowers in the park, talking to a friend on the phone (as long as I don't go into my serious gear mode). Cooking dinner for my family (usually, unless I can't kick myself out of just-another-damned-thing-to-do mode) works.

Once I've moved my focus and gotten a new perspective, I can glance back at the thing—problem, task, relationship—that was causing the worry or concern. It seems smaller, less dangerous somehow.

Choosing what to focus on helps me take my focus off the stressors.

344

"2) Establish a flip-switch topic for each day by finding one new item about *yourself* to appreciate."

And this is the next step.

I know a woman who realized she needed to make major, major changes in her life when she attended a team-building retreat for her job. The assignment was to tell her partner one thing that she was good at in her job. She reports that her mind went blank. She could think of nothing. Her silence brought tears to her eyes and finally she was able to mumble something like "good at meeting deadlines."

This woman ran a large department. She had lots of people coming to her to solve their problems and looking for reassurance, which she always tried to give. Some might say that she gave herself away. She was also very good about telling her employees and her friends and even the cashier in the store that she appreciated something they'd done or said.

Yet she'd let her life get into such a state that she was totally out of touch with what she might appreciate about herself. She tried this—finding one new item to appreciate about herself. And it worked. Today she can tell you what she's good at. And what she wants for herself, the people who work for her (in a very different setting), and the world. And she still uses the flip-switch.

Try it for a week. What have you got to lose?

345

"Some days are better than others, but *all* days hold more enduring joy than I ever thought possible, because I have the keys. Whether or not I use them is my choice, but one thing is for certain, I have no more excuses on which to fall back."

In this passage, Lynn Grabhorn is talking about her discovery of specific tools she teaches to unlock the reservoir of unlimited well-being and happiness that we all have. In her system, the main key is the power of attraction. Whether we call it that or something else, this is our passport to creating the life we want.

A key lets us unlock a door. It does not push the door open. Nor does it whisk us through. And once through, it doesn't tell us which tools to pick up and use. Another way of saying this is that there is no magic key, no one idea or chant or miracle drug that will do everything we want done.

And what there is, is plenty—once we know that we, ourselves, can open to the energy of the universe, can connect with what we desire, can pray or meditate or concentrate our thoughts (whichever word appeals to us), we know we don't have the "normal" excuses. The dog didn't eat our homework. We can't be the victim—of our families, our workplace, our bodies, our world. Because we know better.

Most of all, I know I can choose joy.

346

"Then you know from the very depths of your being that everything really is all right. No matter how it may look, no matter how it may seem, no matter what the media may report to the contrary, you and this precious planet, and most who are on it, will always be all right."

All right doesn't always mean that things are going to turn out the way we expect them to, or that we're in control. There's a Chinese Zen story about a farmer whose son was working in the fields one day with the aid of the family horse. The horse ran away and everyone said, "Oh terrible." The farmer said, "Maybe." Then the horse came back, leading several wild horses behind him. Everyone said, "Oh wonderful." The farmer said, "Maybe." Next, the son was thrown by the horse and his leg was broken. You know the pattern by now—terrible! Maybe. Next, soldiers rode through the village conscripting all the young men, except the farmer's son whose leg was broken. Terrible? Wonderful? Maybe!

This story is, at least in part, about not being quick to judge and not judging on face value. It's also, I think, about what "maybe" or "may be" means—something like "so be it." Things are as they are. And, at base, Lynn Grabhorn and I believe and invite you to believe that they will be all right. That doesn't mean there won't be broken legs or soldiers or famine or drought. It does mean that in the long run, taking the long view, and taking into account the flow of energy that is really important, things are going to be okay.

May I see all manner of things being okay.

347

"Inspired Action is always fun, always easy. It just flows, one step to the next. If what you're doing is difficult, you didn't send your energy ahead first."

Recently, I got an email from a friend telling me to be on the lookout for a box she'd put in the mail to me. It was a box full of sweets that she and another friend baked. Her email was pure magic, conjuring up a vision of my friend in a homemade apron, dancing around the kitchen to a holiday music mix prepared by her husband, wearing reindeer antlers and stirring up batches of goodies filled with organic nuts and butter and fruit.

This friend and her husband are currently dealing with his chronic condition that prevents him working. She is on deadline for at least four book projects and to prepare new designs for a giftware company she works for. Plus, she's setting up her next online classes and finalizing her speaking schedule for next year. She does all this with the help of one part-time assistant and her husband on his good days.

She is very clear about what she's doing, very focused, and the first to admit that she couldn't do it without having her energy aligned. She writes about living with intention. And, more to the point, she does it.

As I plan my projects, I make room for the perspiration of hard work and the inspiration that brings joy and ease to my process.

348

"Does it get easier? Good grief, yes. But if you're going to make a decision to take control of your life, have the things you want, do the things you want, be the person you want to be, and live the way you want with the people you want, there's something you might as well accept: you're in training for good!"

Tiny choices lead to little choices, little choices lead to small changes, small changes lead to more choices, which lead to bigger changes, which lead to more choices. . . . And this never ends. Once we start on a path, we are creating our path and our goal as we walk our path. The choices we make lead to other choices.

I'm reminded of Dara Torres, who in the 2008 Summer Olympics won three silver medals, at age forty-one. This huge accomplishment is accomplished by training—rigorous training—body, mind, spirit. Her story is inspiring. She had a baby, kept swimming; she had surgery, kept swimming; she tried out for the Olympic team after retiring, kept swimming. Odds are that she won't quit swimming any time soon because swimming is part of her training. And when you're in training like that you don't tend to quit just because you've achieved one goal.

In fact, there's one school of thought that says training is for training's sake—we train not because we want to have a bigger house, a better job, a richer spouse. We may, in fact, get those things if we envision our lives as we want them to be, if we make choices that point us toward the positive. And we may well get other things we hadn't even imagined—a chance to travel, to do something good for a neighbor or a friend, a chance to test our mettle up against a hardship of some kind. But what we really get is the practice of making choices and implementing those choices and then doing it again.

May I stick to my path today.

349

"Sure, I know it sounds nearly impossible, but what's it going to take for us to allow happiness? The neat thing about getting into this space of 'I don't give a hoot what you do or did, my valve is staying open anyhow' is that you are automatically allowing the kind of conditions to come in that *you want*—definitely the name of the game."

"I don't give a hoot about what you do or did" does NOT mean I don't give a hoot about you. People sometimes mistake this space for selfishness. For disconnecting from others—family, friends, even the larger community we live in—because we're "doing our own thing." Let me repeat—letting my valve stay open to positive energy, allowing in the kinds of feelings I want in my life, does not isolate me from other people. It does not cut me off. And it does not mean I don't care about those people.

When I have the conditions and feelings and happenings in my life that I want, when I'm living the script I've written, positive energy abounds. And that positive energy attracts and creates more positive energy. So the things that someone else is doing or saying to try to hurt me, hurt less. And the less they hurt, the more I'm able to focus on the positive, even the positive between me and the person who's doing or saying the hurtful things.

If life is a game, the name of it is releasing positive energy to attract more positive energy. And the sky's the limit. The only downer is to let ourselves down, to let ourselves close down. Oh, and one more thing about looking at life as a game—anyone who's a serious student of any game—chess, for instance—can verify this: the more you play, the more you learn. The first time you play, it may seem impossible to move your pieces across the board. It becomes easier, just as it becomes easier to stay open the more we practice staying open. We see the pitfalls and temptations faster. If we close down, we recover faster the more we practice.

I'm playing the game of allowing happiness in my life.

350

"I know, I'm sounding very cavalier about this, like there was nothing to this business of ignoring the actions of some jackass who you're sure is responsible for making your life miserable. Blame is our game, and pointing the finger back on ourselves has always seemed so pointless."

Of course, it's hard to ignore someone bent on getting our attention by making us as miserable as she is—whether that someone is your partner, your landlord, your boss. The question I wish I remembered to always ask is: are you sure? Is this person doing whatever it is they're doing to make my life miserable? Alternatives abound. Some people don't see any other way to build themselves up but to belittle me. (But their main, misguided, maybe subconscious effort is to build themselves up.) They are only doing as their boss told them or what they learned from their dad or . . . In the end, here's a way of looking at it that I came up with: What they're doing, why they're doing it, who they're doing it to is all beside the point to me. What's on-point for me is how I choose to act and react. I can blame them. Or I can look at my reactions to their behavior and choose my actions accordingly. I can walk away. I can choose not to react. And, I might add, I can choose not to blame myself for their bad behavior, which is a response that some people have. That's not self-examination. That is pointing a shaming, blaming finger at ourselves.

Much of the time the people we blame aren't exactly covering themselves with glory, acting like enlightened, upstanding adults. And that doesn't mean we should waste our energy blaming them. After all, we have better things to do with it. Just as you might offer a small child a substitute toy when you're taking away something she shouldn't have, try offering yourself a substitute for blame. It could be walking away from the situation, a time out from that person, a look in the mirror to decide what it is you want.

Where do I want to go instead of blame?

351

"Gradually it sank in that I didn't need to create a multimillion-dollar Steven Spielberg production number, just a moderately believable little story I could tell myself."

Even Steven Spielberg didn't start out being Steven Spielberg. He wrote and directed his first movie *Firelight* at the age of sixteen on a budget of $600. The film generated $100 in profits. And the rest is, as they say, history. But even if it weren't, the point is that almost everybody starts small. Most "overnight sensations" in business, art, theater, literature have been working away at creating their creations and their lives for a long time. And many of them will say that the commercial success and media attention are not what keeps them going after they are discovered.

What keeps them going is what keeps us all going in the direction of the life we want—a "moderately believable little story" we can tell ourselves on a daily basis. The one in which we create our own right work, our own rewarding relationships, our own best selves. The one in which we open up to the universe and the universe returns energy to us in ways we can't even imagine.

By the way, when I did a little research on Spielberg, I discovered that *Firelight* was lost. No copy of it appears to exist, but it did form the basis for the incredibly successful *Close Encounters of the Third Kind* he later wrote. So who knows where my little story can go?

Tell yourself your believable story every night at bedtime for a week. What happens?

352

"Instruction books always accompany inspiration."

I love this quote. I have it hanging above my door so that it's the last thing I see before I leave the house. That way, I'm ready to take on any world I find on the other side of the door, and I'm ready for inspiration, even when it comes at me from some unlikely places.

Pure inspiration is one of the best feelings in the world, right up there with chocolate, winning the lottery, and (fill in the blank). We breeze along, full of anticipation and excitement, brimming with great ideas that maybe never occurred to another soul on the whole planet. Yes, that feeling can happen to any of us, regardless of education or inclination, and it can happen a lot more. We ourselves shut down this great feeling all too often by asking ourselves "what next?" as though we have to have the idea and then we need to write the book of how-tos before anything can even get started. Then the high of a brilliant new idea crashes and burns into a trench of self-doubt and fear.

But here's the deal: the instruction book comes with the idea. You might not be able to read the print very clearly yet, but each idea contains the seeds of its own fruition, and you can put your full trust in that fact. The fastest and best way to speed that process is to keep on enjoying the moment of inspiration and make it last for as long as you can.

Don't worry, the instructions are in the box and there for you the minute you need them.

353

"But we most certainly can learn to allow the contrast, our likes and don't likes, without having to feel and flow so much negativity."

Do you know someone who thinks they have to convince you that their likes are better than yours? Say you're out for coffee with a friend and she wants you to just try the hazelnut-flavored coffee specialty of the house. You know you don't like flavored coffees, and yet she might make such a big deal of it that you feel like you're saying you don't like her if you don't try the darned coffee. So, you have the choice to disappoint her or not have the coffee you want. In this case, I'd try to tell her I loved her but I was going to drink what I wanted to drink. And I'd also like to tell her that we can be different and not have to have one of us feel badly about it. That's what I'd like.

I'd also like to tell myself that I don't have to meet others' expectations for what I should be doing with my life. In fact, I don't even have to meet my own expectations. I'd also like to tell myself that it's okay for me to have my own likes and dislikes—in people, ideas, books, food, in almost anything—and that those likes and dislikes can change over time.

Today is a day to be myself, without judgment and without fault.

354

"If all else fails, smile a phony smile. Just cracking your face moves your vibrations up."

My three-year-old son has a strategy when he knows I'm pretty annoyed with something he's been doing or getting up to. During a tense moment, he tells a silly joke (or tries) and then laughs uproariously at it himself. The laughing is super fake and sounds nothing like his real laugh when something funny catches him off guard. It's so fake that the laugh itself is funny, a strident *haaahh haaaah haaah,* and he knows it will make me laugh every time and it will often get him out of whatever pickle he's in.

Ever notice that when you laugh, the whole energy of a room changes? And when it's two or more people, the effect is exponential? It turns out this works to some degree even if it's totally fake! Just the act of turning up the corners of your mouth or forcing air out of your mouth in a few quick bursts actually starts to change the chemical makeup of your brain, and pretty soon you'll think of something or notice something to actually make you feel that way. Okay, more often than not, you will notice yourself acting like a total freak and that will probably help you get in the groove, but who's keeping score?

If you can't make it, fake it, at least when it comes to smiling and laughter.

355

"Don't give up; don't you ever give up!"

The past is here to stay. It is physically here to stay, in your brain pathways, in the consequences of your actions. It is energetically here to stay because energy never dies. But energy loves to change, recycle, join with other energy. In fact, that movement of energy creates every known process and happening in our world. And we have the power to work with that energy at a higher level than most people could ever imagine.

But, sometimes, the thought that we can't erase what's already here or has come before can lead us to some pretty dark days of worry and regret, if we let it. We all have moments we are not proud of, and difficulties we would rather not have had to face. And as we accept our responsibility for creating what comes into our lives, in one way or another, it can be a real punch to the gut. Consider, however, that any negativity you give to the memory of those things is bringing them along with you into the present, and you have another choice. Those feelings might feel necessary, they might even feel helpful, but they're not going to change the past, and that can be a comfort to you—things have been what they have been, and I don't have to spend an ounce more of my energy trying to change them.

So, what to do? It is never too late (Really! Never!) to make a new path that diverges completely from the old one. You can build new pathways in your brain, you can create outlet after outlet for energy to flow into your life in the best possible ways, and all of that can coexist happily with your past—a past that no longer draws on your energetic resources through guilt and self-blame.

When the past makes you feel like throwing in the towel, remind yourself that the present is yours for the taking.

356

"I'm talking about creating your own utopia, not next year, not in the next decade, but now."

Ten places to go, things to do, foods to try, experiences to have—before you die. That is the theme of at least one recent movie and several best-selling books. Now, I'm not saying it's not good to have aspirations of places to go, things to do, etc., in some future that we take for granted even though we know that there are no guarantees. Now is, after all, the only moment we really have. Yesterday is gone—and regrets or wishes won't bring it back. Tomorrow isn't here yet. Obvious, isn't it?

Then why am I so resistant to the idea that I could be creating my own utopia right now? After all, there's war, poverty, mortgage foreclosures, millions of children without enough food and proper water around the globe. That doesn't sound like utopia to me. So, I look a little bit at the word—the dictionary definition is: an imaginary place; visionary reform that's impossibly idealistic. It comes from Sir Thomas More's book by the same name about a fictional island where perfection reigned, written as a religious allegory for what humans can be and as a way to freely express his views on the political and religious upheaval of the times he lived in. And his word, coined in the sixteenth century, has come to mean an unachievable perfect society.

So, where and what is my own utopia—or yours? That, I realize, is the task. We create our utopias—our visions for perfectly balanced lives—as we articulate them moment by moment. The more consciously we live in those moments, correcting small imbalances, facing fears, correcting the course, the closer we are to our own private utopias—perfectly balanced lives. And as we create those lives in the moment, we open up the possibilities and the energy to send our own utopias out in the world—a step at a time, a day at a time.

I create my own perfect world, in the midst of this moment.

357

"So, from this moment on, never, ever, accept reality as something to which you just resign yourself. Take your thoughts beyond whatever is in front of your nose that you don't like and put them on what you do like."

Go through your life and examine which assumptions are unassailable in your mind. Some of my favorites: "You can't always get what you want." "You have to give something to get something." "There is nothing beyond this physical reality." "Money doesn't grow on trees."

Write down a list of the beliefs that make up your reality. You may find as you write them down that you wish they weren't true, you may even try to mentally toss them out the window, but something nags at you . . . they're still there. They aren't going away fast, and you take that as further proof they must be real, true statements. Phooey. They're just good old thought habits, and they have particular power because of the sheer numbers of folks who believe them and have believed them for eons.

Work through the logic of each of these moldy old beliefs. Why are they so powerful? "You can't always get want you want"—because if everyone did that, someone would end up unhappy. Guess what? You're not in charge of anyone else's happiness (besides, it *is* possible for everyone to be happy—anything's possible!). Hone in on the feelings behind the beliefs—feelings of inadequacy or lack, fear of being alone. If those thoughts are at the core of your belief system, you can bet the accompanying feelings are flowing out everywhere in spades, even when you're not consciously thinking anything's wrong.

Unearth the feeeeelings below some of your stalwart negative beliefs so that you can chuck them once and for all.

358

"Now it boils down to what you want to do with the rest of your life and how willing you are to put forth the feeling-effort to get it."

I just read something about what casting people and corporations are looking for now from models and actors to sell us the latest products we didn't know we needed until we saw them on TV. These folks used to be known as good-looking, but now the type is called "aspirational," and the opposite of this type on television is "real" (e.g., people who look like they were pulled off the street). Ugh, I thought, really?

Since when has aspiration come to this? Looking great under the lights—cooler than us, dressed better—that is the sum total of what marketers think we aspire to?

Aspire. A great word. With a root in Latin that means "to breathe." This is the kind of wanting you do when you're connected to your core energy—with every breath, you are sending out great energy that will come back in spades in the form of desires realized (desires that may include, but probably go far beyond, looking fab in a bikini).

This great word "aspire" has been co-opted for the ugly reason of helping you foster your own feeling of inadequacy. And then, of course, offering the idea that by buying this and that, you can become some other, better, version of yourself. I've got some news: you're never going to become anyone else. And that is reason to rejoice. As your life changes for the better, you will only ever become *more* yourself; anything else would be a travesty.

Breathe in the desire for the real you, in all your glory.

359

"If you want to change something, if you want to improve where you are, if you want that magnificent feeling of fulfillment, or to feel a depth of happiness not normally known to you, if you want to have whatever it is you don't have now, then learn to get your motor running, and turn on!"

Getting your motor running is all about tuning in—to the voice inside you that can give you guidance about what it is you really want and what you need to feel fulfilled—in this moment, and the next one, and the next one.

I ask you to think for a minute about purring—contented, well-fed cats purr, as do well-tuned Ferrari motors. It's the sound of contentment, the sound of true power, ready to take off on a moment's notice, and the sound of beauty. Now take it one step farther. What might you feel like, turned on, champing at the bit, ready to make changes in your life?

Imagine yourself standing tall, strong, striding out toward a day when you do what you enjoy and enjoy the feeling of fulfillment from the process and the outcome. Imagine smiling at people you meet along your way—from your heart. Picture it.

Now turn the key to your motor and go out and do one thing that makes you happy.

360

"Dream the dream of joy, dream the dream of fulfillment, dream the dream of frivolity, but DREAM!"

How many of us were admonished in childhood—stop being such a dreamer? And how many of us took that well-meaning (let's give them the benefit of the doubt) parent or teacher to heart and stopped dreaming? Well, it's time to turn off those old tapes. It's time to wipe the slate clean and remember the last time you had a dream.

Close your eyes. Let it come. What was that dream? Take a breath. Do you still dream it—to learn to paint, to take a trip, to find a different job, to fly an airplane, to discover a cure for cancer, to learn to dance the tango? It doesn't matter in this remembering exercise so much what the dream was as that there was a dream.

Maybe not since childhood have I let myself dream—just dream—without immediately beginning to make a plan to try to make the dream come true. Without immediately tuning in to my internal YOU CAN'Ts radio program and listening to the million reasons that dream will never come true. The point is simply—dream my dreams. And as I dream them, I get better at dreaming, choosing which dream to pursue, and just doing it.

And, if at first you don't succeed, dream, dream, dream again.

"Since what we send out is what we get back, and since what we send out comes from what we've been focusing on, it might behoove us to pay a damn sight more attention to what we're thinking about, ***and how that is making us feeeeel."***

There are at least two sides to every story. More to see in most situations than at first meets the eye. Different ways to look at an elephant, depending on which end you're at. More than one way to skin a cat. And most of the people have a lot on their minds most of the time.

A heavy load those thoughts can be, if all I can think about is how lonely I am. How sad. How I don't have what I need. How other people get more money, love, fun—whatever it is I think I don't have enough of—than I do. Pretty soon I sink under the weight of those thoughts. Into the depths of despair and anger. That's how my thoughts are making me feel.

Should we, could we, dare we try to think a different thought? There's another cliché—I felt sorry for myself because I had no shoes until I met the man who had no feet. Think about that one. If I concentrate on my good strong feet (literally or figuratively) and how they might carry me out of my despair—into a new relationship, a new job, a new body (maybe even literally, because walking *is* good for a lot of things)—maybe I'll feel better.

Feeling bad? Take a walk on the brighter side of your thoughts.

362

"Step 1. Identify what you Don't Want
Step 2. Identify what you Do Want
Step 3. Find the feeling place of your Want
Step 4. Expect, listen, and allow the universe to deliver—and—
(Step Four-A: *Keep your bloomin' focus off those blankity-blank conditions!*)"

In different dance and movement classes and in some martial arts, people talk about a state called "active rest." In bodily terms, it can be as simple as lying with your back on the floor and your knees pointed toward the ceiling. It's a position in which you can relax your muscles, but one not likely to give over to complete abandon and sleep. If you think of it in terms of an animal, like a dog, you can imagine the perfect stillness and calm right before the doorbell rings. But how could the dog leap to its feet in a split second if it were not somehow ready?

Expectation does not have to be about tense, stressful worry. It can be restful readiness. The more restful and the more ready, the better. Both things are equally important.

Is expecting the same as a sense of entitlement? Not in the negative sense. In order to expect, you do have to believe in a very real way that it is okay for you to get what you are expecting. You have to know that you deserve it, not only because of your goodness or your hard work (though those are certainly wonderful qualities).

The best way to expect is to take away the heavy layers of judgment or fear about your desire, and find a way to be ready in a state of rest.

363

"Ask yourself over and over why you want something, and keep asking, and keep asking, and keep asking, even when you think you have no more answers."

One foolproof way to boost your positive vibrational flow is to start asking *Why?* Say you have a want—even a pretty negative one like "I want to get rid of my old car." Asking *Why?* can turn it around and soon you'll be feeling great and magnetizing in that new car and more. It might go something like this:

"I want to get rid of my old clunker."

"Why?"

"Because I hate having to worry about the next time it's going to break down and I'll be stuck on the side of the road."

"Why?"

"Are you crazy? Because I like to get places on time and in one piece."

"Why?"

"Because it makes me feel like an adult—in control of my own destiny. Besides, I hate how people look at me when I get out of that old thing."

"Why?"

"I want to be taken seriously, like when I went on a business trip last month and they upgraded my rental car."

"How did that feel?"

"Oh, I cruised all over, and drummed up more business than on my last three trips combined."

Now you're starting on the road to some nice, positive wants. You can feel yourself buzzing with the excitement of driving around in a beautiful car, making new contacts, and open to new adventures, in control of your own destiny.

Turn around a negative want or start really buzzing about a positive one, all thanks to "why."

364

"It must never, never, be about what is *going* to happen . . . only about what *has* [happened] or *is* happening now."

To tell the truth, where would we be if we spent our entire day in what could be—the future conditional verb tense? A lot of things could happen tomorrow, or the day after that, or the day after that. My house could burn down. You could be walking along the street, look down, and find a hundred-dollar bill. I could answer the doorbell to find those people we see on TV with balloons and a check for a gazillion dollars. (Or as my father, who majored in math, used to say: You have almost as much chance of winning the lottery if you don't buy a ticket as if you do.) So we can spend a lot of time worrying or dreaming about our future—living in a state of "could be."

Or we could be paying attention to our lives in the moment—taking a walk, for example, and noticing the first push of crocus buds, the mother cat lying in the spring sunshine, the smell of the air. Being on the walk when I'm on the walk. It's not that we don't care what's going to happen—it's that we don't daydream, worry, or talk incessantly about it.

One way to look at life is to think about it as writing a script. In a movie is it more interesting to have characters who are involved in their lives, talking to each other in the present situation—whether it's falling in love or looking for a missing person—or sitting around talking about what might happen when?

Today I use what *has* happened to me to help me figure out what *is* happening, and I let what *will* happen take care of itself.

365

"The only place we connect with divine power is in the Now."

There's an old saying: the past is history, the future a mystery, and this moment is a gift, that's why they call it the present. It's a play on words, granted. And I invite you to play with it.

Feel what it's like to be calm, centered, in the moment. Put your feet on the floor. Light a candle. Or close your eyes. Take a deep breath. And another. And another. Feel your connection to your own life. To your own wants and desires. If a negative thought arises, let it go.

Do this three times a day for a week and your connection with the divine power that's inside all of us and surrounding all of us and connecting all of us is bound to increase. Do it three times a day for a month and your life will never be the same.

To connect with the divine power of Now is to know who I am meant to be.

About the Author

Mina Parker is a freelance writer, editor, and mom. Her other books include *Half Full* (2006), *Mother Is a Verb* (2007), *100 Good Wishes for Baby* (2007), *Silver Linings* (2007), and *Her Inspiration* (2007). She has also worked as an actor, a grant writer, and an administrator for several nonprofits. She lives in Brooklyn with her husband and son.

Hampton Roads Publishing Company

. . . for the evolving human spirit

HAMPTON ROADS PUBLISHING COMPANY
publishes books on a variety of subjects,
including spirituality, health, and other
related topics.

For a copy of our latest trade catalog,
call toll-free, 800-766-8009,
or send your name and address to:

HAMPTON ROADS PUBLISHING COMPANY, INC.
1125 STONEY RIDGE ROAD • CHARLOTTESVILLE, VA 22902
E-mail: hrpc@hrpub.com • Internet: www.hrpub.com